ANNE DE LISLE lives with her husband, Ian Russell, and dogs, Topsy and Lottie, in Baddow House, Maryborough, Queensland. She is the author of several internationally successful historical romances and is now working on a contemporary novel about a group of close friends, their lives, loves and heartbreak.

Visit Anne's website at www.annedelisle.com

A GRAND PASSION

ANNE DE LISLE

BANTAM

SYDNEY AUCKLAND TORONTO NEW YORK LONDON

A GRAND PASSION
A BANTAM BOOK

First published in Australia and New Zealand in 2007 by Bantam

National Library of Australia
Cataloguing-in-Publication Entry

   de Lisle, Anne, 1958–.
   A grand passion.

   ISBN 9781863256445.

   1. de Lisle, Anne, 1958–. 2. Couples – Queensland –
Maryborough – Biography. 3. Man-woman relationships –
Queensland – Maryborough. 4. Dwellings – Remodeling –
Queensland – Maryborough. I. Title.

920.02

Transworld Publishers,
a division of Random House Australia Pty Ltd
100 Pacific Highway, North Sydney, NSW 2060
www.randomhouse.com.au

Random House New Zealand Limited
18 Poland Road, Glenfield, Auckland

Transworld Publishers,
a division of The Random House Group Ltd
61–63 Uxbridge Road, Ealing, London W5 5SA

Random House Inc
1745 Broadway, New York, New York 10036

Cover photo by Ashley Smith Photography
(www.ashleysmithphotography.com)
Text design by saso content & design pty ltd
Typeset by Midland Typesetters, Australia
Printed and bound by Griffin Press, South Australia

10 9 8 7 6 5 4 3 2

For Young Lochinvar

FLOOR PLANS OF BADDOW HOUSE

Top floor

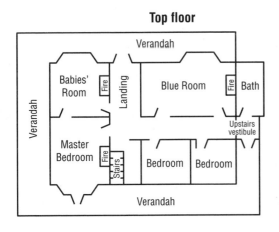

Ground floor

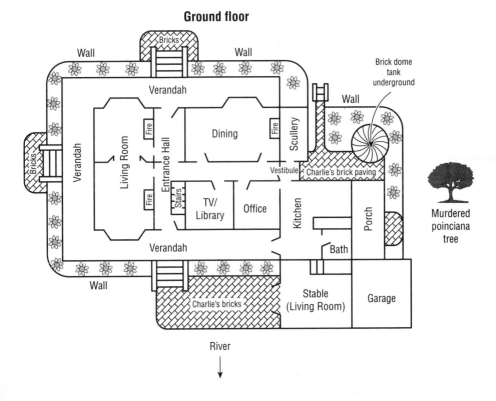

PROLOGUE

IAN AND I WERE determined to escape. The necessity had preyed on our minds and dominated our conversation for ages. Round and round we went, with ideas, questions and words, with words, questions and ideas. But the solutions wouldn't come.

For more than twenty years we had both lived in the small country town of Montville, high on the Blackhall Range in south-east Queensland. Ian had been married to Jenny and I had been married to Chris. But fate chose to play us both cruelly. Within a year of each other, I lost my marriage to divorce and Ian lost his wife to cancer.

We were shambling around in a twilight world, each blind to any plight but our own until one day, lonely, and more than a little desperate, Ian rang me up. 'This is one miserable person calling another,' he said. 'I'd like to take you out to lunch.'

Neither of us wanted a new partner. We were each far too depressed with our lot to recognise wanting anything at all. I didn't even want to go out to lunch, but it seemed churlish to refuse.

We were both hideously nervous. I can't remember what we ate, but I do know we drank a lot of wine. We both vowed not to talk about our pasts. Neither of us succeeded. In the end it was fun; a bright day on an otherwise bleak horizon. We decided to do it again.

In the beginning, our ritual was lunch once a week, but it soon became obvious that neither of us could wait an entire week. We were each others' salve, each others' medication; a miracle cure for the wretchedness. Like adolescents, phone calls were several times a day. When Ian couldn't sleep at night, he'd ring, and our talk would last into the wee hours.

We knew from the moment on our third, tentative date together when Ian grew serious and said, 'I want to spend the rest of my life with you', that we would one day set up house together. But we were two people carrying enough emotional baggage to fill the cargo hold of a jumbo jet. So many issues, so many complications: families to consider, past lives to get over, new lives to come to terms with. Attempting a future together seemed fraught with dangers. Oh, for the simplicity of youth, to be twenty years old and in love for the first time.

Through all the pain, reluctance, indecision, fear and guilt, there were only two things of which we were certain: apart we felt miserable, when we were together we were content.

In our home town we knew everyone and everyone knew us – our business, our respective sadnesses, how we had behaved, reacted, felt, coped. We were two goldfish in a bowl and we didn't like it. Besides, we had both known some very sad times on Montville's hills of pleasant green. Forging a successful future together seemed dependent on escape. But where could we go?

We began to scout around. Business commitments meant that every week Ian would have to return to Montville for two days and a night. We decided that a two-hour journey was the most he should have to do on such a regular basis, but were determined to take the full two hours we'd allowed ourselves, the further the better for our new life, our new beginning.

We looked at the map, we drew circles, measured radii, got quite scientific. Something propelled us to the town of Maryborough.

Maryborough is two hours due north of Montville, an easy run up the highway. We know it to be to be an old town, plump with history and sweet little Queenslander homes. An idyllic cottage began to take shape in my dreams. A neat little cottage, a garden framed by frangipanis and jacarandas, walls shaded by a deep verandah, fragrant with jasmine, honeysuckle and clambering roses.

We couldn't wait to start looking.

>─┤─◄►─⊙─◄►─┤─◄

CHAPTER 1

DISCOVERY

WE DRIVE TO Maryborough on a reconnaissance mission and find ourselves in Queens Park, over-looking the Mary River. Already we can scent the history. The trees are ancient and massive, there is a Victorian-era fountain and rotunda, and cannons point defensively at the river, relics of a time when the new inhabitants of this land feared to lose their precious shores to other foreign colonisers.

We wander about, soaking it all in. We stroll beneath a rose trellis, find a wishing well, toss in a few coins then stroll to the river and on down Wharf Street.

What a bounty of historic buildings. We pass the Court House and its arched loggias remind me of old Singapore in the heyday of Raffles: tennis in the afternoons and Pimms on the verandah. It's hard to believe we're not on a movie set as we saunter past the Customs House and Customs House Hotel, the Port Residence and the Bond Store. We venture inside the Bond Store, and see walls of handmade bricks, an earthen-floored cellar. Astonishingly, some of the original liquor barrels are still there. Wharf Street is the sort of scene you might encounter in one of those places built for tourism, where you pay admittance, see locals in period costume and watch re-enactments. But this is real: normal people going about their daily business, apparently oblivious to the glorious setting.

We go about *our* business. Noses pressed to real estate windows, we begin to hope that we've found what we want. The prices seem reasonable, the houses numerous. Nothing leaps out as The One, but we're enchanted by the abundance of quaint little buildings pictured in the FOR SALE windows. We push open our first real estate agent's door.

➤ ◆ ○ ◆ ◄

Several weeks and several visits to Maryborough later, we slump, downcast, in our dingy motel room.

The garden was too small . . . I say.

That one's already reached its potential, no capital growth there . . . says Ian.

Not private enough . . .

Too run down . . .

Wrong sort of street . . .

Too renovated, too perfect, too finished . . .

Way too small . . .

Midges and mozzies . . .

The road was too busy . . .

I want to see the river . . .

We both know there's *no* chance of that. Our first agent on our first day is abundantly clear on the point.

'We're looking for an old house overlooking the river,' we explain. 'Something with a decent size garden. Something we can renovate.'

There's a brief moment of silence. Then, quietly, almost imperceptibly at first, his shoulders begin to shake. He starts to laugh. Little half suppressed sniggers, that build until he's wiping his eyes. *What's so bleeding funny?* I want to scream but, politely, patiently, we await an explanation.

'If a place like that existed, it would never even make the listings,' he gets out, still wiping the moisture from his eyes. 'It'd be snapped up within fifteen minutes of the owner's decision to sell.'

◅━◈━O━◈━▻

We visit Trevor, our only contact in Maryborough. Trevor is a talented artist who lived for years in Montville and who Ian and I had both known in our previous lives. He looks the archetypal artist: slightly lean and hungry, with dark hair cut in a style reminiscent of the age of flappers and the Charleston – one thick lock flopping over his brow.

Trevor is busy, surprised when we arrive, but far too well-mannered to tell us we are taking up his valuable time. We hadn't wanted to impose, but desperation lowers our resolve.

His home is a gem of a Queenslander on the edge of town in a wide, leafy street near the river. It's the sort of cottage I've yearned for and is filled with Trevor's art and the art of his friends and contemporaries. Trevor is one of those rare artists who actually derives income from selling his work. He receives commissions and his work graces public places. Ian and I are vastly impressed by this.

It is late afternoon. A bottle of champagne seems appropriate. Trevor knows that Ian and I both love old houses, and he knows we have the enthusiasm to take on a challenge. We discuss our plight. We describe our dream of a fabulous old home on the banks of the river.

Ian and I have been extra keen on rivers since we visited Tasmania a year earlier. Salt, sand and surf don't interest us at all. We love country: green, lush, treed country; dry, red, unbroken country. But most of all, since Tasmania, we love to watch the timeless progress of water passing through a landscape. We explain this, and we make clear our willingness, our *eagerness* even, to renovate. We go on to whinge and bemoan our disappointment, the dearth of options.

Trevor is patient and sympathetic. He listens and nods, listens and nods. Somewhere during the second glass of champagne, he says, 'I've heard that Baddow House might be coming up for sale.'

Two pairs of ears prick up. We've never heard of Baddow House, but Trevor's tone suggests this might be significant news.

'You wouldn't want to touch it, of course,' he adds, and takes another sip of champagne.

We wait, agog.

'It's a real dump; an old, two-storey brick and render place on the edge of town. The outside walls are moving away from the inside walls.'

I'm not sure about Ian, but I'm still pretty interested.

'I'll take you down there if you like.'

Glasses are drained. It's almost dusk so we won't really be able to see much, but we're more fired up and curious than we have been for weeks.

⊱━◈━◯━◈━⊰

Two minutes from Trevor's and the three of us pull up at the dead end of Queen Street. The house is huge, towering and black with sooty filth. It looks like the sort of grim building used in Victorian England to house orphans or lunatics. I can't believe what I'm seeing. It's fantastic.

'Are there people living in it?' I ask, rubbing my fogged breath from the side window.

'Oh yes, they've been there nearly twenty years.'

I'm disappointed. I want to snoop, but there are inhabitants.

Ian is more game. 'Let's go for a walk,' he says, and is out of the car before his mouth shuts on the words.

I'm out too, tagging after him. 'We can't very well knock on the door,' my cowardice sneaks in, 'there's no FOR SALE sign.'

'We'll walk round the perimeter,' Ian says. 'No harm in that.'

Trevor is eager too. With the advantage of being a local, he knows the lay of the land. 'This way,' he tells us. 'We should be able to see the other side of the house from the river.'

We are racing the waning daylight, so scramble and

slither down to the river flat as fast as we can. Weeds and vines cling and scratch at us. Mozzies descend in a starving black cloud. But eagerness numbs our senses to everything but the desire to get a better look at the house.

Between us and the house, the vegetation is impenetrable: heavily treed and overgrown with thick, snaking vines. We struggle to catch sight of the towering walls. I'm thinking the house is like Sleeping Beauty's castle, trapped by time and the strangling forest.

We can see the roof and several chimneys, we can see dirty, crumbling masonry. Each tantalising glimpse sends our anticipation escalating.

From down by the river we are looking uphill at the house. It's two very tall storeys, presenting soaring flat walls broken only by a couple of bay windows upstairs and down, but we see an arch here, a big old door there. Excitement makes us heedless of the thorny vines and prickly scrubby things that torment our legs.

As we walk the perimeter of the land, I'm overwhelmed with gratitude to Trevor for bringing us here. I know that even if we never set foot in Maryborough again I won't forget the experience because this place is one of a kind. It's a mystery to me that the care of such a treasure could be abandoned to such an extent. The possibility that I'm looking at my future home tugs at me. A remote possibility of course, and peppered with untold obstacles, but it's there nevertheless.

Trevor explains that we are standing on public land that surrounds the house. 'This is an historic site,' he tells us. 'It's where the first settlement of the village of Wide Bay, later called Maryborough, began. It'll never be developed, never be built on.'

This is all great news. No neighbours. No potential for neighbours. Total privacy.

We are away from the river now, around the other side of the house. The Sleeping Beauty forest still lies between us and the garden, but there is a path of sorts, cut to wind its way through the historic parkland. A small, white cross is driven into the ground beside the path.

The sight of the cross brings us up short. A cross in the ground can only mean one thing, and I'm not sure that I want to hear it.

'An old lady died here,' Trevor explains. 'She suffered from dementia and wandered off. She became disorientated, and was dead a week before they found her.'

An anonymous tragedy, but shocking nonetheless. I look at the house again, a little more thoughtful. The minutes tick by. I know very well that finding the cross is the sort of thing that could easily and permanently put me off a place. Who wants to think of the sadness of a lost and dying woman? And who wants to think of a badly decomposed body being discovered on the outskirts of their garden?

Ian is looking at me with these same questions in his eyes, but I know my enthusiasm about the house is too new and too great to be easily dented. All qualms are firmly pushed away. 'I want to get inside,' I say.

But it's almost dark now, too late for agents, too late to hammer on strangers' doors, however strong the inducement. Reluctantly we leave.

Back at Trevor's, more champagne seems called for.

'So,' asks Ian, 'you think they'd sell?'

Trevor shrugs. 'It's what I've heard. But remember what I told you about the walls.'

I sip my drink. I couldn't care less what the walls are doing. 'How are we going to get inside if it's not listed for sale?'

'I know some people,' says Trevor, 'who might get you in.'

CHAPTER 2

GETTING IN

I SLEEP REALLY BADLY, like a child waiting for Santa. I toss and turn, and spin in the sheets, willing my brain to flick the 'off' switch. If only I can sleep, it will be morning all the sooner. But I can't, and the more I urge myself the more impossible it becomes.

The motel pillows are thin and hard, and require regular pummelling for even a suspicion of plumpness. The room stinks of carpet deodoriser, and we're breathing recycled air from the ancient throbbing machine mounted on the wall. I imagine pools of filthy water in condensation troughs and dust-clogged vents.

Ian is having similar trouble, huffing and puffing and turning from side to side. But we don't speak. Acknowledging we're awake will be the end of hope for both of us. Finally, close to dawn, I achieve thin, weak dozing, then we're up, swigging tea and running for the shower.

Though neither of us has said it, there's a distinct feeling that this could be the first day of the rest of our lives. A day of decision, of selecting the path we intend to stay on forever. Having been pathless for so long, the idea is momentous, the possibility exhilarating. Not that either of us have faltered in our desire to make Maryborough home. It's an appealing town, rich with history and it's the right distance from Montville. It even has connections to Ian's mother who, as a girl on Delubra cattle station near Mundubbera, used to travel to Pialba, adjacent to present day Hervey Bay, for her annual holidays. In their horse-drawn buggy, her family would pass through Maryborough, and she never forgot the beautiful buildings she saw there, years later telling Ian, *you must go to the town of Maryborough, there are so many lovely old houses.* Today, there's a feeling we might discover something that we can't step back from, a feeling that our hearts are going to be committed.

We're both aware that some people might define what we're doing as running away. Perhaps we are, but we don't see the wrong in it. The overwhelming majority of our friends and family have been supportive, encouraging us from the beginning of our relationship, and encouraging still in our quest to make a new start, find a new home, build a new future. But there have been one or two not quite so generous.

Ian is better at ignoring this than me. I find it hurtful and hard to understand. We are two survivors of difficult and sad times. It confuses me that anyone might not rejoice to see a happy ending for such a traumatised pair. I wonder whether my Divorced Status is an issue for more conservative souls, or whether there is a feeling in some quarters that Ian moved on too quickly from his first marriage. It must be stated that Ian's finding someone else with apparent ease and speed is in no way a reflection of how he felt about his first marriage. On the contrary, he and Jenny were very happily married, and it was terrible for him to watch her suffer a long terminal illness. But there are those just not designed to be on their own, and Ian is top of the list.

He is fun-loving, gregarious and easily bored. He can't stand it if I so much as fall asleep on the sofa or in front of the TV, leaving him awake on his own. Ian needs a lover, a soul mate, a companion at his side at all times. He doesn't like me reading books or doing the crossword, he wants me forever awake, alert and participating in his work, rest and play. I must – and do – rap him over the knuckles when I need a moment's peace. It's unimaginable for a creature like Ian to live out his life alone.

I've a suspicion that those one or two raising their righteous eyebrows are all in safe, stable situations themselves. They have no inkling of how it feels to be grabbed by fate and thrown to the wolves. Perhaps, for some, it stretches their imagination to believe that Ian or I could spend so many years of our lives with one person, yet go on to find happiness with another. I have some difficulty getting my head around this. Do they also believe that the loss of a first baby leaves you incapable of loving your second child? Your third? Your fourth?

I try not to think uncharitable thoughts, but it's hard not to be stilted and reserved in the presence of disapprovers. And it's hard not to be impatient to find and follow our dream.

We show up on Trevor's doorstep indecently early.

Trevor takes us to meet Patrick and Elizabeth MacKenzie who, he is fairly sure, know the owners of Baddow House.

The MacKenzies are long time residents of Maryborough and slight acquaintances of Trevor's. They live at Mavisbank, one of Maryborough's oldest houses. It's a classic Queenslander: wooden walls, fretwork, tongue and groove ceilings, charming verandahs, a warren of fascinating little rooms crammed with more treasures than I've ever seen in such a confined space. They've been working on this amazing collection for years and Mavisbank is open to the public as a museum.

Patrick and Elizabeth look the part in their home of yesteryear. Patrick puts me in mind of a nineteenth century preacher from the Wild West: tall and broad, with shoulder-length grey hair and a full beard. He looks strong, but is gentle, quiet and very well-mannered. I can imagine him in a black frock coat, leading his straggling flock in *Abide with Me* on a windswept prairie. We learn later that Patrick likes to do things the 'old way', including the digging of his own well.

Elizabeth wanted a supply of fresh water for the garden, and divined a suitable spot with her willow stick before, shovel in hand, Patrick began to dig. And dig, and dig. When the shaft grew too deep and narrow to manoeuvre his shovel, he attached two empty peach cans to lengths of string. The shaft was only the width of his shoulders, no degree of bending was possible, so he manipulated the cans with his bare feet, scooping them full of moist dirt which was then hauled to the surface.

As the shaft sank deeper, the air grew poorer. But, with ingenious bending of the 'old way' rules, Patrick lowered the vacuum cleaner down to suck out the foul air, thereby displacing fresh air to his level. He dug to a depth of seven metres and was rewarded with a bore so plentiful he was knocked off his feet by the jet of water.

Elizabeth is gentle, gracious and dreamy. She wears her long hair either loose down her back or swept up carelessly to the top of her head when it's hot. Elizabeth always favours long, floaty dresses. She is plagued by the Queensland heat, as I imagine those ladies of yesteryear must have been in their layered clothing and high-necked gowns. Her love of her home and collection is a pleasure to behold.

Patrick agrees to take us down to meet the owners of Baddow House, but first he shows us around Mavisbank. Their collection is a wonder, and Patrick's big paws handle each and every item with reverence as we wander from room to room. It's fascinating, but I don't want to do this now, I want to come back another day, a different time. Selfishly, guiltily, I am driven by the desire to get out of Mavisbank and into Baddow House. I want to shout at Patrick to hurry up.

⊱—◈—○—◈—⊰

At last Ian, Patrick and I arrive at Baddow House. My heart is thudding as we walk from the car toward the house. I've never felt this way about a building before and am a bit confused as to why it matters *so* much.

There's a mature poinciana tree over our heads as we enter the property, and several jacarandas deeper into the garden. I glimpse a familiar leaf here and there in the tangled shrubbery and grow excited when I spot a rondeletia, then a bird of paradise. Neither are in flower so early in autumn, but I recognise their leaves. So many of my favourites. I take it as a sign.

Inevitably, my attention is drawn to the house. The wall facing the street is appalling. We can see that the house was once painted white, but is so black and discoloured we wonder if there has been a fire. Could it really get that way from grime and mildew alone?

The back door is open; relief surges through me. Someone is home. We have a chance of getting in.

A dog barks and a white bull terrier lumbers toward us. It's old and fat, but I still get Ian between it and my calves. A woman materialises at the open door. She is unsmiling, suspicious. I don't think she is used to strangers calling. But she recognises Patrick.

Introductions are performed and Ian, in his element, flashes his legendary smile and says, 'We hear you might be interested in selling.'

Jan Christiansen, the owner, doesn't reply. I get a sense that she hates our intrusion.

He asks again.

'We might.' She's looking from one to the other of us, even Patrick, like we've come to steal her children. Ian, still smiling, apologises for the intrusion and asks, given that the place might be for sale, if we might not take a short look around.

There's a moment of hostile silence. It's obvious she doesn't want us there, but she's hesitating, thinking. I guess prospective buyers are thin on the ground when it comes to houses where outside walls are moving away from inside walls. I hold my breath.

'You'll have to take it as you find it,' she says at last. This is delivered like an accusation. We should have phoned, booked an appointment. I do understand. Anybody would prefer to spruce their place up a bit before potential purchasers take a look inside. What baffles me is how much notice she would have liked us to give, for this crumbling edifice to be brought into an inspectable state. 'You can look round the outside first,' she tells us, 'I'll be in the kitchen.' Then she turns on her heel and vanishes into the dark and mysterious interior.

'There are some rather awful cracks in the walls,' Patrick warns in a low aside as we set off.

Up close, the house looks even more fascinating. There are huge windows filled with rusty iron louvres in the first section we pass. It's a ten-metre-tall, square construction, looking very un-Australian. The flat roof has a parapet with castellated corners. Later, Ian and I christen this 'the Keep'.

We move on. The doors and windows are enormous, everything on such a grand scale. The windows have great stone slab sills. I see cracks here and there; some hairline, some that could be described as rather more than hairline. They fracture the rendered mouldings and snake out from corners of windows and doors, branching in patterns like bronchial tubes. But I'm beginning to inwardly smile. The structural problems of the house have been grossly exaggerated. What brick and render home wouldn't have a few fine cracks here and there?

We pass the pillared portico over the front door. It's ugly: square, flat-roofed and quite out of place. 'That's not original is it?' Ian asks.

'No, a later addition,' Patrick explains. 'There used to be verandahs all around, upstairs and down, but they were pulled down years ago. The porch was added as a new main entrance.'

We nod as we listen to his commentary. *The porch will have to go*, I'm thinking and, all the while, trying to soak in as much as I can in the short time we're going to be allowed. In my stomach there's a tight knot of excitement and fear. It's amazing that something this wonderful might fall into our hands, but I'm terrified that life could be cruel enough to dangle so desirable a fruit then pull it away.

We round the northern corner of the house and my jaw hits my chest. I reel back, dizzy with shock and disappointment. When I finally tear my eyes from the gaping chasm that almost severs the house in half from roof to ground, I look at Ian and see my reaction mirrored on his face.

'This is probably the worst of the cracks,' says Patrick dryly.

There's a short silence. I'm thinking, *well, I guess that's that then, we may as well go home. I might be a maniac who lets her heart overrule her head, but Ian has far more sense.*

Ian, however, is strolling toward the western corner of the house, looking again, eyes running up and down the ten-metre walls. I scamper after him, fresh hope daring to dawn. Ian hasn't given up.

'People in England repair all sorts of ruins,' I say, seizing his moment of madness. 'Think about all those houses that are hundreds of years old, remember Aunty Dorothy's house – that's five hundred years old if it's a day. People renovate roofless barns, they fix up old keeps in Scotland that are just a few crumbling walls without a *suspicion* of a roof . . .' I jabber on in this vein until proximity to the owner, Jan, shuts me up. We are about to go inside.

It's cool but cluttered, dark and filthy. Jan and her husband, Barry, have been living upstairs while downstairs housed their museum. The museum collection is still in evidence, but the public hasn't seen it for a very long time. The place has been closed up for years.

We find a room crammed with a thousand dusty dolls. It's so packed we can't get past the open doorway and have to stand in the corridor peering in. We see a 'pub' lined with shelves filled with old bottles and canisters. We see antiques to boggle our eyes, but there's a real *Marie Celeste* feeling to it all. I'm very sure that Jan and Barry never enter these rooms, that the only things left to disturb the dust and breathe the stale air are spiders and cockroaches.

The windows are all nailed shut and shrouded with heavy curtains. Kept closed, Jan tells us, to keep the light from damaging her valuable antiques.

Jan is thawing, giving a little commentary. As our eyes adjust to the dark, we see that the ceilings are very high. 'Fourteen feet,' she tells us with pride. We are suitably impressed, and we are very excited to see that the doors, architraves, window frames and skirting boards are all made of mature red cedar. But everything is draped in a grey, silken mantle of webs, dust and mildew: an asthmatic's hell, I'm thinking, but luckily neither Ian nor I are sufferers.

We wander from room to room in the sort of hush that overcomes you in the State Library or the British Museum. I think we are overwhelmed by the house, but also much too afraid to discuss anything in front of Jan in case we give our enthusiasm away.

We find ourselves in a vast dining room with a magnificent hearth and deep mantelpiece of carved red cedar. Again the curtains are closed, it's hard to see the details.

'Do you have any ghosts?' I ask. I'm kidding, of course. Who believes in ghosts these days? Ian flicks an *oh my God, I can't believe you just said that* sort of a look at me, but Jan just smiles tightly and says 'No, there are no ghosts at Baddow House.'

I, too, can't believe I've asked such a stupid, immature question and feel slightly embarrassed. Ian continues to cast me penetrating looks; worried, no doubt, that I'm going to put Jan's back up. But I've learned my lesson. My lips are now sealed.

We move on to the living room, location of the Big Crack. Though the walls are a foot thick, you can stand in this room and admire the garden through the gaping chasm. I can also see daylight where the floorboards meet the walls, and realise that the floor slopes downhill in a somewhat alarming fashion. I decide not to mention this to Ian.

Happily Ian has spotted the red cedar staircase and I feel

a wave of confidence return, as I know Ian goes demented with excitement over mature red cedar and is going to have trouble resisting this. The four of us mount the stairs, which are half-covered by an ancient, stained, frayed and moth-eaten carpet runner. *That'll have to go*, I'm thinking, *what a travesty to cover the cedar.*

Upstairs is lighter, the windows less shrouded. This is where Jan and Barry have been living. We discover French doors that open to a sheer, spine-chilling, seven-metre drop to the ground.

'There used to be verandahs upstairs and down,' explains Jan. 'They were removed in 1940, so that the iron could be donated to the war effort.' I'm shocked by the thought of stripping verandahs off this beautiful building to make bullets and missiles. No wonder the place looks so unhappy. No wonder the air of heavy sadness. It's a house in mourning. I think of young men's breasts pierced by bullet-shaped bits of Baddow's verandahs and want to weep.

We move on to the bedrooms. Two are large enough to host a game of football. There are six altogether, but used to be five. One room has been divided into two with a makeshift wall that doesn't even reach the ceiling. Another mental demolition note. There are fireplaces everywhere.

The lone bathroom occupies the top floor of the Keep. I'm expecting a horror but it's brighter, cleaner and more recently painted than any other part of the house. 'There used to be backstairs from here, running down the exterior wall of the house,' Jan tells us, 'the maids' stairs.' Built in a day when master and mistress did not want to be forever encountering servants in their path.

All the while Ian and I are touching doors, examining floorboards, running our hands over the flaking paintwork. The wood is parched from years of neglect. Some of the floorboards are almost grey. Jan tells us that the house stood empty through much of the 1950s, and was badly vandalised. Windows were smashed, letting rain pour through to soak the floor.

We go back downstairs. Our tour has finished. I am certain I want this place more than I've ever wanted anything before. In my euphoria, I couldn't care less about cracks, chasms and sinking floors. I'm not a hundred per cent sure why. Yes, it's an amazing, grand old home that could be made just so again, with enough money, enthusiasm and effort. But my yearning goes beyond that. There's a feeling here that just grabs me and won't let go. The house needs me and I need the house. It's the start of a love affair I never want to end.

But I want Ian to love it too. We are a team. I wonder if I'm greedy, wanting the house as well as Ian.

We farewell Patrick with heartfelt thanks, then we are off.

'Well?' I say, the minute the car moves forward.

'Well what?' says Ian, tormenting me.

'What did you think?'

'About what?'

One of Ian's favourite games is teasing me. I'd hit him if he weren't driving.

'What did you think of the house?' I bite out.

'What did *you* think?'

'I asked first.'

'Ladies first.'

Another favourite game is to make me spill my guts about something before he'll utter a word of his own opinion, so that I'm committed to a confessed sentiment before he has had to expose an iota of his own feelings. I want to tease him back, but I'm too excited to prolong the game. I'm silent a minute, we both know I'll give in.

'I love it!' I blurt. 'I want it and I'll buy it myself even if you're not interested.'

Ian knows I could afford to buy the house, but he also knows I'd have trouble financing the indescribable number of necessary repairs without a partner. He tells me this.

'I don't care,' I say, and mean it. 'I'll live in it as it is, cracks and all.'

'You'd do that?'

'Yes! Yes! Yes!'

'You'd really live in it as it is?'

'Absolutely.'

There's a second or two of silence.

'I'd clean it, of course,' I add. 'I don't mind scruffy and dilapidated, but I don't like dirty.'

More silence.

I look at him, a bit annoyed. This game is no longer novel, and beginning to test my stretched nerves. 'So what about you?'

'I bloody love it!' he shouts so loudly I half-jump off the seat with fright. 'Did you see all that cedar? My God, not just the doors and skirting boards, but the whole stair-case! It's all cedar, never been painted over, do you know how rare that is? For decades people were painting over that quality of woodwork, but at Baddow it has escaped – probably because of neglect, no one's ever renovated the house. Did you see the height of the ceilings? What about the size of the rooms, the view of the river from upstairs – of course we'll have to put the verandahs back on.'

I melt into my seat with delight. Ian is off and running, his brain flying with ideas that are music to my ears. In my head, we're there already, it's all clean, repaired and painted. The garden is a botanic riot of luxurious colour. I'm stepping out of the French doors upstairs and strolling about the verandah, inhaling the sweet jasmine, sipping tea, watching the river flow by.

'Of course we'll have to get geological tests done on the subsidence problem that's caused all those cracks before we consider it further.'

Reality returns with a thump. I know he's right. I know we can't go careering into this thing without due caution. And I know we might get told things that will make it un-acceptable to proceed. Property is Ian's game. He's made a living out of investing in land, shops and houses. He knows heaps more than I do about this sort of thing, and it's obvious we'll need his steady head to stop me running away with the irresponsible enthusiasm I'm currently experiencing.

'Remember how they repair ruins in England,' I say again. 'Remember Aunty Dorothy's house . . .'

'The soil in Maryborough is clay, the worse sort of ground to build such a large brick building on.'

'It's survived a long time, since 1883.'

'Yes, and according to Patrick the cracks only became serious about ten years ago following a very dry season. We'll have to check for termites too, get under the roof, look for dry rot, check the foundations.'

The journey back to Montville flies. We talk nonstop. We don't even stop for our usual chocolate.

CHAPTER 3

NEGOTIATION AND ACQUISITION

BEFORE WE ARE willing to part with good dollars to pay geologists, engineers, building inspectors, termite inspectors and the thousand other people necessary to our peace of mind, we have to know if Jan and Barry will actually sell us Baddow House.

We arrange a date with them.

I'm itching to get into the house again, but nervous about the outcome. We head off at the crack of dawn, and the drive north is a nail biting two-hour drag. We try to buoy each other up with excited chatter, but our nerves are stretched taut, and we keep falling silent. We arrive at Baddow at eight o'clock. Jan and Barry invite us in to commence negotiation.

Negotiation is Ian's forte. I have promised to keep my mouth shut tight so as not to put my foot in it. I'm very likely to betray excessive keenness, and have been told to maintain a meek, hangdog sort of a look.

We soon realise that, though Jan and Barry really do

want to sell, having already bought another house else-where, as professional antique dealers, they are seasoned wheelers, dealers and negotiators. Our one weapon is the dawning suspicion that Barry is a lot keener to sell than Jan.

Ian makes an offer. Jan, as expected, refuses. I stare at the ground. Discussion occurs, cases are pleaded, faults in the house are pointed out. Back and forth we go. Back and forth. Nothing is achieved.

We stop now and again and talk about other things. They tell us about the cellar beneath the old kitchen that's all filled in now and about the legendary tunnel to the river that no one's been able to find. There is an impressive trap-door in the cupboard under the stairs which they show us, but it only gets you into the crawl space beneath the entrance hall floorboards.

They also show us the original water tanks: domed brick structures that, like icebergs, sit mostly beneath the surface. All we can see is the curve of the brick tops above ground. They are huge: six metres deep and almost as wide.

We go back inside. Further discussion occurs. Barry throws Jan the odd pleading look, but Jan won't budge. I begin to fear that pride might prevent both Ian and Jan from backing down. I think the house is worth every cent of the asking price, but have promised not to say so.

We stop for lunch. Ian and I go to the pub in town for an hour.

I'm all jittery. With any other house, I could let myself believe that it's not the end of the world; that if an agree-ment couldn't be reached, another place would come up.

But there isn't another Baddow House and Baddow House is calling me.

We return. Nothing is achieved. Back and forth go the words again. At one point Barry lets out a desperate, 'Do you want to sell this house or not, Jan?'

We stop for a cup of tea. Then Ian says, 'Anne and I need to talk alone,' so we move into the garden while Jan and Barry disappear deep into the house. Much whispering and conferring goes on.

Outside, Ian and I stand under the guava trees at the back of the house. We're directly opposite the Big Crack, and it occurs to me, facing Ian – facing the devastated wall – that over the last few years, between us, we have done danger, loneliness and hardship. We've done fear, struggle and loss. Acquiring and mending a broken house is a very minor thing against all these earlier trials. It is simple, a matter of some trivia, and the dollar difference at this stage of our negotiations is small. I voice my thoughts.

Suddenly we're smiling, clasping hands. 'Whatever it takes,' says Ian.

I nod. 'Whatever it takes.'

Sealed with a kiss.

We find the others. Negotiation recommences. We're close, I'm scenting victory, trying not to smile. Ian suggests paying the price Jan and Barry seem stuck on if they throw in a couple of pieces of the old furniture. There are a few items in their possession that belonged to the family of Edgar Aldridge, original owner of Baddow House. It seems appropriate that these pieces stay.

It is the catalyst.

At four in the afternoon, eight hours after our arrival, we are shaking hands with Jan and Barry. There are smiles all round.

I almost dissolve with relief.

><+◆>-०-<◆+><

Back in Montville, we ring our children. Ian has four: Dinie, Georgie, David and Annabel, I have three: Andrew, Elizabeth and Robert. They descend in age in that order, from Dinie, Ian's eldest at twenty-seven, to Robert, my youngest at seventeen. If they all still lived at home, we'd be bigger than the Brady Bunch, but the entire seven have flown their respective nests. Four are in Australia, three are overseas, five are now working, two – my youngest, Elizabeth and Robert – are still at university.

Our discovery of a huge and unique old wreck of a house is not our only piece of news. We have to tell them all that we plan to move in together. Ian and I have been a couple for some two and a half years at this stage, engineering every possible moment in that time to be together, seldom passing a day when we haven't seen each other. But this is not the same as Moving In.

I'm a bit nervous about telling my children. My eldest, Andrew, is over in Italy, teaching English at a language school in Venice, the university students are in Brisbane. I call the Brisbane ones first, then spend two days tracking down the elusive Andrew.

I'm not sure why I'm quite so nervous. My children have known Ian slightly since childhood, have come to know him much more over the past couple of years, and are, happily for me, genuinely warm in their acceptance of him in my life. Perhaps there's a sense of guilt that I haven't managed to follow the straight and narrow path that my own parents followed, that I'm not married to my children's father, presenting a united and solid front of respectability to the world. I've made mistakes, been impetuous, muddled along, done my best but been imperfect.

None of my children have ever given any indication that they wished things could have been different. They've been loyal, supportive, my best friends as well as my children. It's a huge relief when they welcome the news. They just want me to be happy and, if living in Maryborough with Ian is what I want to do, then they are right behind me. I'm proud of their mature and selfless attitude, and can't wait to show them Baddow House.

Ian is nervous too. His children took the loss of their mother very hard, it hasn't been easy for them to watch him move into a new life with someone else. He makes his calls, and believes all the children are accepting. But it's hard to tell, hard to know what's really going on in everyone's heart of hearts.

>-+·+>-·0-·<+·+-<

Ian and I have to drive to north Queensland for the twenty-first birthday of his niece. Ian wants to stop in Maryborough on the way, to meet our local councillor and find out what plans are in the pipeline for the Baddow House area. Though Trevor has told us the land surrounding the house is deemed an historic site, never to be built on, we know we should get official confirmation of this.

It's a month since we signed the contract, another month till the house is ours and we can move in. We've already commissioned a multitude of building, termite and soil tests, but this is our first trip back up to Maryborough.

That we arrive a little early is not entirely accidental. The pull of Baddow is magnetic. How could we contemplate driving all this way and not sneaking another look at the house? It's unlikely that the Christiansens will welcome this visit, which is understandable, given that they must be busy packing and sorting decades of their lives into boxes, but we show up anyway.

When we reach the house we see that both their car and van are missing. This is good news and bad. If they are out we won't be able to get inside the house, but at least we will be able to wander about the exterior unwatched. We can take our time, soak up the feel of the place, and we can peer in windows.

We do exactly this. It's wonderful to saunter unhurried about the garden, identifying trees and shrubs, deciding what will stay and what will go, making wild and extravagant plans, listening to the birds in the park, acquainting ourselves with our new environment.

Unlike Ian, I feel very much a trespasser and, despite my happy contemplation of the garden, can't help throwing regular nervous glances toward the road. Ian's attitude is, as always, more cavalier than mine. 'Don't be so English about it,' he keeps telling me, 'the house is as good as ours anyway.' I try to relax.

Ian loves to bait me about my English background which, in his eyes, renders me a correct, polite, law-abiding little citizen worthy of regular teasing. That I was raised in a military environment exacerbates this Englishness in me: excessive punctuality is in my genes, playing by the rules, telling the truth, holding justice and good manners as utterly sacred. The wild colonial boy at my side believes rules were meant to be bent, and gets a kick out of bending them. I know he'd be inside the house in a flash if there had been a window left open. Thankfully they're all nailed shut.

On the western side we can see the river clearly. Having a view of the river is an immense bonus, one that seems almost too good to be true. I have an intrepid, tight-knit, lap-swimming group of friends back in Montville, who love to test uncharted waters. Every year when our local pool closes for winter, we take ourselves to the deep, black vast-ness of the Baroon Pocket Dam. Some days we just round a few buoys, but some days we swim to the other side. What a startling sight we must present to shivering, rugged-up picnickers as we emerge: wild women in our togs, caps and goggles, water weed and blue-green algae clinging to our ample forms. Creatures from the black lagoon.

Today it occurs to me that the Mary River is *particularly* murky and I am aware of a slight wavering of my river swimming keenness. I push it aside to focus on other, more exciting things.

Strolling the environs of my soon-to-be home, I'm expe-riencing a flicker of hope that I might be able to write again. Writing has been one of the greatest joys of my life, but the words dried up along with my marriage.

My last novel, *The Legend of Creag Mhor*, translated in Europe as *Der Schwarze Highlander (The Black High-lander)*, took a tortuous four years to produce; four times as long as my previous books. Every sentence, every word, was wrung out of me with sweat, tears and not a little blood. It was like giving birth with everything going wrong: the baby too big, upside down, sideways, cord round its throat, no doctor, midwife out of town. Even the consolation of being told it was the best work I'd ever produced didn't enable me to continue as a writer.

Divorce, with all its unfortunate trappings, plus the death of a parent, the loss of a close friend, juggling single motherhood, trying to make a new home, to fend for myself, earn a living when the words had dried up: these are all problems for the head, or so I thought.

It came as a massive shock to me when I discovered how emotional dramas could manifest as physical symptoms. Fit, healthy, invincible me, watching my blood pressure soar, my hair come out in clumps, waking up in the morning with every muscle and sinew so stiff that walking downstairs was a slow, painful experience. I'd always believed I was above and beyond such frailties. Strong in both mind and body, better equipped than most to triumph over adversity.

A close friend and staunch member of the swimming girls, who is also a general practitioner, told me that I was one of the sanest people she'd ever known. I hugged those words tight through the bad days. When Ian burst into my life and the smile returned to my face, she admitted she couldn't understand why I hadn't gone under. 'We've all been waiting to catch the pieces,' she told me.

But I know I'm on the road to recovery and have been since Ian and I teamed up. I sense that Baddow House is going to complete that recovery. Can a house be a muse? I'm not so sure about that but when I look up at the soaring, battered walls of Baddow, I feel such a tug of affection and inspiration, I believe she could be mine.

Away from the road, in the back garden, Ian grabs an empty terracotta flowerpot and says, 'here, if you stand on this you'll be able to see inside.'

His words snap me out of my introspection. I eye the flowerpot, tempted. Most of the windows are heavily draped and afford no peeks, but a couple of panes in the living room are obscured only by thin netting.

Ian up-ends the flowerpot near the best window. I hang back. Fear of being caught wars with an almost overwhelming desire to get another look inside the house. He prods me in the ribs. 'Go on,' he says.

I can't resist. With my nose pressed to the glass and hands cupped to block out the light, I can just make out the interior of the living room. Excitement dulls my apprehension and sense of guilt and I'm soon visualising the joyful furnishing of the room.

But a solid edifice the size of Baddow House is extremely soundproof, and from the far side of the house we don't hear the Christiansens' van return home. It is the intensity of their stares we sense first. Then I'm off the flowerpot, nearly breaking my ankle in the unwieldiness of my leap. My face is burning with shame, my throat too tight for words.

Ian comes to the rescue. 'Barry! Jan!' he says, and strides toward them, hand outstretched as though we'd expected them all along. 'Thought you'd be home soon. Hope you don't mind us dropping in to see you. But we've driven up to see Councillor Hovard. Pity to come all this way and not say hi.'

Barry is relaxing a bit, but Jan's entire being is throbbing with hostility. I really don't blame her. I'd be a bit annoyed if I caught someone climbing on flowerpots to look inside my house. All I can think of is escape, but to bolt now would only confirm what they're already suspecting: that we shamelessly seized our chance to snoop.

'If we'd had your number,' I say, 'we would have tried to call you, but I'm afraid we left it in Montville. This was all very spur of the moment.'

Jan still hasn't spoken, but Barry and Ian are starting to chat. Ian is asking about stormwater drains and underground pipes, all relevant questions to be asking of Barry. Our visit starts to seem more legitimate.

'I expect you'll be sorry to leave this garden,' I say to Jan, desperate to appease, 'I can see you've done a lot of work here.'

To my relief, Jan starts to unbend. We chat for a respectable few minutes, then make our excuses and leave for Barbara Hovard's house.

Barbara is the Maryborough city councillor for Division Four, the suburb of Baddow. She later becomes our mayor. Barbara was born and raised in Maryborough. She loves her town and is truly passionate about caring for its future. The hospitality she shows us is appreciated, considering we don't yet live in Maryborough, and she is more than happy to discuss what's earmarked for the farmland adjacent to the park and Baddow House.

We learn that, though some of the farmland beyond the park will one day be developed for housing, as Trevor said, the park itself won't be touched, being the site of the first township, the village of Wide Bay, settled in 1848. Barbara tells us that shortly after first settlement, the village of Wide Bay was renamed Maryborough by order of Governor Fitz Roy to commemorate his wife, the Lady Mary, killed in a carriage accident at Government House, Parramatta.

In those early days, the township consisted of a cluster of slab huts, several inns and a few sly grog shops. There were pits for sawing timber on the river flats and a shingled-roofed church further up the hill that doubled as a school house during the week. Today, none of these buildings remain, however the site is of great historic significance and will never be developed. This is exactly what we want to hear confirmed, because it is the park, wrapping around Baddow House, that gives such a feeling of peace and privacy.

Barbara is pleased and grateful that someone intends to renovate Baddow House, and tells us all of Maryborough will feel the same way. Ian and I are fast realising that the decline and neglect of this Maryborough icon has been a huge source of grief for the locals. 'Of course you have your very own ghost,' she adds, all blithe and smiling.

Now, Ian and I are far too mature to believe in ghosts but *we don't want to hear this*. I think our faces express how unwelcome the words are. It is not mentioned again. Barbara would not like to scare us off. She loves her town, is justifiably proud of its history, and who knows how long it would be before someone else was willing to take on Baddow House?

⊢⊣⊹·○·⊹⊢⊣⊂

'What did you think about the ghost thing?' I ask.

We're back in the car, heading north.

'It's rubbish,' says Ian.

'You don't believe in ghosts, do you?'

'Of course not. Do you?'

'Of course not.'

'Remember "the Deal".'

I nod vigorously. 'The Deal' is that I enter into our future at Baddow house in the full knowledge that once a week Ian has to drive to Montville for business commitments. His commercial property investments in Montville and adjacent Maleny are Ian's bread and butter. They need constant attention. Every week I will be on my own for one or two nights. If I can't promise to hack it, the whole Baddow House adventure is off.

'It's just that it's a big old house with long dark corridors, and it's all neglected looking,' I say, more to reassure myself.

'That's right. Any fool might say it was haunted.'

'It looks like something Norman Bates might live in,' I add. For people with children less keen on scary movies than mine, I should explain that Norman Bates is the guy with the dead mother who stabs a woman to death in the shower scene in *Psycho*. I explain this to Ian.

We change the subject.

Test results start to filter in. The north-western end of the house has subsided approximately five centimetres, which is a lot, hence the shocking cracks. As Ian pointed out, the house is sitting on clay which expands and contracts with fluctuating moisture levels. Underpinning is necessary to be sure the foundations are sitting on the stable load bearing soil that has been found two metres down.

We learn that the removal of the verandahs was disastrous for the house. It exposed the clay to the full impact of the elements: the long dry season, the flooding rains of summer. Structural problems were inevitable.

Removal of the verandahs also condemned doors and windows never meant to face the weather to be continually drenched and sun-blasted. Many window frames are totally rotted out. Restoration of the verandahs is strongly recommended.

There is evidence of termite activity, but none living. It has been dealt with in the past, but could reoccur. Annual checks are recommended.

The roof is reasonable. We might get five years out of it. More importantly all the batons and trusses beneath the roof are in good condition.

Something called 'tie rods' are recommended by the engineer to control the bowing of the walls triggered by the subsidence. This means we have to thread metal rods from one side of the house to the other and clamp them to plates on the exterior walls. These can be tightened as much as we like to grip the house together and stop further spread of the walls.

The cracks will have to be repaired inside and out, the house will have to be repainted inside and out, much of the wooden joinery will have to be replaced or repaired, the floorboards will have to be repaired, sanded and oiled, the house needs rewiring and a new kitchen will have to be built.

The job is huge but not impossible.

Craven ideas tempt us, of getting major work done before we move in. It's enticing to avoid living in untold amounts of mess and debris, inhaling paint dust that's probably laced with lead.

But we know there is only one way to get things done the way we want them done. We have to be there.

CHAPTER 4

MOVING IN

It's Friday, 29 August 2003, moving day, and I'm almost beside myself with excitement. I've been packed for weeks, counting down the days. Now I'm counting down the hours, the minutes.

We have decided to camp in the empty house for a few days to give it a good clean before the furniture arrives. Much easier to clean an empty house.

We travel up in Ian's ute with our cleaning gear in the back. Also the fridge, stepladder, two fold-up chairs, a couple of bottles of champagne, some bread and cheese and a chamber pot. It pours with rain all the way up and I make Ian stop on the highway to put a tarp over the fridge.

When we arrive in Maryborough, the sun comes out just as we drive under the poinciana tree. *Our* poinciana tree. It's another sign.

There is a minor crisis when Jan and Barry break the news that settlement is delayed because of a legal hitch their end and that we will have to go away and wait another three days.

We point out that we *have* to be there: we have cleaners lined up for the weekend; we have a termite killer lined up; we have packed and driven all the way to Maryborough, for heaven's sake! Eventually they weaken and give us the keys, emphasising all the while that the house is not officially ours till Monday. Ian and I don't care. At last we are alone in Baddow House. It's indescribably thrilling. We run around exploring rooms, bolting up and down the stairs, hanging out of windows. It's the first time we've seen the house more or less empty and the first time we've been allowed in without an escort.

We examine our new pieces of Baddow furniture. There is a large washstand with a thick marble top and little wooden spindles running along the back above the tiles. I wonder how many people have leaned over its marble surface to splash water on their faces in the hundred and fifty or so years since it came to Maryborough. A mulberry and white wash jug and bowl have been left with it.

There is an inlaid octagonal table in the dining room. Its proportions are fine, the pattern of the inlay intricate. I decide this is a ladies' table and later am excited to spot it in a grainy photograph of the ladies' drawing room taken at Baddow in Aldridge days. In the entrance hall is a mirrored, red cedar sideboard that didn't belong to the Aldridge family, but has been included in the list because it is an early Maryborough piece. Ian particularly loves this. Its proportions are hefty, a more manly item than the delicate inlaid table, with chunky, ornate corbels supporting its weathered cedar surface.

Lastly there's a piano in the dining room, complete with

patterned inlay and brass candle holders. We learn it was made in the 1860s. My youngest son, Robert, who makes music on anything, be it animal, vegetable or mineral, will be delighted with this acquisition. I experience a stab of pity for this piano, which has surely been enjoying a quiet retirement – it's in for the shock of its life.

Our exploration of the house continues into the afternoon. There are some surprises, but nothing too dire. The interior walls are in a worse state than we realised. There are huge damp, mouldy patches exposed by the removal of Jan and Barry's furniture. Doors are sagging on hinges, there are doors missing, one door has been cut in half, windows that won't open, rotten windows, missing skirting boards, loose skirting boards, missing mantelpieces, vandalised fireplaces and everywhere – *everywhere* – cracks and holes in the walls and chunks of loose plaster. But I'm in a state of euphoria and offer up a silent prayer of thanks to Edgar Aldridge.

⊳·⊹⊱·○·⊰⊹·⊲

Edgar Thomas Aldridge – 'ET', as he is affectionately known in Maryborough – built Baddow House in 1883. Aldridge's Castle, some called it, and it must have seemed like a castle compared to the rough bark shelters Aldridge would have known in 1848 when he first came north with the Palmer brothers and founded what was then known as the village of Wide Bay.

Henry Palmer later wrote: 'The arduous work then soon commenced of erecting buildings, and as labour was very scarce then, a good deal of the laborious work devolved on the pioneers who had to work like the Israelites of old *"with sword in hand, and so they builded".'*

Baddow House was Aldridge's third house on the site. He started off in a little earthen-floored hut made of wooden slabs with a shingled roof. But Edgar was astute, ambitious and hard-working. He quickly prospered and, when the first land sales were made in the village, he invested heavily and before long had built wharves, wool stores, the popular Bush Inn, a trading post and a number of other small buildings which he leased to less established settlers.

As he prospered, Aldridge built a second house for himself and wife, Maria. This was a long low-set building, much larger than the first, with wraparound verandahs and a detached kitchen. Quite palatial for its time and place.

Years slipped by and Aldridge's empire continued to expand. Before long he owned countless inns, hotels, houses, wool stores and wharves. He took up extensive pastoral leases at Toogoom, Booral and Fraser Island, where he bred Arab horses for the British Indian Army. Soon he was the largest employer in town.

Edgar's third and final house was a monument to his life of success and prosperity, and it was a gift for his Maria. But Maria died before Baddow House was completed. Edgar himself died less than two years later. Heartbroken, they say, unable to live without his adored Maria.

The house passed into the hands of Edgar's son, Harry, who, according to an article published in the *Sunday Mail Magazine* in 1989, was a 'lean and handsome colonial boy with a wild black beard and a lusty appetite for tinted gels and good horses'.

The story goes on to suggest that back when his father was still alive, Harry had seduced two Aboriginal girls and that when the girls told him they were pregnant, he 'saddled up the best horse on Baddow and bolted'.

According to the article, the girls had both been tutored by missionaries. They were Christians and they were familiar with European ways. Abandoned and pregnant, they went to Edgar.

Edgar had come from a well-to-do family in England. They were merchant bankers and Anglican clergy, and had an ancestry that could be traced back to Alfred the Great. Since arriving in the colony of New South Wales in 1839, Edgar, with his proud lineage, had set about building his own small empire.

The Aldridges were 'toffs, part of Maryborough's Anglican Establishment'. Edgar's reaction to the pregnancy situation was, therefore, the last thing the 'Establishment' expected. He astonished his world by demanding his boy marry one of the girls. It was a reaction that proved Edgar not only an empire-builder, but unusually humanitarian for his day and age.

Some details of the *Mail* magazine's story are clearly inaccurate. Records show that the first pregnancy happened many years before the second, for example. But it is fact that the pregnancies occurred, that the children were born, that Harry Aldridge married one of the girls, Lappie, and that the second girl was sent to another Aldridge property, where she and her daughter, Jessie, were cared for.

It is also fact that Harry Aldridge's marriage to Lappie was not easily achieved. In Maryborough, no minister would unite the mixed race couple. Harry and his bride were forced to take a ship to New Zealand where, I can only suppose, mixed marriages (such as between the Maoris and white settlers) were more common and easier to obtain than in the fledgling state of Queensland. Harry and Lappie returned to Maryborough as man and wife.

At first Harry and Lappie lived well at Baddow House, the Aldridge name ensuring Lappie was treated with the courtesy and respect she might not otherwise have received in a day when attitudes toward black skin were so marred by bigotry.

Sadly not all remained well. Whether Harry was less astute than his father or whether it was as a result of the great bank crash in the 1890s we can only guess, but after Edgar's death in 1888 the fortune he had amassed began to wane. Harry died in 1910 with a reputed nine pounds to his name. Two years later the banks repossessed Baddow House. Lappie and the now grown children were forced out.

Rumour has it that Harry's eldest daughter, Esse, was broken by the grief of having to leave her beloved home and wept bitter tears at the forced eviction. The story goes that as she wept she wandered the rooms of the house she would never enter again and wiped her tears onto the walls.

Today, surveying the cracked and crumbling walls, it's as though Esse's tears have melted the plaster.

Ian and I spend the day setting up our camp and getting organised. We've bought a new bed in Maryborough, to be delivered that day. It's a king-size bed. Neither of us have had a king-size bed before, but feel the proportions of the bedroom demand it. The deliverymen arrive just after lunch and kindly enquire if we know we have bought a haunted house.

We realise there is going to be no escape from this sort of thing. A few days before moving, a friend in Montville tells me she has grown up in Maryborough. 'Baddow House!' she exclaims, on hearing our news. 'I can't believe you have bought Baddow House. That is the Ghost House of my childhood!'

It is mid-afternoon. We have four people booked to come the next day to help clean, but tonight we just want to get down all the frayed and ragged curtains that pollute the rooms. Out comes the stepladder. There are thirty-eight windows in Baddow House, every one curtained. We are racing the clock and the last of the daylight. We know it will be all but impossible to work after dark. The light fittings are few and far between. And besides, though neither Ian nor I have mentioned the Approaching Night, each is aware of the unacknowledged thing we have to face. It lies between us, a tangible dread we try to conceal with our determined chatter, our busy hands, our cheery demeanour. We want to be finished, cleaned up and snug in our new bed at a safe, early hour. So we are quick, efficient, united in our purpose.

Some curtains appear to have once been red velvet, but now hang in faded, tattered, pink ribbons. Other, lace, curtains are less ruined but so clogged with dust, webs, dead insects and mould spores that we have to hold our breath as each is gently lowered to the ground. Ian stands on the stepladder and passes them to me one at a time. I am terrified I'll drop one and send clouds of choking muck into our lungs.

Daylight is beginning to fade as we drag the last of the curtains outside into the garden. Tomorrow they can go to the tip along with the garden gnomes we've discovered inhabiting the shrubbery.

I'm determined not to let darkness fall without locating every light switch in the house so as twilight descends I run around flicking them all on. The dusty, bare globes seem pathetically dim.

We are exhausted, filthy and starving. We decide to have showers before it's completely dark, then go out and get something to eat.

The nearest food is Red Rooster. As we pull up at the door, a woman in the car park starts yelling at us. We are befuddled and bone weary, and we have no idea why this total stranger is so angry with us. Ian winds down his window.

'You're in a handicapped zone!' she is yelling.

Shamefaced, we re-park and slink into the restaurant, hoping no one inside overheard the encounter. But I'm hopeful suddenly: if we're too tired to spot a handicapped zone maybe we'll be tired enough to sleep soundly through a night in the Ghost House of Maryborough.

'Hello Baddow!' shouts Ian, flinging open the front door with awesome force.

Lots of noise and movement are the key to confidence, we've decided, but our words echo in the hollow rooms, they disappear along passageways and are sucked up the stairwell. Though arriving before the furniture was a great idea so far as the cleaning goes, we begin to realise that entering a dimly lit, derelict, haunted house is a hundred times creepier when that house is bare and echoing.

'Hello!' roars Ian again and again. I know he's as scared as me, but he marches boldly forth, being all manly and brave. 'HELLO!' he bellows and I'm afraid if he 'Hello!'s one more time, he might provoke an answer.

We mount the cedar staircase talking and laughing, but our hearts pound and quail. What's wrong with us? Two sensible adults and we're spooked just because the house is old, decrepit, and everyone keeps telling us it's Ghost Central.

Are we men or mice?

Men, we are determined to be – at least one man and one woman.

I remember a dream I have had many times in my life, both as a child and an adult. I find an amazing old house for sale. It has turrets and grand staircases, great chambers with murals, reliefs and frescos. There are domed ceilings adorned with Renaissance art. But it's haunted. No one will buy it and it's oh so cheap. The dream becomes a battle of my will against my fear. I want the house, if only I can conquer the fear. There are some rooms I just can't enter. I open doors and try to cross thresholds, but there is always a wall of resistance so powerful I can't force my way through. I know this wall is constructed of a malignant evil and I'm terrified, but if I don't overcome my fear, I can't have the house.

Mounting the staircase at Baddow I sense no evil, but I am wretched and sweaty. I remember the Deal and wonder how I'm going to keep my part of the bargain.

We go to the only bathroom – such a long, long way from our bedroom – and clean our teeth. I can't bring myself to look in the mirror for fear of what I might see behind me. There is no way on this earth or another that either of us is going to be visiting the bathroom alone at night in the foreseeable future. Hence the precious chamber pot, safely stowed beside our new bed.

Ian falls instantly asleep. I control the urge to hit him. I was supposed to be allowed to go to sleep first, but now I'm alone in my wakefulness, rigid and perspiring, ears straining. I'm five years old again, believing in the pack of wolves beneath my bed. It's the same routine. Eyes tight shut, sheet up to chin, vulnerable arms and legs not allowed near the edge of the bed where danger lurks. But it's no longer wolves I fear, it's the weeping of Esse and the laughter of a lean and handsome colonial boy.

CHAPTER 5

SWEET MORNING

WE WAKE TO A glorious sunny day. Ian has had a slightly better night than my few hours of thin dozing, but we're both too excited to feel hungover or jaded and there is work to do so we spring out of bed. We have four people booked for two days to help us clean and we know they won't be late. There is a fresh skip in our step this morning. We have survived the night. If we can do it once, we can do it again – and again and again.

As soon as we've had a cup of tea, we dash into Andy's Foodstore, which is open all hours, and return with a bootload of powerful light globes. Ian is soon up the stepladder replacing and discarding what last night seemed like five or ten watters, if you can buy such things. Tonight we'll have the comfort of normal levels of brightness. Just as Ian is fitting the final globe, two cars pull up outside and we know the hard work is about to start.

Darren and Diane run a cleaning business in Maryborough and have bought along two others to help:

Diane's aunt, Nola, and Nola's husband, Cyril. There are greetings, handshakes, expressions of gratitude that they are willing to work on a Saturday, then the six of us commence the big clean up.

We scrub walls and fireplaces, wash chandeliers, kitchen cupboards, floors, doors, skirting boards, windows and every other available surface. Of course, our efforts are a Bandaid: with total renovation to face, the house is soon going to get worse than dirty, but we need to get the caked-on grime and stale, musty odours out if we are to live here during the renovation.

It's amazing how fast you can get things done with so many helpers. Twelve busy hands are cutting through this seemingly insurmountable task at a cracking rate. The first morning, we attack the living room. Darren and Diane are doing tricky, professional stuff up on ladders. Ian, Cyril and Nola concentrate on the finer details: skirting boards, doors, mantelpieces and chandeliers. I'm doing windows, dragging the extension ladder from one end of the room to the other as I go.

We've decided I'll just do the inside of the glass at this stage, which makes the job much easier, though the inside is a hundred times dirtier than the outside which has had the benefit of an occasional wash by the weather. I'm almost needing a garden trowel to shovel off the muck and suspect the glass is wearing the grime of decades. It takes several cleans of each window to get through the accumulated black grime, but I'm loving the satisfaction of making the glass sparkle then throwing open the windows to let in the first fresh air these rooms have enjoyed for years.

'We're going to need a general handyman,' says Ian, halfway through the morning. 'Someone who can fix all those little problems, not part of the main overhaul. Someone patient. Someone who understands old houses.'

Ian, although strong in the arm and always willing to work till he's the last man standing, knows he lacks the patience, skill and finesse to carry out these sorts of jobs.

'Sounds like you're describing Cyril,' says Darren.

'Cyril's a perfectionist,' adds Nola.

Ian and I beam at Cyril. Cyril, we already know, was once in the Air Force. Retired now, he has the sort of time on his hands we might need.

'There's just one problem,' says Nola, glancing at her husband.

Cyril looks down from the chandelier he's meticulously attending to, 'I only work for family,' he says, with an apologetic shake of the head, and returns to rubbing each and every dusty crystal till they are all glinting and gleaming.

Only family. We are disappointed. We've watched Cyril at work for hours. He's methodical, careful, with gentle hands and a keen eye. We know he's fascinated by the old house, drawn to it, as we are. We press him, but he will not bend his rules.

We work on, dragging our equipment from room to room, upstairs and down, stopping for tea breaks, returning to work, stopping, returning, but always chatting. It's wonderful to feel the house growing cleaner. It still looks an absolute fright, and will until the walls are repaired and painted, but it's beginning to smell fresh and the clouds of dust in the air have diminished.

On the second day we are all in the dining room, chatting as we work. I'm up my ladder doing more windows. Darren and Diane are also on ladders, balancing buckets on trestles, looking frighteningly like the main act of a Chinese circus as they wipe down our walls. Cyril is at the fireplace, caressing the ornate woodwork with a soft cloth and a touch of oil. Ian and Nola are crouched doing skirting boards. I don't like being up my ladder much. There have been a few wobbling incidents this morning that have challenged my nerves. I've got my eye on Ian's crouching-at-the-skirting-boards job. I know I'm better at crouching than Ian, whose chunky build seems to get in the way of useful flexibility, and am just about to ask him to swap jobs when I hear him ask Nola if she's always lived in Maryborough.

Nola shakes her head. 'We were in Mackay before we came here.'

'Hot up there,' remarks Ian.

'We've lived all over really,' she says, 'but originally I'm from Mundubbera.'

'A Mundubbera girl?' There's a grain of surprise in Ian's voice. 'Small world. My mother grew up in Mundubbera.'

'Oh,' says Nola, 'what was her name?'

'You wouldn't have known her,' he says, dunking his sponge back in the bucket. 'She'd have been a good forty years older than you. She left Mundubbera when she was married, but her maiden name was Bloxsome.'

Nola laughs. 'Bloxsome? My sister's niece is married to a Bloxsome. Richard Bloxsome. She's his second wife.'

'Richard Bloxsome is my first cousin,' says Ian, and Ian and I both shoot looks at Cyril. 'Guess that makes us family, eh, Cyril?'

Cyril shakes his head in disbelief, smiling. None of us can quite believe the coincidence, but all are delighted by it. Ian and I have found ourselves an ally who time will prove we could not have done without.

Early in the week we have to drive back to Montville to supervise the removal of my furniture. I don't want to go. Already I'm experiencing a huge, tugging wrench at the thought of leaving Baddow. Ian is keeping his house in Montville, along with most of his furniture, seeing as he'll need somewhere to stay when he's down there once a week. But I've sold my house, so everything I own will be migrating to Maryborough. Of course I have to go.

It's a massive few days. My house is built on three awkward levels, some of the steps are steep and narrow with tight corners, which means that larger items of furniture have to be trussed up and lowered over the balcony. Half way through the process, the men realise they can drive their truck right up to the base of the balcony, and everything – cushions, paintings, mirrors, boxes crammed with my existence thus far – gets hurled over the railings and caught by strong hands below. I can't watch. I spend the day lugging clothes and pot plants out of the back door, filling my little car and Ian's ute.

We drive in convoy up to Baddow, unload and stay one night, then drive back again because the removalists slightly underestimated the quantity of my belongings and a second journey is necessary. Then it's down to Montville for a third time, to clean my empty house before, finally, the move is done. I'm ill with exhaustion, the final journey north is a blur punctuated with constant stops to take in caffeine.

But back at Baddow my flagging spirits soar. Every particle of me recognises this as Home, as the place I want to be for ever. The house is a pile of furniture, boxes and strewn clothes, but I know there's no hurry. I can sift and sort in my own good time. With so many rooms, for now we can shove all the mess into places we don't need to use.

Furniture is not the only late addition to Baddow. Topsy, Ian's solid old cattle dog, comes north to live. We've avoided bringing her until now, concerned that all the mucking around back and forth might unsettle her. Topsy is nervy, distrustful of people, grumpy, greedy and lovable. She hides at the first hint of danger, at any sudden noise – the crack of a whip, the slam of a door – yet is fearless when it comes to killing snakes. A coward with killer instinct, Topsy's psyche is too complex to fathom. But today, jumping out of Ian's ute, taking a first sniff at her new home, she seems both excited and content.

Days tick by. The nights aren't great, but they are better than the first one. There is still much accompanying each other upstairs after dark, shared bathroom visits, and plenty of leaving lights on everywhere. However the lights are now dazzling and, with our furniture in place, the echoing emptiness that was once so disturbing is no more.

But I still can't *conceive* of even *considering* thinking about being here alone.

We don't mention the Deal, but Ian postpones going

away so he can help me with settling in. I'm unspeakably grateful.

My night fear is a strange contradiction to the way I feel about the house at other times. It is anathema to the warm envelopment I sense whenever I step inside Baddow's walls, a mystery that something I love so much should have the power to frighten me, but it does. Every day, when dusk falls, there's an unwelcome shift. Colours fade, shadows deepen and the birds in the garden grow quiet. It's all too easy to imagine the rustle of a long skirt on the step, or the tap of a booted foot on the staircase.

I know I'm a victim of my overactive imagination, and yearn for the security of commonsense, to have been born with a steady, plodding head, incapable of such flights of foolish fancy. Perhaps one day surgeons will be able to lobotomise that part of a person's brain. A quick hit with a laser and *zap: reality rules.*

Then Ian admits he couldn't face a night on his own either just yet, which makes me feel a bit less foolish, seeing as Ian is far more of a risk-lover than me. But his confession has the unfortunate side-effect of giving credibility to my fears, of feeding them, of making them real and legitimate. If Ian is afraid, I reason, there must be good cause.

So, for now, there is no Deal. We are babes in the same wood and must stick together.

During the day, however, I'm content in my pottering, unpacking and sorting. We're having bright clear weather, the rooms are awash with more sunlight than they've known in decades, and I throw open every window in the house to let the fresh spring air pour through.

Already I'm planning colour schemes and running to the paint shop in town for colour charts and tester pots. But I must be patient. Our first real job is the underpinning of the subsided north-western end of the house. We've had quotes, booked workers, and are now awaiting their arrival. In the meantime, there's a sense of kicking our heels, of biding our time. There's not much we can do before the underpinning, which will cause some movement to the house and probably create a few more cracks. But we can explore, discover and plan. And perhaps plenty of planning time is good: we are less likely to make mistakes.

We grow increasingly conscious that in Baddow House we have taken on more than a family home. It's a unique and vital part of Maryborough's history, the home of Maryborough's 'Founding Father'. We want to get it right, to do the job better than well. We want to give the house the restoration it deserves, to return its appearance to that which Edgar Aldridge desired and so meticulously planned for.

I feel deeply drawn to Edgar and Maria Aldridge. Perhaps because their dream has become my dream. Edgar succeeded in creating something astonishing in his time and I wonder what drove him. Perhaps it was ambition: the desire to own the grandest house in town and show all the other pretenders who was the real king of the heap in this blossoming corner of the new colony. Aldridge's Castle. I'm sure this name was facetiously coined, and can only speculate on the spirit of competition, the envy, that must have existed in a time and place where a poor man, with enough hard work and acumen, could make his fortune fast.

But I wonder if it was all one-upmanship with Edgar. There's a tale that Baddow House was modelled on a house in his childhood village of Little Baddow in Essex, England. A house he admired and hankered after and, when fortune permitted, built for himself. When you look at the six fireplaces he installed in this, his new, sub-tropical home, you get a sense of just how deep his pangs of home sickness must have been.

⤐┄◈┄○┄◈┄⤙

We begin to encounter wildlife.

The back door is seriously ill-fitting and leaves a gap of about fifteen centimetres to the ground. This doesn't keep out much of anything smaller than a wild pig.

The cane toad menace begins.

Now, I'm not a complete wimp who's going to jump onto a chair and scream at the sight of anything that scurries, hops or crawls, but I *don't* like cane toads.

I've read that if you touch them they can squirt enough poison in your eyes to blind you for life. When my children were little, their favourite bedtime stories were such things as *Dangerous Australians*, *The Unexplained*, *Weird and Wonderful Facts*, *Ripley's Believe It or Not*. My brain is still a font of how-you-are-most-likely-to-die trivia. Ask me which dinosaur had the longest claws, I can tell you. Ask me how many millilitres of poison a Taipan can drip down its fangs in a five second penetration, I can tell you. Believe me, I *know* about cane toads.

If Ian's around when a toad ventures under the door,

I yell for him to do the deed. If not, I fetch the dustpan and brush, scoop the toad up and pin it down with the flat end of the brush, shut my eyes and bolt outside. Then I lob it as far as my best throwing arm can lob a toad. As I don't find concussed toads littering the lawn each morning, I imagine they cope well with this airborne experience. That, cat-like, they spread their limbs, land lightly and make good their escape.

But of course they return – why, we don't know, but come they do. Light as a cat. Cunning as a cat. They hide under shrubs, wait till I'm gone, then hop in again. The evidence is clear in their droppings that I have to clean off the kitchen floor every morning. Luckily there is another door that separates the kitchen from the rest of the house. This door fits flush to the floor and we close it every night to keep the toads at bay. This door becomes known as the 'Toad Door'.

I'm really surprised that we don't have a serious rodent problem. If ever you saw a house likely to be teeming with rats and mice, it would be our house. There is the fifteen centimetre gap under the back door for starters. Then there are the gaps in the floorboards, the gaps between floorboards and skirting boards and, of course, there are the cracks in the walls. If I can get my arms through these cracks, they are not going to keep rats out.

But we don't see rats or mice. We don't hear any, and we don't find any droppings. I'm delighted, but amazed and confused. Perhaps they are scared of the ghosts.

One morning, sitting in the kitchen, we hear scraping sounds from the ceiling overhead. Ian says, 'there's your answer'.

'*Pythons*,' I whisper.

'Only one, I expect,' says Ian.

And of course I *know* about snakes. I know they are territorial. But my bedtime-story-gleaned scientific knowledge is at odds with the suspicion that no one python could consume the number of rodents that surely must want to populate our house. I imagine colonies of writhing coils above our heads. The only pity is that they don't devour the cane toads.

⊱─◈─○─◈─⊰

Before the end of the first week Ian goes into town on an errand. It's my first time in the house totally alone and, though it's broad daylight, I'm not one hundred per cent comfortable. I try to be. I wander about; I go upstairs, then down again. I hang out of windows and look at the brightness of the day.

I try to exude confidence, to give out a proprietorial *this is my home and isn't it all just wonderful* sort of air. It's not working. I want to go outside. I want to escape to the safety of the great outdoors where birds are tweeting and grass is growing and clouds are scudding across the sky. The stillness of the house is almost crushing. It's the silence of the mausoleum; thick, thick walls keeping out the pulse of life. I want music, I want noise, any noise. I go into the airy, sunny living room, sit on one of the sofas and plonk my feet on the coffee table. 'Hello,' I say out loud. First sign of madness, talking to yourself. Or so we always said at school. 'Hello,' I say again. I'm not sure who I'm talking to, but suddenly it seems like precisely the thing to be doing. 'If you can hear me,' I say, 'listen well, because this is important.'

I pause for effect, waiting for any listeners to gather, to tune in. I'm very aware of the lunacy of my behaviour, but have no intention of stopping. 'I love this house,' I say. 'If you want to stay here, I understand, because you love this house too.' I'm searching for the right words, wanting my words to have the desired impact. 'I don't mind at all if you stay,' I say, which is not strictly true, 'in fact, I welcome you. But there are conditions.' I pause again, making myself believe my words. If I don't believe them, how can I expect anyone – or any*thing* else – to? Sincerity is essential. 'My conditions are these: I never ever want to see you. And I never ever want to hear you. Abide by my terms and we can all be happy.'

I leave the room feeling somewhat foolish but very much better.

CHAPTER 6

DODGING THE DEAL

IAN'S SISTER ANN ARRIVES to stay. It's brilliant to have someone else in the house which still seems far too big and echoey for the two of us. Ann doesn't mind braving the splintering floorboards with her bare feet, or eating in a kitchen that has been condemned. Nor does she mind having no curtains and being woken at dawn by a laser of sunlight slicing into her eyes.

I'm very excited to welcome Ann to Baddow. I pretty up her room as best I can. There's no disguising the cracks in the walls, which are awesome in this corner of the house, but I unpack and wash sheets and a bed cover. Though it's the first week of September, a time when the garden should be a riot of spring colour, there's not much flowering in our neglected beds. I find a meagre few freesias – poor, drab specimens, but their scent is sweet and I pick them all for the mantelpiece in Ann's bedroom. Ann is wonderful. With Ann there is no sense whatsoever of pessimism about our relationship. She loves our new house, she loves us and she loves what we are doing.

Ann is fun-loving and happy, naughty but nice. She's a female version of Ian, though she's far, far prettier. Her visit gives us a huge injection of confidence. She oohs and aahs at the devastated splendour of the house, is suitably shocked by the Big Crack and suitably excited at the prospect of the restoration.

We tell her about our ghosts, about Esse's tears and the many sightings of a woman on the stairs. When her eyes grow round, we're quick to assure her that we haven't seen anything. Yet. We don't confess that, once our contract was signed and unconditional, the previous owners told us of the woman on the stairs, and that it is 'only a matter of time' before we, too, will see her.

Ann and her husband Ted live in a town called Miles, four hours drive west in the sort of territory I consider the Outback, but that Ian insists is not the real Outback at all.

I love visiting Miles. It looks like the Australia I learned about in geography classes at school but failed to discover when I moved out from England and found myself in the lush, green hills of Montville. Miles is set in flat, dry, sparsely treed country. There are cattle properties and wheat properties, scattered evidence of human settlement on wide, wide horizons.

The sky at Miles is astonishingly blue and at night the stars are brighter and more numerous than I've ever seen in my life. The first time I stayed at Miles, Ted took me out under the stars to show me the Southern Cross. I'd seen it before, of course, but not like this. For every star I'm used to, there seems to be another hundred. The entire night sky is a living, glittering mass. I could live at Miles . . . if it weren't for Baddow House.

We venture into Maryborough with Ann.

The main street, Kent Street, is dominated by the magnificent City Hall built in 1908. A brass cannon sits at the entrance. This is the Time Cannon, once used for accurate time-keeping. Every day at one pm the cannon was fired, reputed to be audible more than twenty miles away. It must have been startling to unsuspecting passers-by.

The shops in the old streets of town are sparsely tenanted. We're told this is because Station Square, an air-conditioned shopping plaza, opened only three years before. Half the stores in town moved into it.

It's a shame: the old streets are beautiful. Row upon row of lovely old shops with ornate façades built in an era when the town was wealthy, labour was cheap, and pride in the blossoming colony ran high. But some businesses have doggedly remained. There's the department store, Dimmey's, looking like a relic from the nineteen-fifties, with merchandise spread on tables, a few slow moving ceiling fans stirring the humid air. There's a sprinkling of cafés and bakeries, a couple of shoe shops, a chemist, newsagent, framing gallery and a jewellery shop or two.

There is also St Paul's Anglican Church, with an enormous belltower built by Edgar Aldridge in memory of his beloved Maria. The tower is brick with decorative cement facings and battlements. It is twenty-seven metres high and houses nine bells, all cast in England. The bells were shipped out on the *Eastminster* in 1888 which, though arriving and delivering her cargo safely, was lost in a cyclone on her voyage home. The largest bell weighs one thousand and sixty-seven kilos, the smallest two hundred and ninety-five. All nine are inscribed: *'To the Glory of God and to the Memory of Mrs Aldridge, 1886'*. To this day, the nine bells peal out in Maria's honour on the anniversary of her death. That this falls on St Patrick's Day must be a matter of confusion for any unsuspecting Catholics in town.

So much grandeur, so much history, so much potential. I fantasise about buying all the shops in town and renovating the lot of them. But with Baddow House to bleed us dry this is clearly not going to happen.

There is a corner store called The Inconvenience Store, evidence that wit is alive and well in Maryborough. We pass a butcher's shop advertising roo, emu, crocodile, goat, camel and buffalo. Not for the fainthearted or semi-vegetarian me. There is, of course, a pub on almost every corner, with rows of private little rooms upstairs; standard architecture for a town that was once a thriving port teeming with lusty, thirsty sailors.

We can't get enough of Wharf Street. We pass the Criterion Hotel, a three-storey pub, rebuilt after a fire in 1878. It's a stunning monument to the architecture of that era, loaded with iron lacework and elaborate Victorian touches. We discover that it now houses a popular nightclub and that every Friday and Saturday night, its patrons disgorge at closing time, to rampage loudly and destructively along our precious Wharf Street, targeting the delicate, rusting lacework of the verandah of our favourite, the Customs House Hotel.

The Customs House Hotel is a long two-storey brick

building, with battered iron lacework decorating the verandahs upstairs and down. It is seriously run-down, there are holes in the rusting gutters and bits of rotten boards droop from the upstairs verandah. But this is part of the charm: a façade entirely unspoilt by over-eager renovators. This building is supposedly haunted too, which makes us feel a tug of the kindred spirit kind, but also an iota of jealousy. *We* are the official Ghost House after all, and we don't want any pretenders to our title.

We learn that the hotel has a tunnel to the river, used in the nineteenth century to float kegs of beer and other fare up to the cellars. An ingenious saving of man power. But today's proprietor of the hotel tells us that, though their tunnel was built for purposes of convenience and storage, it soon degenerated into an opium den and illegal gaming hell, along with many other cellars in town.

We read early newspaper reports of the stifling heat in the opium dens, and the 'stenches as thick as a main sewer mingled with opium fumes'. Opium was still a legal substance in those days, so the police could do little to close these places down, unless they could prove gambling or serious health concerns.

The Gympie gold rush played its part in Maryborough's turbulent, prosperous past. Though the fickle goldfields made some men rich, many others were ruined. A far more reliable source of income was to milk the miners. Plenty of traders in Maryborough did just that, making a fortune supplying the miners with the tools of their hopeful trade, food, tents and every other necessity.

What a hot-bed of hard drinking, opium smoking, brothel-patronising vice our town was in its frontier days. But in George Loyau's book, *The History of Maryborough*, published in 1897, he writes that by the 1880s *'the orgies, revelries and devilries of ancient times'* were a thing of the past.

Clearly Maryborough was moving on to a golden age of trade, expansion, respectability and prosperity. The town became a centre for the fledgling wool, timber and sugar industries of Queensland. The port grew busier and larger with every passing year, until the jetties extended for more than two kilometres.

There was timber, wool, sugar and cotton to export, and there were people to import. More than twenty thousand new immigrants first touched Australian soil in Maryborough. They trudged up Wharf Street, laden with children and worldly belongings, to be processed at the Customs House.

Today, Muddy Waters Café occupies the only scrap of remaining one hundred and fifty year old timber wharf and we quickly realise we have discovered our favourite eating place. The food is great and it's a perfect spot to watch the river slug by and imagine those early bustling days.

After sustaining cups of tea and friands, Ann, Ian and I wander back to the top of Wharf Street. On the corner of Richmond and Wharf streets, we find the Maryborough Heritage Centre. Here, the three of us examine grainy pictures of immigrant ships and lists of passengers, recognising some contemporary Maryborough names amongst the new arrivals. We discover that the author of *Mary Poppins*, P.L. Travers, was born in Maryborough. That Maryborough was once one of the busiest ports in Australia, second only to

Sydney, and that back in the eighteen-fifties, when Queensland was on the cusp of becoming independent from New South Wales, it was a toss up between Maryborough and Brisbane to be declared capital of the new state.

We flick through leaflets and buy a couple of little books on Maryborough's glorious past.

Ian can be guaranteed to get chatting with strangers every time he's let out of the house. Today is no exception. He's gossiping with the lady behind the counter.

'Baddow House, you say?'

'Yes,' he tells her, 'we moved in about a week ago. Splendid old home. Amazing no one has brought it up to scratch before.'

'People were afraid,' she says to him, and I fancy I see her eyes dart about nervously. 'I went there once, years ago now. Took my mother . . .' she shakes her head, as if the memory is too painful.

'Back when it was a museum?' suggests Ian. Though I don't know why he's encouraging her.

She nods. 'There's a room,' she says.

'Yes,' I can't help joining in at this, 'there are several.'

My sarcasm is lost.

'To the left after the entrance. A big room.'

'That would be the dining room,' I say.

She nods. 'That'd be it. Well, could we set foot in that room? Never,' she says, 'something terrible happened in there, and that's a fact.'

'What sort of something terrible?' Ian asks.

'I couldn't tell you,' she says, 'but there's no one and nothing'd make me go in there.'

Great. I'd been rather proud of our grand dining room, with its lofty ceilings, magnificent cedar fireplace and deep bay window. I had exciting plans for it. Now I'm going to be scared of it.

><del>·><del>·O·<del>·<del>·

'You can't take any notice of that sort of talk,' says Ann bracingly.

We're strolling back to the car, heading home. Though she's far too young to be my mother, Ann manages to make me feel all mothered, nurtured and cared for. It's a universal thing with Ann. In Miles she's known throughout the community as 'Mummy'.

'I know,' I say. 'It's superstitious garbage but sometimes, when you're alone in those cavernous rooms, it's hard to remember.'

She presses my arm. 'In time it'll get easier. You'll paint the walls, you'll make it your own home and, when that's done, you'll laugh at all this Ghost House stuff.'

Ann has to return to Miles and her Ted. Ian's business commitments in Montville are screaming for attention. Apart from the tenancies and shops that need attending to, he is up to his neck in his 'Rangeview' project in Maleny, close by Montville. This is thirty hectares of an old dairy farm that Ian is developing, with the intention of on-selling for housing. The success of Rangeview is really important if we are to be able to handle the expected costs of renovating. But it's going to mean three days and two nights away each week. The moment the Deal is to become a reality looms. I need a stay of execution and invite Scott Bain, an old friend from Montville, to stay.

Ian and I have known Scott for years. Scott isn't fanciful, Scott doesn't believe in ghosts. I can remember a time when Scott house-sat for some ghost-believing friends in Montville. He stayed in their 'haunted' house for weeks while they were in England. He scoffed at their ghostly claims. He is the man for the job.

Ian farewells us, and I sleep really soundly, knowing that only a wall separates Scott the Unbeliever from me. We joke together during the day, do a bit of gardening, eat lunch at Muddy Waters, laugh at the nerves of a tradesman's apprentice who refuses to come into the house.

I'm more relaxed than I have been since we arrived. Increasingly, I realise that Ian and I set each others' fears off. My wild colonial boy, I call him, and he loves it; loves to think he's an untamed adventurer: flouting rules, running risks, dodging danger with aplomb yet loyal and chivalrous to the end. And he is all of these things, but he's also as imaginative and fanciful as I am.

I'm pleased with my diagnosis, because a problem identified and acknowledged, is a problem on its way to being solved. Together we will kick this ghost thing and, in the meantime, I have Scott.

Scott is small, neat and dapper. An absolute gentleman, with the quaint and perfect manners of another age. He has a fierce wit and a fountain of amusing trivia stored in his smart little head. He seems to be related to half the population of Queensland and knows everything about everyone. A veritable oracle when it comes to Queensland history, gossip and lore. Scott is also a keen and expert gardener; he inspires me hugely.

So while Ian is away, we begin to plan the garden. Maryborough sits on a latitude of twenty-five degrees south, more tropical than I've become used to, and I can't grow a lot of my favourite plants from Montville which, being slightly south of Maryborough and high in the hills, has a cooler climate. But many of the trees and shrubs of my childhood in Malaya thrive here.

My father was a Gurkha officer in the British Army, in the days when the Gurkhas were always stationed in the 'Far East'. Life was a nomadic existence between Malaya, Singapore, Hong Kong and Brunei. A tropical, exotic childhood of privilege and recreation. We swam, holidayed in the cool, jungle-covered highlands and, at home, played mah-jong and tennis and enjoyed the garden that we didn't have to tend with our own pale hands.

I'm determined my hands will toil long and hard over Baddow's garden. Frangipanis, bougainvilleas, allamandas, gardenias. Our garden will take me back to my lush, rich, scented, bright and tropical childhood. If only we can find enough water.

The river is tidal and salty. We're told that drilling a bore will probably result in water too salty for the garden, that our chances of finding fresh water are slim. I remember that Elizabeth from Mavisbank is an accomplished diviner and the day Scott leaves I invite her up to wield her rod.

I'm a bit sceptical but fascinated nevertheless. Elizabeth strolls about the garden with a forked piece of willow clasped in her gentle fingers. Every now and again she stops, the willow twisting as though tugged down by unseen hands. 'You have plenty of fresh water here,' she says, and strolls on, locating numerous possible sites.

How does she know the water is fresh? I ask. 'I've never divined salt water,' she says, 'only fresh. Why, I don't know, that's just the way it works.' At one stage she holds out the willow to me and says, 'Here, you have a go.'

I laugh, go all coy and shake my head.

'Go on,' Elizabeth urges.

So I do. And weirdly I feel a strange tugging when I pass over certain parts of the garden. I try to grip the willow so it can't move, but some invisible force outdoes me and the stick turns, almost burning my skin. 'Keep it,' she says, 'show Ian when he's back. I have plenty more willow.'

Now, I'm not going to say that all of a sudden I can find water with the wave of my special wand, but there is no doubt in my mind that something turned that stick in my hands.

Later that day Ian returns and, when he hears the story, gets excited and has a go. He walks up and down for hours with no movement whatsoever in the magic willow. He's disappointed, jealous of my new talent. I'm secretly quite pleased that he can't do it. It makes me feel gifted and special. I grow very smug, but we decide not to take on the expensive risk of drilling for water until we have finished our renovations.

⊱━◈━○━◈━⊰

Scott's scepticism has rubbed off on me. It's only two weeks since Ian started his runs down to Montville but I know

I'm getting braver. However, in an act of cowardly procrastination, the next time Ian goes away, I invite my sister-in-law, Delia, to stay. Delia is married to Ian's younger brother Bruce. They live at Gympie which, at only an hour's drive south, makes them geographically our closest relations. I've only known Bruce and Delia for a couple of years, from the time Ian grew bold enough to start introducing me to his extended family, but Delia and I have clicked since our first meeting. Reliable and straightforward, she has my trust as well as my liking.

Though Delia has lived in Australia for more than thirty years, she was born and raised a Scot. Perhaps it's the Celtic blood in her veins, but Delia has been known to 'sense' things. I want her company, but I don't want her sensing anything at Baddow.

It's the first night of her visit and we are curled up in the living room, which is a bizarre juxtaposition of Ian's and my favourite antique furniture, big squishy sofas and jagged, gaping chasms in the devastated walls, so open we can feel the wind whipping through the cracks.

Delia is dark haired and petite, small enough to make me, at a respectable one hundred and seventy centimetres (five foot seven), feel like I've evolved from a different species. She's conservative-looking in her glasses and neat clothes, and she's pretty: a cute little librarian. We're sipping wine by the light of the dim chandelier, cosy together in our draughty luxury. The company and wine make me reckless. I know I'm mad. I know I will regret it later, but the morbid fascination is just too magnetic to resist. I press Delia to tell me about her 'sensing' moments.

She tells me of a house she and Bruce once lived in. Unbeknownst to them, a young man had committed suicide in the house some years before. Hanged himself. Sometimes, especially when she was home alone, she would glimpse the figure of a young man standing in the doorway of one of the bedrooms, out of the corner of her eye. Only much later, when she learned of the suicide, did she connect the tragedy with what she was seeing. Her sightings were occasionally confirmed by visitors who would ask who was the young male guest in the bedroom at the end of the corridor.

Listening to her, I get that goosebumpy feeling. Stories like this always leave me excited, but scared. I believe Delia totally, I know she'd never make up something like this, yet I can't quite believe in ghosts. Clearly she saw something but I tell myself there's got to be another explanation. Just as Neanderthal Man might have run screaming from a solar eclipse believing it was the end of his world, we don't yet understand why people sometimes see things that aren't really there. That's my theory, anyway, and I'd rather not budge from it.

Delia tells me that from childhood days in Scotland she has always had feelings about houses that she visits; a sense of happiness, of sorrow, of fear.

Buoyed by both the wine in my hand and Delia's company on the sofa, I ask the inevitable question: how does she feel at Baddow?

'I would not like to stay a night here on my own,' she admits.

There's a moment of silence. I fancy I hear wind whipping through the cracks in the walls, a tinkling in the chandeliers.

'But that is mostly because of the size of the house. It's too big for me to be comfortable in. If there is something here . . .'

'Yes?' I'm slurping at my wine, edging closer to her.

'It's something good,' she says. 'Yes, definitely. I feel that quite strongly. It's a sense of relief and rightness. I think they must be pleased you are here.'

CHAPTER 7

WILD LIFE
AND WILD CORPSES

I AN RETURNS AND I tell him Delia's reaction to the house. We are walking Topsy down by the river. It's late in the afternoon, the end of a perfect, balmy day. Ian laughs off my conversation with Delia, but I can tell he's listening hard, hanging out for the verdict she delivers at the end, relieved when he hears it.

The eucalypts are turning amber in the dipping sun and the grass looks unnaturally bright. I've always found the light at this time of day the most beautiful by far. Everything looks richer: intense colours, contrasts well defined. Flocks of white birds follow the river home at the end of every day. We see them now, in a wedge formation, flying so low they almost skim their reflections on the water. At moments like these I can hardly believe my good fortune, to live somewhere so idyllic. Underpinning delays are far from my mind. I'm awash with calm, happy thoughts.

From the river the house with all its dilapidation is hard to see. It's close by, but the Sleeping Beauty forest blocks our view. Sometimes I worry that when we have restored the house fully, it will lose its romance. Not that I would keep the awesome fissures in the walls. They worry the hell out of me and would be gone this instant if I could wave a wand and heal them. But the crumbling masonry on the chimney stacks, the rusty edges of the roof and the stained exterior walls excite my imagination. I don't want the house to be bland and flawless, shiny like a new penny. I don't want to erase the fingerprints of time.

We take the path back up the hill toward the end of Queen Street, Topsy is running miles ahead. 'Topsy!' Ian calls, for she shouldn't really be unleashed. Like everyone else, we turn a blind eye to this particular by-law when we are down by the river, but once we near the road we know we must obey.

Topsy ignores Ian. She's a dot on the horizon, showing unusual verve and speed for a dog that generally struggles with a lumbering gait. Ian calls again – shouts, more angrily this time. 'I don't know what's wrong with her,' he says, 'she's not usually this disobedient.'

As we climb the last bit of path to the road, Ian strides ahead of me, ready to chastise his wayward dog. We turn into our driveway in time to see Topsy disappear across the lawn and down to the far reaches of the garden. We follow as fast as we can, both now calling her crossly.

'Wait,' says Ian, 'I think she's got something there.'

As we approach, I can see Ian is right. There is a very large object in her jaws. Too heavy for her to lift from the ground, she's endeavouring to drag it.

'Perhaps it's a big fish or something from the river,' I suggest.

'I don't know, but whatever it is, she knew it was there. She couldn't wait to get back from her walk to retrieve it.'

Topsy's hauling efforts grow more frantic as we approach. There's desperation to protect and keep the trophy she's sure we mean to deprive her of.

We're still baffled. The closer we get, the more certain we are that it is not a fish. It's round, like a basketball, only larger. There's no doubt in my mind that we are dealing with organic matter, else why would Topsy be so excited? I stop in my tracks. 'I think you can handle this,' I tell Ian. 'She's your dog.'

I watch from a distance and see Ian, with the utmost difficulty, separate Topsy from her prize before dragging her away and tying her up. He then fetches a large plastic bag and returns to the site, gathering the mysterious item into the bag before dropping it in the wheelie bin.

'What was it?' I ask as he wheels the bin out to the road. Luckily it is collection day in the morning.

He turns to face me. 'A pig's head,' he says.

'*You're joking.*'

'No, take a look if you don't believe me.'

'I believe you!'

We return to the house, discussing it all the way.

'How the hell did a pig's head get on our front lawn?'

'I have no idea.'

'Someone must have chucked it there,' I say, thinking wildly of *The Godfather*: horse's heads, vendettas and all that.

'I expect someone must have.'

'That's a very scary thought.'

'It is.'

'Someone mustn't like us being here.'

'Don't think like that. There's bound to be another explanation.'

'I can't think of one.'

'Perhaps Topsy found it elsewhere and carried it here.'

'But you saw her. She couldn't even lift it.'

'True.'

'And it's not as if there are any abattoirs or butcher's shops just up the road.'

'True.'

'So what are we going to do?'

'There's nothing we *can* do,' he says. 'It'll be gone in the morning. Try not to think about it.'

But I do think about it. I am certain there must have been human involvement. It couldn't have just materialised in the garden, someone had to have put it there. But why? What possible reason could someone have to hurl a pig's head into our – or anyone else's – garden? I think about it all evening. It keeps me awake for ages that night and I'm thinking about it the minute I wake up in the morning. I know the ghosts are not the only thing we're going to have to keep quiet about when the children come to stay.

Ian is a long time fetching the paper from the letterbox. When he finally appears in the kitchen, he's grinning hugely.

'I have an answer for you,' he says.

'Oh?'

'I've been exploring. There's a stormwater drain under the road. A big one. It must come all the way from town. It emerges into the creek at the bottom of the garden. There's a huge pipe half-hidden by all the vines and weeds there. The offending item must have been washed down with all that rain a couple of days ago and Topsy dragged it up the hill.'

'Explanation accepted,' I say, and offer a silent prayer of thanks to Ian for being such a good, exploring, problem-solving type. I'm not sure I like the idea of a town with pig's heads floating around in stormwater drains, but at least I can sleep tonight.

⊱┄⊷┄○┄⊶┄⊰

Sleep. Always an optimist. I do sleep at first, tired from the previous night's cursed imaginative journeys. But it's hot and the mozzies are buzzing. I twist in the sheets and toss on my pillow. After a while I get up and turn the fan on full. It helps, but some sneaky mozzies hide in the lee of my head and bite my ears.

Ian, of course, is fast asleep. He has spent the day chain-sawing and loading the ute with great boughs of dead trees.

I am spinning in the sheets, seeking a cool inch of linen when an almighty THWACK – THUD! has me half off the bed with fright. I grab Ian.

'*What was that?*'

He's heard it too, and jumps up, reaching for the light switch. We both blink, blinded by the sudden brightness. I can hear my breath harsh in the frozen silence. The only movement is the steady whirring of the fan. I look up. 'It sounded like something hitting the fan,' I whisper.

Ian rounds the bed, eyes scanning for evidence of intrusion. Suddenly he stops.

'What is it?' I say.

He's pointing at the floor.

'*What is it?*'

I hang over the end of the bed and see the corpse of a huge bat, dribbling blood onto the floorboards.

David Attenborough is missing a good few opportunities at Baddow House.

⊱──⊱◈⊰──⊰

A friend gives me a book called *Orchid Bay* by Patricia Shaw. It's set in nineteenth century Maryborough and she thinks I'll be interested. I am. It features a man getting eaten by a crocodile in the Mary River. Normally I would have taken this as artistic licence employed by an author desperate to inject excitement into an otherwise tame plot. But *Orchid Bay* has a well researched air about it, prompting me to ask around a bit.

'Oh yes,' say two kids I meet fishing on the jetty near the house. 'There's a couple of big salties living up on them mud flats.'

'Oh yes,' says a neighbour, 'you should see the size of the croc in the pub at Tiaro. Stuffed it is. Shot not far from here. A while ago now, but.'

A fellow doing some bobcat work for us has even better stories. He tells us of a mate who's fishing for barramundi one night on the river bank. It's late, the best time for a good catch, and he's sitting on the mud flat with his dog at his side. He hears a thump and a splash and the dog is gone. It's the last fishing trip he ever makes.

Another story is of a farmer up-river from us, whose cattle were disappearing. He staked out the river and shot a six-metre crocodile. That these incidents are reputed to have taken place years ago is little comfort.

I suspect the locals get a kick out of scaring the new-comers. Perhaps their stories are wildly exaggerated, perhaps they are total fabrications. I have to know the truth, so ring the local council offices. They put me on to a cheerful young town planner, Jamie Cockburn. 'Certainly,' he informs me. 'Not so many as there once were, of course, a lot of them have been shot out now, but it's still possible you might see one. We get sharks too. Small bull sharks.'

I eye the murky waters of the Mary with increased respect. My plan to host river swimming parties for my friends from the Montville swimming club evaporates faster than a snowflake in hell.

I make the mistake of ringing my mother in England. Her daily newspaper seems to specialise in deadly Australian wildlife stories. I get frequent alarming phone calls from her advising me of such horrors as a killer locust plague sweeping Queensland or the discovery of the new and previously unheard of flesh-eating ant of New South Wales that is marching north. I'm forever promising to shut the windows and wear gloves in the garden.

Now she has visions of me being stalked by monster crocodiles while mulching the camellias or pruning the roses. I've done my best to reassure her, telling her that the sightings occur only once in twenty years, that the river is one hundred metres from the house and that there are not one, but two, solid embankments between it and my rose garden, both far too steep for such short-legged beasts to negotiate. She's not convinced.

⊱─◈─○─◈─⊰

We decide to install gates across the old driveway. This entrance is a lovely feature but seldom used, there being another, newer, more convenient way to reach our parking spot. This original driveway deserves a majestic entrance, and a set of bolted gates should also deter the steady stream of curious locals who wander in. We get kids taking short cuts from the park through to Queen Street. We get whole families – mum, dad, grandparents with walking sticks, babies in strollers – all sauntering in for a look. We get strangers knocking on the door asking to do a tour of the 'museum'. Most accept with good grace when we tell them the place hasn't been open to the public for a decade and is now a private home, but we encounter the odd one who gets belligerent.

'But I've heard it *is* a museum.'

'No, I'm afraid not. It used to be, but the previous owners closed their business many years ago. Now it's just a private home.'

'But they say it's worth having a look round.'

'Yes, that may well be, but I'm afraid it's not possible.'

Silence. Lingering. Trying to peer over my shoulder.

'Some mates of mine said that they had a look. They said the place is still a museum.'

Topsy, where are you?

'Well, no, I'm afraid they are wrong. Or perhaps they were here ten years ago.'

More lingering.

'We'll pay admittance.'

'I'm sorry. Really, this is just a private home.'

And on it goes.

A young couple knock on the door and tell us they plan to have their wedding here at the house.

'I'm sorry,' I tell them, 'we don't do functions. This is just a private home.'

'But we know you do weddings. Some people told us they were married here a couple of weeks ago.'

'That's not possible,' I say, 'we were living here then and I think we would have noticed a wedding taking place. Perhaps you're thinking of Rosehill Homestead across the river, they do functions.'

'No, it was definitely Baddow House. They said so.'

We also get visitors at night.

We wake up one night to the sound of talking and laughter on the driveway and hang out of the window to try to make out what's going on. In the moonlight we can see a couple of figures wending their way toward the house. From their voices we know they are girls. We suspect they are out with boyfriends and have been dared to approach the Haunted House.

'Get the torch,' Ian whispers.

I rummage in Ian's bedside table where he keeps his brand new spot-a-predator-a-kilometre-away-strength spotlight. He aims it at the shadowy figures and flicks the switch. Trapped like the proverbial bunnies in headlights are a pair of clinging, cringing teenage girls. Their screams are worthy of Hollywood. Ian and I giggle as we watch them bolt back down the driveway. When we hear a car roaring off we get back into bed.

A minute later we hear the car engine again and know it's coming up the driveway. Ian repeats his torch trick. There are more screams and the car reverses out, fish-tailing all over the place. We don't see them again. But we know we need gates.

⊰┈⊱◈⊰┈⊱

Graham Morrison comes from a long line of blacksmiths. We're told he can make and shape anything out of metal and that he works with a patience and skill that's all but lost these days.

Graham is obviously chuffed to be asked to make new gates for Baddow House and the three of us pore over design ideas together. His workshop is inspiring: a hothouse of hissing cauldrons and leaping naked flames. Everywhere there are sections of half-constructed gates and grilles, and there are moulded twists of iron: spindles, bars, rings and arrowheads; all pieces of assorted puzzles waiting to be assembled.

We choose parallel vertical bars for our gates, crossed with a swirly, deco pattern. The curved top will have little arrowheads running along the edge, and we decide to powder coat the whole thing in charcoal grey. It takes Graham a month to make them. Achieving something, *anything*, goes a long way to appeasing our frustration at the continued absence of the underpinners.

Because of the height of the gates and the width of the driveway, they are going to be very heavy, but Graham assures us he can get hinges that will cope. He crafts and hangs the gates perfectly and we are ecstatic both about their beauty and by our ability to lock ourselves in. Ian hammers a PRIVATE PROPERTY sign at the entrance.

CHAPTER 8

GEORGIE

J UST WHEN I THINK the Deal is about to become a reality, I get a massive stay of execution. Georgie, Ian's second daughter, comes to stay. Georgie has been living in Sydney but is about to go overseas. She has three months up her sleeve and decides to spend it with us at Baddow. It will help her to save for her trip.

It is not long since her father and I began living together. It must be a very strange feeling to move in with your father who's just moved in with someone who's not your mother. Even at twenty-six years old. I think Georgie's very brave.

It's little more than three years since her mother died, and everything is pretty raw still. A delicate situation: I know I must tread warily. Georgie is particularly sensitive to the loss of her mother. Ian is nervous about the visit too. None of the children, mine or his, have yet spent a night under a roof with us. We know we will soon get weekend visits from those of the children who are in Australia, but Georgie is the first.

I am aware that there were tears when Ian and I first started seeing each other which, though understandable, is bad for my hard-won confidence. Georgie and I are going to be alone for two days each and every week till she goes overseas and I have no idea if she is still upset about my being with her father.

Ian and I intend to be together for the long haul. We are going to marry one day, but we need the time to be right, and for everyone to be happy about it first. We discuss tactics. We know that I must be relaxed with Georgie; friendly without fawning. We know that trying too hard will make it worse, but trying too hard is a real danger when it is so important that this goes well, for my sake as well as Ian's.

I'm so nervous when she arrives, I'm almost talking gibberish. Conscious of how foolish this is, I try to get a grip. After all, I remember Georgie from when she was a little girl and I've seen her quite a few times in Montville since Ian and I became a couple. But this is different. We're all living together now. I'm sharing a bedroom with her father. We'll be seeing each other first thing in the morning, in pyjamas, cleaning our teeth. We'll be together twenty-four hours a day.

I suspect she's nervous too.

Georgie settles into the Babies' Room, so named because it has a connecting door to our bedroom and I imagine a family using it as a nursery, given the proximity to Mum and Dad. We know that any of our own 'babies' who are scared of our ghosts will opt to sleep in there – my own daughter, Elizabeth, included.

When Georgie moves into the Babies' Room, she moves in with her mother. Besides the cluster of photos I had expected, there is a cushion on the bed with her mother's face superimposed onto the fabric, and the book written by a family friend detailing Jenny's battle with cancer takes centre place on the dressing table. I'm not sure whether Georgie really needs these props, or whether she is simply sending me a message.

We are all in new territory, thrown into a situation none of us have encountered before or had ever expected to encounter. We all tread carefully, negotiating the eggshells, but secretly I'm optimistic about the future. We are all adults. We are all sane. Nobody wants to be miserable. I can see no reason why things will not travel smoothly.

I knew Georgie's mother through my many years in Montville. Ian's happy life with her made him the cheerful sort of man he always will be and for that I'm very grateful. I have no problem talking about Jenny with Ian when he needs to, or with anyone else for that matter. Wendy Ellerker, my oldest friend from school, set me straight on the subject before I'd even had time to fully consider it: 'If you want someone without baggage, Anne, you'll have to find a twenty-year-old virgin.'

She's so right, but then Wendy always is.

The only time my confidence in my relationship with Ian wavers is when someone makes me feel that I am where I shouldn't be, or that I have usurped the place of another, more valued human being.

I feel immeasurably sad for Jenny that she died. The last time I saw her, she told me that the one thing she couldn't bear was the thought of not seeing her grandchildren. Even today, this memory is enough to choke me with sadness. All the more so given that, though neither of us realised it at the time, it would be I, not her, who would know her grandchildren. It fills me with a great sense of responsibility. Sometimes I can't help wondering whether she did somehow know what would happen. It was odd that she mentioned her future grandchildren to me when we didn't really know each other that well. It came as a comment out of the blue one day when I hadn't seen her for more than a year.

Twice I've had graphic dreams about Jenny.

Once was a sweet, calm sort of dream, in which she and I were sitting on a wall together, arm in arm. No words were exchanged, but there was a huge sense of comfort and unity. I woke from this dream awash with confidence and contentment.

The other time, following a rare argument with Ian, I dreamed I was shouting at Jenny to come and sort him out. I remember feeling furious with her for leaving and letting him become my problem.

I discuss these dreams with Ian. It's strange that I'm the one to have the dreams of Jenny when Ian does not.

>—+—◆—+—O—+—◆—+—<

The first few days go well. Ian is with us and we muck around the house, make good food, swig champagne and mutter our daily lament over the absence of the underpinners.

Wednesday looms. Ian will be gone for two nights and three days. Georgie and I stand side by side waving Ian goodbye. Suddenly he's gone and it's just us. Ian's really worried and I've promised to ring him as soon as I'm able.

I wonder what we're going to do all day. Of course there is always sanding and painting. The old scullery, first on our list, beckons, plus the other trillion and a half things to do to the house. But overshadowing this there is Us.

We go inside for a cup of tea. We have something to eat. We chat. We quickly discover a mutual love of food, a fear of getting fat, a history of yoyo dieting. We decide to go for a brisk walk together every morning.

Day one rolls on. We start to giggle, to tell each other things. I'm amazed at the speed of our opening up to each other. Perhaps it's nerves, perhaps it's the mutual desire for things to work out. I'm more buoyed up than I have been for ages.

>-+-+>-0-<+-+-<

Before leaving Montville, I lost my best friend. It wasn't that she died, but I lost her nonetheless. It has gone down as one of the biggest sadnesses of my life. What happened was simple enough, and has probably happened a million other times to a million other women, but it seemed to me at the time that none could have been as unhappy as I was.

My friend's husband was the possessor of a somewhat roving eye. Mine was the shoulder she cried on when his eye was caught by a pretty face. This had been going on for

years, and it was an education to me to see how unfaithful-
ness did not have to involve acts of sex. It was awful to see
how much pain could be caused by his casting of an
admiring glance or by his voicing one misplaced compliment
too many. There was nothing my friend could do to stop
these tendencies but shun those women who had caught her
husband's eye. The list of the shunned was not a short one.

I hated him for making her so unhappy. I never dreamed
the dreaded eye would fall my way. I didn't even notice it
when it did. But my friend noticed. All of a sudden, the
wonderful, eccentric, volatile, creative creature I had so
loved, turned in all its fury on me. She did not accuse me of
acting to encourage the eye, yet could not bear to have me
in her presence. I was cut from her life, told never to cross
her path again. When her daughter invited me to her
wedding, I was told to stay away.

It was bewildering. It was agony. She had meant the
world to me, had supported me through my divorce, was
my best friend, my sister and my mother all rolled into one.
I felt as though my mother had cast me aside because my
father had looked at me inappropriately.

It was a double agony for the injustice of it all.

She left a gaping hole in my life. Now, this gaping hole
has been filled by Georgie.

⊳⏵◦⏴⊲

Georgie and I decide to take Topsy with us on our morning
walks. Topsy is a blue cattle dog, an outdoor working-in-
the-paddock-with-Ian sort of a dog. Belying her age and

weight, she's comfortable jumping in and out of utes, hunting snakes, being on the run and loose all day. She's not used to being on a leash and doing domestic dog stuff.

We find a rope and slip it through her collar, to act as the leash we haven't yet got around to buying. Georgie and I take turns holding her as we set out on our circuit of the nearby golf course.

Topsy is heavy, strong and totally unaccustomed to the restraint. She's also unaccustomed to the other dogs we pass on our path: good, obedient little pets, trotting neatly at their master's heels. Topsy, who is strangely timid of anything on two legs, reveals a hitherto unsuspected desire to lunge at and kill anything on four.

It gets embarrassing. We brace ourselves every time we see someone approach with another dog. We get four hands on her rope, flex our muscles, ready ourselves for a tug-of-war.

A man approaches with the biggest rottweiler I've ever seen in my life. Its head is about a foot across, its shoulders as thick as Ian's. We try to steer clear, clutching Topsy's hastily shortened rope. Rottweiler Man must read panic on our faces and smiles reassuringly as he and his leashed monster draw near. 'Don't worry,' he says, 'my dog's not aggressive.'

We are almost past, almost breathing again when Topsy, with great cunning, astonishing athleticism and perfect timing, leaps, twisting in mid-air to land on the rottweiler's back, her teeth at its throat.

The rottweiler is so startled by this unprovoked attack it doesn't retaliate; just stands there while Topsy, in a frenzy of teeth, saliva and rabid growling, does her best to rip its trachea out.

Georgie and I are screaming at Topsy and tugging on the rope with all our might to prise her free, which we eventually manage, suffering rope burns to our hands and shame on our faces.

We stammer apologies to Rottweiler Man, who just stares open-mouthed at us. We slink off. It is Topsy's first and last walk round the golf course.

⊱┈━┈○┈━┈⊰

'Keegan's got his eye on you,' I tell Georgie one morning. Keegan is the floor sander's apprentice who won't dare remain in the house alone. He always waits outside, safe from ghosts, if his employer has to duck into town for something.

We giggle and carry on. I know that Georgie has met someone in Sydney who no number of hunky or un-hunky apprentices will tempt her away from, but I'm experiencing a second adolescence and loving it. I can't resist teasing her and she teases me back.

She laughs at what she sees as my strange ways. My habit of never stepping outside for so much as a second without a broad-brimmed hat and a long-sleeved shirt. My excessive punctuality, my fear of authority and getting into trouble. She doubles over in hysterics when we're out one day. We are supposed to be at home painting but, when Ian is away, Georgie and I develop the habit of making illicit excursions from our duties. We've driven the half-hour to Hervey Bay

– which, as a bigger town, is home to more shops than Maryborough – and are in a chain store's lolly department, where you can pick up a carton the size of a potato sack and fill it to overflowing with assorted treats packed with fats, sugars, colours and other delicious poisons.

She dares me to eat one before my carton has been weighed and paid for.

'Go on,' she urges. 'Dad and I do it all the time.'

'I can't,' I bleat self-righteously. '*Your* father might encourage such dishonesty, but *mine* would roll in his grave if he suspected I'd do such a thing.'

'Just one,' she prods.

I look over my shoulder. I'm tempted. I know I'm going about it all wrong, drawing attention to myself by looking guilty. I eat one.

The next second the P.A. system barks out: '*Security! Security to Aisle 3!*'

I choke on my caramel and almost drop my precious carton. 'What aisle is this?' I croak, caramel cube lodged against my larynx.

Georgie is weeping with laughter, totally beyond speech, and I quickly realise that it's just a horrible coincidence.

I slink to the check-out and pay for my remaining lollies, making a mental note to keep out of the shop for a good six months.

><+>−◦−<+>−<

Ian, Georgie and I start to host lunch parties in our cracked, peeling dining room. My Englishness makes me amazed that people are willing to drive the two hours here and two hours home just for lunch. My mother thinks twice about the forty-minute drive from her Cotswold village to Oxford once a year to do her Christmas shopping. It's a major excursion. A long haul. Not to be undertaken lightly. Two hours for lunch? Imagine driving for two hours and having a cheese sandwich shoved in front of you. It instils great responsibility in me to produce decent food.

Luckily Georgie is a keen cook too and between us we create feasts for our friends. We get lots of visitors from Montville, including the swimming girls, who make up for disappointment over the predator-riddled nature of our river with an extra glass of wine and slice of pudding. But our first lunch guests are David and Allie.

David, Ian's nephew, is a fit, muscly, sporty young man, so we make him earn his lunch by helping Ian carry the piano out of the dining room in anticipation of the day we start painting.

Not that we can paint until after the underpinning, but I've already plastered the dining room walls with the contents of about six tester pots of red paint. I've been determined from the start that the dining room should be red, and luckily Ian's just as keen. But which red? I don't want it maroon or plummy, and the bright pillar box reds look awful. One red looks like we've daubed the walls in blood. My secret favourite is the colour of raspberries but next to the others it looks almost pink. There have been murmurs of disapproval from Ian over the possibility of pink walls. We live with our assorted red splodges for weeks, so get plenty of opportunity for feedback.

All these lunches finish up with rich puddings so Georgie and I keep going with our morning walks. We talk and talk as we do our circuit around the golf course. She asks me about my family, the years surrounding my marriage break up. We talk about her mother a lot, about the happy pre illness days, about Georgie's childhood, about the tough years of her mother's illness. We talk about death, we talk about reincarnation and whether we want to believe in it or not.

We decide we'd like to believe in it, but are not sure if we can. It's also a bit of a worry, we agree, about where and with whom you might get reincarnated. We know we've lived safe lives with families who love and are loved. It's a big, bad world out there, and if reincarnation is totally random, we shudder to think of the possibilities. 'Perhaps people who've known each other once cluster together,' I suggest. 'Perhaps we all pop up in each others lives again and again and again. Maybe you and I have known each other before and that's why we felt natural together from the start.'

We find this a happy thought.

I tell her of a weird dream I had about meeting my father, who died about a month before her mother. No doubt some would say I had experienced more than a dream.

It happened in the midst of a very difficult time of my life. My father had just died, I was newly divorced, I'd just lost my best friend and was being plagued by several other, more minor dramas. I'd had the worst of bad days, battling feelings of being unable to cope with all that was being thrown at me. Sleep was impossible. Thoughts tormented me into the early hours when, on the cusp of sleep, I felt as though I was floating up and out of my body. I was sure I was conscious, yet couldn't move or control what was happening. Briefly, I looked down at my sleeping body before floating up and out of the window.

The night sky dazzled, and I was soaring toward it. Suddenly I was in amongst the brilliance, stars zooming past me like an asteroid shower. It was an amazing feeling, one I would do anything to recreate. I was up in the mists of Orion's belt, conqueror of the heavens, nothing could touch or harm me again – when everything abruptly went still, the zooming stopped and I was surrounded by an ocean of shadowy faces. Across the throng, I saw my father's face and I stretched out one arm. His fingers caught mine and, for an all too brief moment, we clung. Then his hand slipped away and everything happened in reverse. Back through the asteroid shower at astonishing speed, back home and back to my supine body.

I woke in the morning feeling strong, calm, and capable of taking on the world.

I begin to realise that Georgie and I cope with grief in very different ways. I don't need to surround myself with the physical trappings of my grief, the photos and mementos, as much as she does. With me it's all locked up in my head. There is, I feel sure, no right way or wrong way. It's an individual thing, perhaps influenced by age, perhaps by personality. I am no longer bothered that the Babies' Room has become a shrine to her mother.

With so much time to talk, Georgie and I leave no stone unturned. I believe it is really therapeutic for us both.

CHAPTER 9

ELECTRICS AND OTHER MATTERS

T HREE WEEKS LATER, we're still waiting for the underpinners. Ian finds the frustration harder than I do
because he was born with a desire for everything
to be done yesterday. He's like a caged beast, pacing the
house, making phone calls, huffing and puffing and stamp-
ing his feet. We console ourselves by getting on with what
little we can.

Cyril, our new-found relation-in-law (thrice removed) is
a regular presence. He's been chipping away at endless
repairs since we moved in. He has fixed loose skirting
boards, replaced missing skirting boards, repaired vandalised fireplaces and rotten window frames. He has mended
the cut-in-half door.

Countless times when an apparently insurmountable
problem arises, Cyril says, 'let me think about it,' and every
time he comes up with a solution. Perhaps his brain is stim-
ulated by the numerous cups of tea we share.

Nothing can be hung on the walls. We learn this very

quickly when our largest and most valuable painting comes crashing down, taking a fist-sized lump of plaster with it and smashing a precious Chinese bowl on the sideboard below that had belonged to my mother. Miraculously the painting escapes serious damage. It slams down onto the sideboard then slumps forward onto the back of a sofa. There is minor scratching to the canvas from shards of the shattered bowl, nothing that can't be repaired. We are slow to catch on. We hang it again with a bigger hook. This time it lasts for a week before crashing down, nearly collecting Georgie.

We discover that, though the brick walls are solid, the plaster covering them is extremely thick and extremely crumbly. Even the lightest of pictures has to be attached with a mammoth Dynabolt driven deep into the solid brick-work. Cyril hangs our oversized painting by driving about six Dynabolts through a wooden mount and into the depths of the wall, before attaching the painting to the mount.

We can't do a great deal else. We know the underpinning will crack the plaster, maybe even break a window or two, but there is one other thing we can tackle, and that is the electricity problem.

Apart from the need to re-wire, there are nowhere near enough power points in the house. Some rooms have none. Baddow was, of course, built before the days of domestic electricity supply. But even though the house was later connected, it's as though when those early electricians first came to Baddow they took one look, threw their hands up and said *too hard let's not bother here*.

Calvin Hannam, electrician extraordinaire, enters our lives.

Calvin is slender, agile, ingenious and brave. He's willing to negotiate the darkest, scariest places. He smokes like a chimney, but only outside the house, and drinks his coffee very black and strong enough to stand the spoon up in. He *needs* his coffee so, in the interests of both human kindness and of a task well done, I make sure a steady supply is on tap.

The job is a nightmare for him, but he never complains. He performs acts above and beyond the call of duty, squeezing through tiny crevices to get under the floor and dragging himself around on his elbows like a commando, tools of the trade clamped between his teeth. He goes where no man has gone for a very long time and discovers hundreds of metres of mysterious wiring that seem to have been placed without logic or method. These have to be traced, identified, removed if they are obsolete, replaced if in use. It's pitch black down there, so we feed torches and lamps to him, but we don't join him.

Ian doubts that he'd fit through the hole in the floor. He might lodge halfway and never get out. I suspect I'd fit, but there's no way on earth I'm entering the bowels of Baddow House. God knows what could be down there. I'm thinking trapdoors to tunnels, rats, pythons, toads, cockroaches and a trillion other creepy crawlies. And I'm thinking the body of Baby Joey Aldridge who, we've been told on good authority, is buried under the house somewhere. He died at six months of age and was buried in the part of the garden that our house was later built on. We admire Calvin hugely.

We start to notice that every day when Calvin comes to work, there's a guy driving the car for him.

'Greg's a mate,' Calvin tells us. 'He's doing the driving for me till I get my licence back.'

Bad luck for Calvin, getting done for drink driving. But good luck for us, as we discover Greg, who turns out to be such a treasure.

Greg becomes our regular 'outdoor guy'. He lives at Mungar with his wife, two daughters, two dogs, cats, numerous chickens, budgies, cockatiels and assorted guinea pigs. We do a headcount one day over morning coffee and work out that Greg is responsible for ninety-eight souls. Make that one hundred, if you count Ian and me, for we rapidly learn to count on Greg.

Greg's first serious test is to build a retaining wall on the embankment between the house and the river flat. This bank is thickly overgrown with guava and macadamia nut trees, bougainvillea, various ferns and, unfortunately, the noxious cats' claw vine which tightly trusses up all. Eradicating the cats' claw is on our list for next winter, by which time, we hope, the urgent work in the house will be done. For now, we want to gain a bit of extra ground at the house level, hence the wall, which will enable us to fill a new stretch with fresh soil and plant a hedge.

It's tough work, digging post holes into a steep bank, pouring concrete and setting vertical posts into place. But after the first few days Greg gains an unexpected apprentice. Ian's son David returns from a two-year stint in England and Europe. Twenty-five kilos lighter, pale as a witchetty grub, he looks an unlikely figure to be thrust out into the tropical sun with a crow bar in one hand and a mattock in the other.

Though he's too polite to say so, Greg probably wonders what sort of help he's going to get from such a wan-looking lad. Summer is fast approaching and the days are heating up, but David readjusts to the climate of his native land within hours and between them they throw up the retaining wall with impressive speed and skill. By the time David leaves for Brisbane he's as brown as the macadamia nuts.

I'm excited about this wall because I've been itching to plant a hedge. My collection of frail little camellias and rondeletias wait patiently in their pots. The plan is to alternate them all along the edge of the wall. The rondeletias will grow faster and give us a fairly instant effect with their broad, glossy leaves and sweet-scented blooms. But it's the camellias that will make my hedge a real treat once a year. Planted in loose fill, they love their new home and reward us with plenty of flowers in their very first season.

⊱──◈─○─◈──⊰

We get our first heavy rain of the summer and it pours really hard while I'm in the shower. I jump out, grab a towel and race to find Ian. 'There's a burst pipe,' I tell him.

'Where?'

'I don't know. But I could hear water gushing while I was in the bathroom.'

We sprint back upstairs, expecting floods and chaos. There's nothing. We stand in the bathroom listening and can clearly hear tumbling, spilling water. But the house is dry.

'Could it be inside a wall?' I wonder aloud.

'I don't think so.'

We follow the noise and realise it's coming from a mystery pipe that enters the bathroom through the ceiling above the shower cubicle and disappears out through one of the exterior walls. It's a fat pipe, built to take plenty of water, and there's plenty of water in it right now.

'It's rainwater from the roof,' Ian deduces, 'it must be from the Swimming Pool.'

The Swimming Pool is our name for the flat, open water tank on the roof of the Keep, directly above the bathroom. It is concrete lined, about four metres by five. This is also the haunt of one of our rumoured ghosts, a young girl who is said to have drowned in it and who, we're told, can still sometimes be seen during thunderstorms.

Since hearing this, I try not to think about the Swimming Pool when I'm standing underneath it naked in the shower. Nor am I keen to loiter in the bathroom during thunderstorms.

We can't work out why water from the pool would be drained inside the house. It is a mystery that needs solving and so we go to see Patrick and Elizabeth at Mavisbank.

'Gravity-fed water for use in the house,' Patrick explains.

'Ah,' say Ian and I in unison.

'That's why they would have put the scullery beneath the bathroom. They're the only two rooms that would have required water.'

'Ah,' we chorus again.

'The kitchen was a separate building,' Elizabeth adds. 'They would have drawn water for the kitchen from a different tank.'

This much we knew. The old kitchen had stood quite a distance from the house, above the cellar. Above the tunnel too, if those theories are to be believed.

The innovation of all this amazes me. I imagine Harry, his wife Lappie, daughter Esse and her siblings all washing in plentiful fresh water in their second-floor bathroom. No need for a poor little maid to trudge up and down with pitchers of water. Many decades later, when mains water was connected to the house, the pipe was simply re-routed out through the wall and down into the underground stormwater drain, into the territory of pigs' heads and other souvenirs from town. It seems a shame to waste so much good water. Perhaps later, when the new roof and guttering have been fitted, we can collect our rainwater in one of the underground tanks. But for now, there are too many other priorities.

<hr />

Calvin tells us we should vacuum out the attic space above the bedroom ceilings. Apparently it is standard practice in houses of this age, especially when the ceilings are made of tongue and groove boards. Otherwise all the accumulated muck of the ages can work its way through the ceiling and keep the rooms below showered with fine dust, ad infinitum.

We hire a man with an impressive industrial vacuum cleaner. The floor space up there is about two hundred and forty square metres and it takes him and his apprentices two days. He vacuums out over *nine hundred kilograms* of accumulated dust. Almost a tonne! We take photos of the massive sacks he keeps dragging down the stairs.

There's a set-back when the final sack is almost full. It's sitting on the upstairs landing, as tall as me and considerably fatter. Its bulging mass throbs and pulses as a hose as thick as an elephant's trunk sucks the last of the attic detritus into its belly. I've just come upstairs to see how they're going when without warning there is a devastating rupture. The bag explodes and its contents, under pressure from the powerful hose, erupt with the force of a Mount Vesuvius. Suddenly our upstairs landing, adjacent corridor and stairwell are Pompeii before the archaeologists moved in.

There's a stunned silence. Then the operator stammers apologies and dispatches apprentices in all directions to get brooms, mops and buckets.

'No problem,' I say, 'I'll do it.'

The operator scratches his dusty head in surprise. 'You?'

'Yes, me. I'll clean it up.'

'You're sure?' His eyes are the only living thing visible through the volcanic ash.

'Absolutely,' I say.

I am not being generous. Nor am I being a martyr. I have seen apprentices at work with brooms and I don't want this calamity spread any further than it has already.

Luckily the bedroom doors are all closed and while the French doors at the end of the hallway are open it's not a windy day. I want to yell *Don't breathe! Don't sneeze! Don't move! Just go!* 'I'll be fine,' I say, forcing myself to sound calm. 'I'm used to this sort of thing, what with all the renovating.'

He hesitates a moment or two, then nods to his boys and in a flash they've extracted the hose from the manhole in the ceiling, gathered up the equipment – including the fragments of torn bag – and gone.

I see them off, then return to Ground Zero. First I carefully shut the French doors, then I fetch bags, buckets, a broom and a shovel. I gather up the cushions off the day bed on the landing and take them outside where I smack them vigorously before returning to my shovel and broom.

I start with the architraves, doors and window sills. It takes hours – there is just so *much* of the stuff. I'm constantly up and down the stairs, taking bucketfuls to the wheelie bin. I'm a bit scared to open the bedroom doors but when I do, discover it could have been far worse. Inside each door there are a few square metres coated with the extra fine dust that managed to leak between door and architrave. I gather this up then wash the floors.

The clean-up takes half a day. But, after all, it's wonderful to know that the attic is now pristine. I look up at the manhole cover in the ceiling. According to Maryborough lore, Harry Aldridge once spent two days locked in our attic.

The story of Harry's sojourn in the attic begins with his Aboriginal wife, Lappie, hearing that some of her people were out to get Harry. The Aborigines of the day were no more enthusiastic about mixed race unions than the Europeans and Lappie – so the story goes – held grave fears for Harry's safety and for that of her children. Knowing a raid was imminent, she urged Harry and the children, Esse, May, Daniel and Harry Junior, to conceal themselves. With the help of a long, long ladder, the manhole cover was removed and Harry, with the children, duly climbed up into the attic.

Lappie assumed she'd be safe from her own kind, so she didn't hide. But when the raiders came, they would not be placated. Perhaps frustrated to find their true quarry missing, they knocked Lappie on the head and carried her away. It was a blow she was said to never fully recover from.

Harry had no way of knowing what had happened and he had no way of getting out of the attic without help. No one but Lappie knew he and the children were up there. So for two days and nights they languished in stifling heat without food or water.

The story goes on to suggest that it was the workers in the fields who came to his rescue. Known as Kanakas, they were Pacific islanders, brought to Queensland to work in the spreading sugarcane plantations. Some came willingly, on the promise of money, but many were coerced aboard ships and carried to Queensland in what was actually a slave trade. The practice was known as blackbirding and was one of the most shameful events in Queensland history.

The islanders at Baddow had their duties in the fields and their own quarters some distance away, so would not normally have gone near the big house. But they must have noticed that the place seemed deserted and dared to creep in. The rooms were empty and silent. There was no sign of their employer and his wife. There was no sign of the four children. Clearly all was not well.

They called out for their master, and presumably heard

weak cries for help. Harry and his children were discovered and released and a search party was sent out to find Lappie.

Somewhere, not far away, the party of islanders caught up with the kidnappers. Lappie was rescued and taken home to her family. But the fate of the kidnappers was not to be envied. Legend has it that the islanders killed and cannibalised them. Standard practice for a defeated enemy.

><+>−O−<+><

Ian and I love the stories we're told. No doubt some are true, some are nearly true and some are gross distortions of the truth. We don't mind; we love them all, and we love that our home has such a fascinating past.

A passion for history was one of the first things we realised we shared. On some of our early outings, long before we moved to Maryborough, we'd babble on so much about times gone by that we'd forget to eat, drink or notice the passing of the day. I love the social trivia of yesteryear, the behaviour, the manners, the intense formality that had sons calling fathers 'sir' and wives calling husbands by title. And I'm agog at the extraordinary stoicism of women.

I fascinate Ian with lurid tales of the sexuality of Queen Elizabeth I, with the implication made by many historians that her anatomy was 'not like other women'. So just what did she have down there? It's hard to believe she'd been born a hermaphrodite. Knowing how desperately her father yearned for a son, you'd think the midwife would have been mighty swift to declare the baby a boy if there had been a hint of male genitalia. A mystery that will never be solved.

Ian loves the glory of battles won against amazing odds, of bravery, chivalry and derring-do. He likes the trivia too, and once told me about the pickling of Nelson's body.

Generally, those who die at sea are buried at sea, which is logical when you consider the evils of transporting rotting bodies back to port in the days before refrigeration. But Nelson was a hero, deserving a grand funeral back home. So in order to preserve his body until they reached port, his crew dropped him into a barrel of rum which, in some circles, is still known today as the Blood of Nelson.

This was a story I'd never heard before and will never now forget. Unlike Ian, I'm just a tiny bit put off drinking rum.

Most of all, we both love Scottish history. Early in our relationship, we were out driving when Ian asked me who my greatest hero was.

'Fact or fiction?' I said.

'Both. Either.'

I didn't have to think for long.

'Mmm . . . fiction is more compelling at the moment. It's got to be Young Lochinvar. Walter Scott's Lochinvar.'

Ian took his eyes off the road for a heart-stopping, accident-inducing instant and stared at me.

'Watch out!' I yelled. We swerved back onto the straight and narrow. Luckily we were on a little-used stretch of country lane.

Ian apologised, confessing his passion for those particular verses. Suddenly we were both laughing and quoting lines like mad.

So faithful in love, and so dauntless in war,
there never was knight like the young Lochinvar.

Ian admitted that in another life he'd like to have been Young Lochinvar.

Lochinvar is the character who hears his beloved is being forced by her father to wed *a laggard in love, and a dastard in war*, and rides his charger up the steps at the wedding feast, swings the fair Ellen onto his saddle and makes away with her.

For the rest of the day, Ian called me Ellen and I called him Young Lochinvar. Instantly we agreed that when the time came to set up house together, we'd call our home Lochinvar.

Thus Baddow House has another, secret, name. Baddow House is our Lochinvar.

CHAPTER 10

GEORGIE'S GHOST

SINCE WE HAVE BEEN living at Baddow, we have been subjected to an escalating number of ghost stories, but my courage is maintained by the continuing presence of Georgie. She comes and goes, visiting friends and getting organised for her trip to England, but she times it so she's always with me when Ian's away. I'm very grateful for several reasons, but Ian and I are agreed not to tell her one of them: my dread of being left to spend my first night alone in the Ghost House.

We get strangers walking in off the street, knocking on our door and asking, 'Do you know your house is haunted?'

Tradesmen, deliverymen, neighbours, raffle ticket sellers and every other person who has cause to come to our front door reiterates the news until it's almost laughable. Almost.

When I get the car serviced, the girl from the garage drops me home and sees where I live. 'Baddow House!' she says, '*creeeepy . . .*'

'Yes,' I say dryly, 'so people tell us.'

We are told repeatedly of the girl who drowned in 'the Swimming Pool'. I can never imagine why she was up on the roof.

A popular story is that if you walk down to the river and look up at the house, you can see faces at the windows. We try this, but the only images we see in the glass are reflections of trees in the park.

There are voices, footsteps, glimpses of the past, the woman on the stairs. You name it, we've got it. I think I'm starting to get cured. It's like being treated with immersion therapy for a phobia: you fear moths and they shove you in a room full of moths. You weep and wail, your heart pounds, your pulses almost erupt but, eventually, exhaustion and the realisation that the moths have not the power to eat you alive sets in.

But I'm to learn that daring to believe in progress can be a dangerous thing.

⊢•◈•○•◈•⊣

Ian is away again. Through my sleep, I'm vaguely aware that Georgie's bedroom light is on. It glows through the glass panel above our connecting door but I'm too groggy to do much wondering and soon fall back to sleep.

In the morning we meet downstairs as usual, to get ready for our fat-busting walk. 'Did you sleep well?' I ask routinely, tugging on my running shoes.

'Actually I had a really bad night,' she says, sitting down.

I pause in my lacing, remembering. 'Come to think of it, your light was on late.'

'Yes. I turned it off when I went to bed and had almost gone to sleep when something made me open my eyes. I'm surprised you didn't hear me scream.'

She's got all my attention now. Lacing forgotten, I'm riveted.

'I saw a woman lying on the bed next to me,' she says.

'You saw *what*?'

'She was just lying there, on her side, staring at me like this.' Georgie opens her big eyes wide in a parody of a hideous zombie-like stare.

'You must have been dreaming,' I say.

'No. I swear she was there. The light was off but I could see her clearly. She was sort of glowing, and just staring at me with this fixed look.'

I'm getting sweaty listening to this.

'I grabbed for the light switch and then she was gone. I left the light on all night. I nearly got into bed with you.'

'You should have,' I say. 'What did she look like?'

'Actually, she looked a bit like you, Anne, shoulder-length hair and a fringe. But her hair was dark.'

I immediately think of Esse, part Aboriginal, dark-haired Esse. Esse, who wept a lot and who couldn't bear to leave Baddow. Esse, whose bedroom Georgie is unwittingly inhabiting. I mustn't tell her. Besides I know my thoughts are foolish. Ghosts don't exist. Clearly Georgie was dreaming. I attempt to rationalise it with a dream analysis I am unqualified to deliver.

'You say she looked a bit like me, except for the colouring.'

Georgie nods.

'Well I think you were dreaming and it *was* me you saw. Think about it. Suddenly I'm thrust into your life. Twenty-four hours a day, seven days a week I'm in your face. Your subconscious had me there in the most intimate place – your bed. My head on your pillow. Even in your sleep, you can't escape me.

She laughs a bit and I am relieved. We go for our walk. Death and reincarnation dominate our conversation.

Ian returns and we hurry to tell him about the episode. He dutifully laughs it off.

⊱──⊰

One of the things I like most about our early weeks in Maryborough is that virtually no one in Maryborough knows us. In the small town of Montville it was impossible to post a letter or buy a newspaper without running into people you knew, which is all very fine when you are happy and in a people mood but when life has grown rugged, sometimes you want to slink in and out of town without having to talk.

Maryborough is an anonymous delight.

I can go to the supermarket in my most unflattering, grottiest gear, smeared in garden or house muck, confident that no one's going to say, *Anne's been looking a bit rough lately*, and wonder why. I can explore every corner of town, knowing I won't encounter a single familiar face or provoke a single curious comment. It's immensely liberating.

But all too soon things start to change. 'Baddow House captures heart of Romance Writer' says one headline. 'An Epic Romance', says another. The problem is the fame of Baddow House. Everyone in Maryborough wants to know what's going on with this iconic building and, for some, my history as a romance writer adds spice to the tale.

I have no idea how my writing past has become general knowledge and cast accusing looks at Ian, who's not known for his secret keeping powers. He's quick to swear innocence.

I find myself wishing people wouldn't focus on my writing career, as it draws the inevitable question: *So what are you writing now?*

'Nothing,' I'm forced to admit time and time again. 'The renovations keep me too busy,' I explain, by way of an excuse.

But in my heart I know that I'm still in a period of convalescence, that I can't write again until I regain my sense of equilibrium.

The body, I've discovered, heals more quickly than the mind. Hair grows back, energy returns, but regaining confidence, courage and belief in oneself takes much, much longer. Hopefully this will happen before I run out of renovations to excuse myself with.

>—+-◆>—○—◆+—<

Georgie and I get serious about painting the scullery. This we can do because it occupies the downstairs area of the

Keep which will not be affected by the underpinning. If the underpinning ever happens, that is. The scullery is a dirty, shabby mess, the walls layered with multiple coats of old paint. But when there are two of you, and chatting can occupy the hours, no task ever seems quite so arduous. We put on our painting clothes, turn up the CD player and get started.

I'm the fascinated recipient of daily news reports about Georgie's budding relationship with Tom Carroll. Theirs is a story that excites the romantic in me. Years ago, Georgie and Tom went out together briefly, but extreme youth and Georgie's unreadiness to throw herself into a serious relationship stalled their progress as a couple. Tom never forgot her. He waited patiently, bided his time, and some five years later he's wooing her again. This time it looks like his efforts will be more successful.

Though Tom is in New South Wales, there are lots of phone calls to punctuate the tedium of our painting. It's exciting to be in on the beginning of something I just know is going to be big, and it's wonderful to see Georgie looking so happy.

But we also talk plenty of trivia. As my mother would put it, we talk about anything and everything and nothing of importance. The hours zip by. At one stage Georgie asks me, 'what's your favourite song ever?'

'That's hard,' I say, 'there are so many. Give me a minute.'

We paint in silence.

'*Eternal Flame*,' I tell her after an age, 'The Bangles.'

Georgie nearly drops her paintbrush. 'You're not serious?'

'Why not? I love that song. I could listen to it any time, in any mood.'

'I don't believe it,' she says. 'It's mine too! You ask any of my friends. Anyone who's ever met me. When that song comes on the car radio, I turn it up full volume and belt out the words. I know them all.'

We laugh. But somehow I'm not surprised. Georgie and I have bonded so thoroughly and easily, shared tastes and experiences seem to occur all the time. It's easy to get all fatalistic and believe you are destined to encounter certain people in your lifetime, even to believe that you've known them before.

⊱⊰

Bit by bit we get visits from the other children. Ian's youngest daughter, Annabel, is still travelling in England and Europe, but his eldest daughter, Dinie, who works for a travel agent in Sydney, comes north on a trip to visit us. David comes again, which is brave of him, considering the forced labour he was subjected to last time when he was fresh off the plane from England. David is good natured enough to laugh when we tease him about being Greg's apprentice.

My eldest son, Andrew, is still in Italy, and won't be due back for another year, but my younger two, Elizabeth and Robert, come up from Brisbane.

Elizabeth and Robert are both at university doing science. There's been some subject swapping, so their degrees are dragging a bit, but they both seem fixed now on completing what they're doing. Some of Robert's subjects sound a bit mysterious: bizarre and intangible fields of physics. We laugh when he tells us he's studying Chaos this semester. I imagine a lecture hall of anarchy: students hurling rubbers and screwed up bits of paper at each other.

Elizabeth does the sort of subjects that involve handling dead body parts, which is really strange considering she's so scared of ghosts and the dark and anything remotely spooky. But Elizabeth has had an un-queasy stomach since she was a toddler. I remind her of the time we took our dog to be spayed, and had to drag her out of the vet's screaming in fury because she wasn't to witness the opening up of the dog. 'I want to see Lucy on the inside as well as the outside!' she howled.

An eclectic mix of young people. But the vote seems to be unanimous: they all love the house.

We notice that most of the young think the house is great, that what we are doing is great, but a lot of our contemporaries, those in the safety of middle age, think we're mad. They can see that the house has once been magnificent, they know Ian and I love old houses, but the thought of taking on such a massive old wreck makes their more conservative blood run cold. Probably most of them have dabbled with renovations themselves at some stage in life and have a realistic idea of what we're faced with. They understand the pitfalls, the dangers, the expense, the sheer hard work, and would never willingly put themselves in our shoes.

Kids don't seem to mind living in mess. They don't mind that the walls are peeling and the floors are cracked and rough – and they don't even notice how foul the kitchen is. In fact, Robert probably feels quite at home given the squalid student accommodation he's been inhabiting.

We love having all of them to stay; the sound of young voices and laughter injects life into the house. The patter of not-so-tiny feet running up and down the stairs and along the corridors accompanies the music of Robert hammering away on the ancient piano in the dining room. Sometimes it's Beethoven, sometimes its Cradle of Filth or Marilyn Manson – we don't care; our house is built for music. I wish Maryborough wasn't quite so far for them and the house could hum more often.

CHAPTER 11

UNDERPINNING

EVEN WHEN GEORGIE IS away, I keep up my circuit of the golf course each morning. Actually *playing* golf holds zero interest for me, the closest I've ever come to playing being sessions as my Aunt Dorothy's caddie in school holidays. But walking the circumference of the club grounds is the perfect distance for a morning fat-busting session. It takes about forty minutes, striding out at my maximum pace, and is easy walking in all weather because there is a narrow bitumen path the entire way.

The path takes walkers past the Ululah lagoon which is a haven for ibises, swans, geese and wild ducks. Ululah was the best fresh water supply in Maryborough's early days, the Mary River being tidal and salty, and it was a regular camping ground for the local Aborigines.

Massive shady trees: figs, jacarandas, albizias and others I haven't a hope of identifying, grow along the edge of the path, so you never have to walk too far in the sun before you gain the shelter of the next canopy. It's a beautiful walk, and I know how lucky I am to have it on my doorstep.

I see the same people every morning. There seems to be a walker's etiquette that has us all saying 'Hello!' or 'Good morning!' to every person we pass. Sometimes you fall in with another person if you happen to start out at the same time. I don't know their names, but we chat about the weather, each other's gardens and we make smug comments about all the other residents along the street who don't get up at the crack of dawn to walk, but who lie snugly, lazily abed.

I meet another English lady who is an avid gardener. In winter she wears gloves and a woolly hat and gathers kindling as she walks. She's been living here many years and can identify everyone we pass, with added, interesting titbits. One morning we pass a tiny, sparrow-like woman I've seen plenty of mornings before, and my new friend tells me this lady is past ninety years old but walks everywhere, even into town to do her shopping. I'm impressed, and experience a stab of determination to make myself do this for another forty-five years.

Most mornings another elderly woman zips past me on her bicycle. She's quite plump and always wears a loose-fitting dress that flaps dangerously around her spinning pedals and wheels: an outfit at odds with her safety helmet and bike-riding confidence. It's one of those bikes with a little basket and tinkling bell, and on her return journey the basket is always full. I imagine she goes out every morning to buy the newspaper and a litre of milk or a loaf of bread, and has been doing so her entire life.

There's something immensely satisfying to me about people sticking to their habits and routines, about so much regularity. Seeing the same people doing the same thing every day, year in, year out. It's a security, an assurance, that the clocks will keep ticking, the world will keep turning, and that the tides will keep rising and falling. Perhaps I need this assurance more than most because of the nomadic nature of my childhood.

My parents met and married in Malaya in 1955, and throughout my childhood lived in South-east Asia. We would be two years here, two years there; moving from Malaya, to Hong Kong, to Singapore, to Penang, back to Hong Kong then on to Brunei. These house moves were also peppered with the extra journeys my sister, Jane, and I took back and forth to school in England. From the ages of nine and eleven respectively, Jane and I were put on a plane to London's Heathrow, flying west for the school term, then doing the whole trip in reverse for the holidays.

We made this journey twice a year: for Christmas and for the Northern Hemisphere summer break in July/August. All other holidays were spent in England with our Aunt Dorothy, Uncle Eric and cousins Pat and David.

Usually we flew to Singapore, where we would overnight at Raffles Hotel, then catch a little, propellered plane the next day to Penang – or wherever our mother and father were at the time. Back and forth. Back and forth. Long, long journeys in those days. More than thirty hours from London to Singapore and I used to throw up all the way. Luckily Jane was a good traveller and had the presence of mind and sleight of hand to be nifty with the air-sick bags.

Jane still is the most switched-on, clear thinking person I know. Absolutely the best to have at your side in a crisis.

People used to wonder that we were sisters: Jane, with her dark hair and nut brown eyes. Eyes as big and thickly lashed as Bambi's. Me, with my pale skin and snowy hair. Jane, competent, alert, decisive and totally reliable. Me, easily distracted, too busy talking to listen.

In recent years, Jane has told me of the great burden of responsibility she felt in getting, not only herself, but her younger sister from one end of the planet to the other: to be sure that we boarded the correct plane, we had our luggage, our tickets, our boarding passes, to have to deal with my air-sickness and get me safely home, time and time again. I had no idea. Belatedly, I am humble with gratitude.

It was an exciting life spent in exciting, exotic places. Days on the beach dominated our holidays, but there were also trips to the hills, to temples, to fascinating markets before the days of mass tourism. We would see living snake and frog meat for sale, spices, incense, batik fabric, wonderful costume jewellery. We'd dodge mangy dogs, beggars, and try to keep at bay the hordes of locals trying to touch my cap of bright hair, a blonde-haired child being a symbol of good luck in some cultures.

Jane and I loved it all. Sand and surf, the snake temple – where we happily let snakes coil round our juvenile throats, the spicy food, the tropical fruit, the games of mah-jong, Monopoly and pontoon. But the nomadic nature of our life left me the legacy of a craving for sameness, of needing the security of staying in one place for a very long stretch of time. So far my adult life has not worked out this way.

There have been eleven house moves since I married and came to Australia. It would be easy to believe the gods are conspiring to keep me on the move for their own amusement.

Now is the time to fight back, to dig in my heels for the peace and stability I've been seeking for years. I want to be able to plant a tree and stay put long enough to see that tree grow to maturity. I want my rose bushes to thicken and age alongside me. I want to know my home so intimately that I am familiar with every leaf and blade of grass, and with the reach of the sun on any given day at any point of the season. I want to find my own patch of dirt, put down my own deep roots and cling to that spot until I die. And then I want my ashes scattered there.

I recognise Baddow House is that patch of dirt.

The underpinning team are due today, and the irony is not lost on me that, just as we are underpinning Baddow House, so Baddow House is underpinning me.

<hr />

It's been a two-month wait for the underpinners and we're raring to go. Young Lochinvar's been up since dawn, inspecting his castle, measuring cracks, looking at levels. The underpinning process has been explained to us, but it's too big, too daunting, too specialised for us to fully get our heads around. We have to wait, watch, trust the team, and hope the house doesn't fall down.

They arrive in a flurry of utes, trucks and unfamiliar equipment. First they excavate around the foundation wall of the section to be underpinned. This is almost half the house. When the foundations are exposed, I'm surprised to see they're comprised of little more than a continuation (though thicker) of the exterior wall of the house. 'Strip foundations', they are called. Ian and I are picking up plenty of jargon.

Our strip foundations have a fierce crack running through; an extension of the Big Crack above ground. We are a bit shocked to see that it has travelled all the way to the bottom of the foundation wall, but at least we are on the brink of fixing it.

As the men dig, I worry about Baby Joey Aldridge's grave. We've been told that a headstone was once sighted underground near the northern corner of the house, which is the very spot receiving most attention from the underpinners. But all that gets dug up are some remnants of original verandah footings.

Spring has turned into summer and the days are heating up. The men are working on the hottest part of the house: the north-western end. They labour shirtless in shimmering heat without a leaf to shade them. The air is still, the ground dry and dusty and the glare of the sun bounces off the white walls with the force of a solar flare. We offer the men cups of tea, glasses of water, biscuits and cakes, but they always bring their own supplies.

Unlike Cyril, Calvin and others who have helped us, these men seem bent on keeping to themselves. Communication is minimal. Ian gets frustrated because he likes to know what's *going on* at any given time of the day. Underpinners are a breed of their own. It would take the

Spanish Inquisition to get information out of this lot. All we can do is watch and wonder as they work.

The men excavate down about two metres below the foundations until they reach the load-bearing soil and rock that our geologist tested for and found in the days before we moved in. Fresh concrete is poured into this hole, just enough to form a slab that the men will be able to place their jacks on.

They then go away for a week to let the concrete cure and we are left with our foundations hanging in mid air. It's really very scary. If ever the end of the house was going to drop off, it would be now. I try to avoid going into that part of the garden because looking at the suspended walls is just too disturbing for my psyche. We try to joke about it, saying how we'd better not carry anything *really* heavy – like a coffee mug – at that end of the house, but it's not very funny and I find myself keeping out of the most vulnerable area of the living room.

I'm so relieved when the men return.

Twenty-six fifty-ton jacks are positioned on the newly cured concrete, and fitted to the underside of the suspended foundation wall. The idea is to work all the jacks simultaneously and get some reasonable levels back to this end of the house. Ian hopes to be allowed to operate one of the jacks.

We get quite a crowd on jacking up day. We've always known this would be a momentous occasion. A day when disaster could strike or a day when we would realise our dream of a straight, stable house. Georgie is away, but Cyril and Nola come to watch. So do Trevor, Elizabeth and Patrick, plus half the neighbourhood.

Men are positioned on jacks. Ian gets his wish. He's operating a prime jack, right on the northern corner. The order goes up and the foreman stands back. The men pump the jacks. All eyes are on the Big Crack. Topsy runs for cover.

One . . . two . . . three . . . One . . . two . . . three . . . the pumping must be done in unison. There is utter silence from the crowd. Nothing much seems to be happening. *One . . . two . . . three . . . One . . . two . . . three . . .* I see a small piece of plaster fall from high up under the eaves. I bite my lip.

'Rest!' calls out the foreman. He strides around the house, examining with eagle eyes. 'Again!' he shouts.

One . . . two . . . three . . . One . . . two . . . three . . . Trevor nudges me. 'Look at the Big Crack,' he says.

I look. It's definitely a fraction smaller, a fraction less gaping.

One . . . two . . . three . . . One . . . two . . . three . . .

A couple of plaster chunks drop to the ground from above the Babies' Room bay window. I don't say anything. The foreman has seen them, but I feel sick.

One . . . two . . . three . . . One . . . two . . . three . . .

More plaster rains down. A couple of fresh cracks appear above the bay window. I'm expecting the window panes to shatter at any second and am poised to duck for cover.

One . . . two . . . three . . . One . . . two . . . three . . .

The Babies' Room cracks spread wider. A chunk of plaster and brick big enough to kill a man plummets to the ground. I open my mouth to yell a warning.

'Stop!' shouts the foreman and I quickly shut my mouth. He strides about inspecting. 'That'll do,' he says. 'That's enough.'

Measurements are taken and levels are done with a little beeping machine. I look at Trevor. 'Is that *it*?' I can't believe the whole thing only took about ten minutes.

Ian comes over. He's all sweaty with effort and flushed with excitement. 'We're still an inch lower than the rest of the house,' he tells us, 'but that won't be visible to the naked eye. Any higher would have caused too much damage.'

'It caused a bit as it is,' I say. 'Have you seen that bay window?'

He looks up at the Babies' Room and winces. But we both know that you can't pull or push a big solid mass in one direction without it giving in another. The trick is to strike the best balance that you can. The Big Crack is much less gaping. Loose bits of plaster have fallen out of it, or been ground out by the pressures exerted, and I can see that the levels are not as uneven as they once were. Even with my naked eye. This is very reassuring.

The party over, most people go home. Trevor, Elizabeth and I go inside to drink tea, eat cake and recover from the trauma. Ian is far too worked up to relax. He's pacing about, examining walls, measuring cracks, needing to be outside with the men, doing as they do. I tell him not to stand below the Babies' Room window.

Now that we're jacked up, they bolt metal 'pins' – which actually look more like solid iron posts – between the cured concrete slab and the base of the old foundation wall. Then the jacks are removed and the wall, neatly propped and pinned, sits solidly on its row of metal stilts. Concrete trucks form a queue in the driveway. The whole excavated area has to be filled with concrete. I lose count of the number of trucks that come to disgorge their loads. Ian later tells me that fifteen truck-fulls were needed, which means that more than one hundred and fifty cubic metres of concrete now sit below us. Sounds good and solid to me. I dare to re-enter the living room at last.

Even better, we can now get serious about our interior restoration. Friends and lunch parties must be put on hold. Trips to the movies, to the shops and Muddy Waters are a luxury of the past. Up until now, we've only been playing at renovating. The real work is about to begin.

CHAPTER 12

PLASTER, PAINTS
AND PUD

Now that we have our levels, Cyril can do more. All the stuck windows and unaligned doors can be re-hung. This involves taking doors off, shaving bits off them here and there to make them straight, then rehanging, getting levels, taking them down again, shaving a bit more off, and so on.

The windows are all sash windows, opened and closed with the aid of counter-weights. These are long metal sausage shapes that hang concealed inside the wall beside the window. The heavier the window, the bigger the counter-weight. Half our counter-weights are missing, strings are broken, or wrong weights have been put in that don't balance the windows. Cyril repairs all this, making new weights out of concrete he sets into cylinder shapes.

We have advanced to the stage of painting rooms. It's brilliant to think that we will soon have a room or even two completed. Georgie and I have already painted some of the easy areas, including the kitchen which is just a temporary paint job seeing as we're going to have to pull it down next year, but we know the main part of the house is well and truly beyond us. The ceilings are over four metres high for starters, and there's no way I'm getting on that sort of ladder. Even worse is the state of the walls. The plaster is loose and powdery and we have been warned that without proper professional preparation we will never get paint to stick to it.

But before a lick of paint goes on, we have to find a plasterer to repair those cracks.

The town supplies a unanimous recommendation. Neville 'Pud' Cockburn is the man for the job. 'Pud' is the *only* man for the job. Not far off retirement age, Pud is a master of his art. He has experience, patience and is trained in techniques of the old school that have all but died out today.

Unfortunately most of Maryborough and the Fraser coast are also after Pud, who has learned to keep a close guard on his whereabouts and phone number, so as to avoid being harassed day and night by desperate renovators.

Rumours are rife that he has moved to Hervey Bay, thirty minutes drive from here. Some even think they know which street he's in. But Ian, canny and determined as the best of them, is close on the scent. The young town planner at the council we've had contact with has the same surname as Pud. Jamie Cockburn is the one who filled me in about the Mary River crocodiles, and he's the one Ian rings if he has any queries to make with the local council. He's a very helpful and well mannered young man and, given the singularity of the surname, Ian feels there's a good chance Jamie and Pud are related.

Ian's hunch proves correct. Pud turns out to be Jamie's uncle. Ian has Pud in his sights now. It's only a matter of time.

A precious phone number is obtained. But no one ever answers it. We suspect that Pud's got one of those call-vetting phones where the number of the person calling pops up. Perhaps it is Ian's persistent ringing, perhaps his nephew puts in a good word, but, finally, ecstatically, we make voice contact with Pud. He takes pity on us and comes around. But Pud can only give us limited time. He repairs one room then disappears. It's always touch and go to lure him back.

We do the dining room first. Not too much work for Pud here, as the dining room is not in the underpinned, most damaged section of the house. He taps and bangs at the walls, scraping out any loose plaster from the cracks and around the architraves. Then he packs anything that needs filling with new plaster, smoothing it down to blend with the old wall. He's soon gone and the rest of us can move in to finish the room off.

Finishing off involves repairs to woodwork, courtesy of Cyril, sanding and re-oiling woodwork, which is my job, and any extras that need attention: a spot of reglazing here – that's Cyril again, an extra power point there from Calvin, painting the walls, then sanding and sealing the floorboards.

Cyril and I get to work. Cyril repairs windows and floor-boards while I start on the cedar. I have volunteered to sand and re-oil all the cedar joinery in the house. So today is day one of Cedar Duty. First I have to sand the muck of the ages off the wood. The trouble is there's so much. Muck *and* cedar, that is.

I do the skirting boards first. I'm not an experienced sander and, as I don't want to risk gouging great chunks out of the precious wood, I don't use a power tool but pieces of hand-held sandpaper. But even this can leave uneven tracks and scratch marks if I'm not careful. The skirting boards are good to practise on because I know they'll be mostly hidden by furniture. It takes days. I work my way around then up to do the window sills, window frames and architraves. Then I do the fireplace before, finally, the most dreaded part: the doors.

The doors, with their large flat panels, are going to show any irregularities a mile away. I know how much Ian loves this cedar, that it matters even more to him than it does to me. I do leave scratch marks and have to sand deeper to get rid of them. Sweating, I have visions of having to sand ever-deepening sweeps to erase my errors and ending up with spoon shaped panels. It's a nightmare, like when I trimmed Jane's Barbie doll's hair without asking. The cut was horribly crooked so I kept cutting to try and even it up.

Today there's the added pressure of Cyril the Perfectionist working in the same room. I sneak furtive looks at him to see if he's noticing my clumsy, amateurish efforts. But he's always engrossed in his own fastidious work.

Days later, I'm finally finished and can toss out the reams of sandpaper, wash down the woodwork and start oiling, which is pressure-free. It doesn't even matter if I slop it on the walls because they haven't been painted yet.

Just as Cedar Duty has been my toughest job, going to

the tip becomes Ian's. There is so much rubbish here, both from the garden and from our renovations, that Ian travels daily, sometimes several times daily to the local tip. At first, we keep count of his trips in amazement but, as they mount into the hundreds, the novelty wears off.

He becomes intimate with the men running the place: their most familiar face. They wave him in time and time again, never charging him admission. I wonder if they ever speculate about where he's getting all his material from.

⊳─◆◇◆─⊲

We discover house painter Tony Benecke – 'Benji' – and plead with him to take us on. He's very busy – as are all the tradespeople in town – but, like Pud, he takes pity on us and agrees to paint a couple of rooms. Little does he know that it'll be two years before he escapes.

I assume Benji must be a throat cancer survivor. His voice is hoarse and rasping, and there is a faint scar across his throat. Several weeks and several dozen tea breaks later, we discover that in fact he nearly lost his head in a car accident.

Benji is intrepid. Benji is fearless. He climbs the tallest of ladders and teeters on trestles balanced up high in the soaring stairwell. He outdoes Darren and Diane as the main act in our Chinese circus.

Together we paint the dining room cherry red. Blood red, I tell visitors when I'm trying to scare them, though really it is the luscious deep pink of ripe raspberries, the exact colour I've yearned for from the start. I love it with the dark cedar woodwork and our old pieces of furniture.

We've acquired a beautiful cedar dining table by a stroke of great good fortune and happy timing. Old friends of Ian's, Scotchie and Pepi Walker, no longer have a use for the family table that has stood proudly in the Glenlyon dining room for generations. It is too large and cumbersome for most modern homes, but we know it is exactly what our dining room at Baddow deserves.

On a scavenging trip to the antique and junk corners of Brisbane, I find a vast chandelier with twenty-four lights and about a thousand crystals. It's a bit dodgy, crystals falling off and hung all lopsidedly. I have to remove half the crystals and twist hundreds of minute bits of wire to reattach them correctly.

Calvin mutters unspeakable things when he sees it, but a cup of coffee thick as tar and he's willing. Soon it's hanging in splendour. We're a bit shocked by the amount of light it throws. The dining room is as dazzling as the Versailles ballroom, but a dimmer switch gives us the atmosphere we seek. We are ecstatic.

We cover the dining room chairs in apple green velvet, which might sound alarming with the cherry red walls, but the room is huge enough to cope with the colours, and everything is toned down by the quantity of dark wooden fixtures and heavy furniture.

Ian buys a set of decanters for the sideboard and fills them with the usual whisky, brandy and port. He saves the largest till last, and fills it to the brim with the Blood of Nelson.

We are champing at the bit to start on the garden. I come from a family of green-fingered, keen gardeners. Well, I'm not sure about the green-fingered bit where I'm concerned but I'm certainly keen. I want to build wide flowerbeds all around the outside walls of the house but know I must wait until the verandahs are on. The verandahs are going to involve massive earthworks and much tramping about of big-booted men. Any garden I build would swiftly vanish. But we can plant in areas well away from the house.

There is a lovely, mature poinciana tree overhanging the driveway. We see lots of very healthy poincianas around town so are confident that they do well in our soil and climate. The bonus is that they are Ian's favourite trees. We plant eight of them in various spots, well away from the house and the builders' trucks. With little else to care for yet in the garden, we throw all our loving efforts into these trees.

Never have trees been so well mulched, fed, watered and hugged. Our reward is the sight of them springing vigorously skyward, with ever multiplying foliage. One tree has been placed as a centrepiece in the front lawn. How gratifying to see that this one outdoes all the others. We are astonished at its rate of growth. Ian inspects it daily, often summoning me outside to bear witness to its splendour. Before long it is twice the height of Ian. We speculate on how glorious it will be the following summer. Then Ian walks into the kitchen after one morning's inspection with a deep frown on his face. 'That tree's looking a bit off,' he says, 'not as green.'

I look up from my crossword. I don't need to ask which

tree. 'Perhaps it's starting to yellow off. They are deciduous,' I suggest.

'Too early for that,' he says. 'Besides, the others all look healthy.'

'Could we have over-watered it?'

'Unlikely. These trees do well in the steamiest of the tropics. It shouldn't mind a heavy-handed watering.'

We ponder the problem but all we can do is hope to find signs of recovery the next day.

It looks worse.

Days pass. Ian stands by his tree, fingering the yellowed foliage. He's perplexed, disappointed, but mostly he's upset.

'I've been thinking,' he says.

'Mmm?'

'Do you remember a couple of weeks ago when I was poisoning cats' claw on the bank, I rinsed out my spray kit up here on the driveway.'

'Mmm.'

'I think I've poisoned the tree.'

My stomach lurches. I know Ian's going to be crushed about this. 'Is it too late to save it?'

'Probably, but I'll try. I'm going to flood it, try and dilute the poison.'

He drags the hose out and his favourite tree sits in a lake for the next several days. It loses all its leaves. The other poincianas spring defiantly upward.

I try to cheer him up. 'They're pretty tough, you know. It might grow again next spring. Just sit dormant for a while.'

Ian is far from cheered. He's looking like a man who's

just murdered his favourite child. 'We'll have to wait and see,' he says and slouches off.

⋗⋯⊶⋯○⋯⊷⋯⋖

D Day dawns. Deal Day. Georgie has gone to visit friends, Ian must return to Montville and I am finally going to be on my own overnight.

'Are you sure you'll be all right?'

Ian's quite worried for me. He's already confessed that he wouldn't want to have to face it.

'I'll be fine,' I lie, knowing I have to keep this promise of promises.

After three months, Baddow House is well and truly home. I'm a thousand times more comfortable than I was in the beginning. The rooms are full of familiar furniture, some are even painted, and I'm accustomed to all the little tweaks and creaks the place makes.

But I know that when the shadows grow long and the sun dips over the horizon, my imagination will transport me to another realm.

Ian leaves after breakfast and rings several times during the day. I've banned him from mentioning The Night, knowing I have to psyche myself up and mustn't be reminded by the jitters of another. I have to school myself not to think, not to care, not to imagine a sloe-eyed Esse standing at the window, weeping into the moonlight.

I make preparations. I have my shower when it's still daylight. I turn on lots of lights upstairs. I bring my toothbrush downstairs, so I don't have to make the trek along the passageway after dark. I play music, I have the TV on loud. I hum around the kitchen in my pyjamas preparing food, taking larger than normal swigs from my wine glass.

Being the Last One Awake has always been a problem for me. At home. At school. At Aunty Dorothy's house, Latimer House. That was the worst. Five hundred years of human existence between those four walls. Rooms packed with antiques, and with paintings of beady-eyed Tudor types, lace ruffs around their necks, hair drawn back from pale, plucked brows. Latimer House, so called because Bishop Latimer, a Protestant bishop, delivered his last sermon from her very steps before being arrested by those loyal to the Catholic queen, Mary Tudor. Bloody Mary.

Latimer was taken away to be burned at the stake opposite Balliol College in Oxford. His final words were: *'We shall this day light such a candle, by God's grace, in England, as I trust shall never be put out.'*

Some might interpret these words as his belief in the power of his martyrdom to the Protestant faith. To me, they smack of wanting to stay, of having no intention whatsoever of venturing forth to the Hereafter. *Let my force be with you and let it never be extinguished. I'm going to hang around.*

'It's the Bishop,' my cousins would say, every time a light flickered, or a floorboard creaked, or a door inched open of its own accord. Sometimes when my sister, Jane, with her precocious palate for literature, sat absorbed in Balzac, Dante or Voltaire, my cousins, Pat and David, and I would go down to the cellar and inspect the floor for signs of disturbance; signs that a body was entombed below the worn flagstones. We'd make dens, camps and lairs. We'd explore the attic, reached by a twisting wooden staircase. Later David, intrepid boy, made one of these attic rooms into his bedroom.

It was fun, a game, some of the happiest times of my life, but it was not so funny when the shadows grew long, the sun dipped under the horizon, and I was sent to bed. Especially not if I was Last One Awake.

Seeing as I'm the only one in Baddow House tonight, being LOA is clearly my inescapable fate.

But there's Topsy in the garden, and there are houses further along Queen Street. In these houses, I tell myself, there are TVs going, babies crying, people arguing, laughing, parents reading bedtime stories to their children. I draw comfort from this. So many beating hearts, so much pulsing, living flesh only a stone's throw away. With the windows open, sometimes I hear distant traffic, even a siren or two. These are good, wholesome thoughts.

I try not to remember Ian's brother, Bruce. Intrepid Bruce. Forward scout of the Vietnam War Bruce, for whom the bullets of the Vietcong held no fear, saying that no way could he sleep alone between these four walls. Outside, he declared, wrapped in a swag on the grass, he'd be fine. But not inside. Never inside. Bleak, uncomforting words.

I'm certainly not about to do the swag thing. I consider bringing Topsy inside, then dismiss the idea when I remember the time a friend told me she'd been woken up by her dog in the bedroom barking furiously at an empty corner of the room. She could see nothing and no one, but the dog persisted, hackles up, growling at the bare wall for ages. I wonder if Edgar had dogs . . .

Bearded Edgar with a stockwhip in his hand.

But these are bad, bad thoughts. I shove them away, annoyed with my head for straying down such dangerous paths.

I form a plan to go to bed really early. Eight p.m. isn't a fraction as scary as midnight, the witching hour. Maybe if I get to sleep early enough . . .

At quarter to eight I hop in the car and check into a motel.

This scene is repeated the second time I'm left alone. But on the third time, I make it.

CHAPTER 13

SCREAMS IN THE PARK

I'M PRETTY COCKY ABOUT my courage. Ian has never slept here a night on his own. I delight in teasing him, and when Delia and Bruce visit for Ian's birthday in November Delia and I threaten to go to a motel so that the brothers have to face a night in the Ghost House without our protection. Not that I really believe Ian is so easily frightened. He's probably just making me feel better about my own stupid cowardice by pretending to be the same.

But one evening, about a week after Bruce and Delia have gone, we are upstairs. It's just on dusk. We're mucking around, as we do. Ian has chased me up the stairs, I've outrun him and I'm laughing at him for being so slow.

'Maybe,' he says, 'but at least I'm stronger.'

'Prove it,' I challenge.

We are like a pair of ten year olds; daring each other, chasing each other and, now, wrestling like a couple of idiots. Ian pretends to be overpowered. I playfully punch him. 'Edgar!' he calls out, '*ouch!* Maria! Help me Edgar!'

I go very still and, in my best theatrical voice, intone, 'Don't . . . invoke them.'

At these words Ian freezes, but only for a split second – then, to my astonishment, he's downstairs and out of the front door.

I follow him.

'I can't believe you just said that,' he says. He is standing on the garden path in the twilight, taking deep breaths.

'It was only a joke.'

'Maybe, but it struck a nerve. It was chilling. Evocative. Don't say anything like that again.'

'Okay,' I agree, 'but don't you shout for Edgar and Maria again like that.'

'Done.'

We're both smiling now, but I am more aware than I've ever been that Ian is just as easily spooked as me.

In so many ways we are amazingly alike. We find the same things funny, the same things scary. History fascinates us. We are both capable of immaturity: it's fun to muck around, to play games, to laugh. We both have the potential to annoy, yet our ways don't annoy each other. We love nothing better than being together and tag after each other all day: he follows me to the washing-line, when I go to the bathroom I see the shadow of the toes of his boots outside the door. He might be there to chat, or he might be lurking in silence to pounce when I emerge.

We both have a love of the Gurkhas: mine bequeathed to me from my father who knew his Gurkha men were matchless, Ian's from his days as a teenager when he witnessed a visiting company of Gurkhas participate in a military parade. His fascination became total: he admired them beyond anything, dreamed of becoming a Gurkha officer one day.

In fact I joke that he only pursued me for my connection to the Gurkhas, that he's fulfilling his fantasy to chase the daughter of the commander of a Gurkha regiment.

Teasing happens regularly between us. But best of all is working together on the house, which is our grand passion. It's our common goal, our common dream, to build our Lochinvar.

⋗⊶⊶○⊷⊷⋖

Pud has been lured back to replaster the living room. It's the biggest room in the house and also the most damaged. It is, after all, site of the Big Crack. We're still in awe of Pud, still living in fear of him leaving for other, more important jobs. Every morning when he arrives, whoever spots his ute first will rush in and tell the other, 'Pud's here!' Sighs of relief all round.

We attempt to ply Pud with cups of tea and home-baked biscuits, we hope to bribe him, to sweeten him and tempt him into seeing this as a cushy job, but he never accepts, just sets up his ladders and trestles and gets to work.

First he scrapes out the cracks till they're gaping and huge, like a surgeon excising an infected wound. After that he mixes up wheelbarrows of magic 'mud', a secret mix that can expand and contract but hopefully will never crack. Then he climbs the trestles with his buckets and special tools and creates seamless smooth walls for us. We are speechless with gratitude.

When Pud has finished, Cyril and I move in. There are two fireplaces in the living room that have been vandalised in the past, and Cyril's first job is to rebuild their mantels and surrounds. They end up a Frankenstein's creation of old and new parts, but so cunningly fashioned by Cyril that it's impossible to tell that they've ever been tampered with.

He re-hangs the bi-fold cedar doors that divide the living room in half. These doors have been missing from Baddow House for years, taken down so that the room would be one huge open space. We're told that John Hastings, who owned Baddow House in the nineteen-seventies, located them on a garage in Maryborough, cut to size and painted white. Thanks to John's detective work, we've been able to restore these magnificent panelled doors that are some three metres tall and made of glorious, aged, red cedar.

Cyril attaches a few centimetres of wood to their bases to make them full height again. When the doors are sanded and re-oiled, you can barely tell they've been altered. But it's a nightmare to rehang them. They are incredibly heavy and sag on their hinges, scraping the floor. So Cyril goes into his routine again: adjusting and rehanging. It takes all day. Without Cyril's inexhaustible patience it would never have happened, but by dusk we have perfectly hung, smooth-swinging doors that respond to the touch of a fingertip.

The next day he moves on to the windows, while I get on with Cedar Duty. There are nine large windows in the living room with varying numbers of panes. Some need puttying, most have no counterweights, and a few are totally rotten and need replacing.

It takes days. Summer has hit hard and it's hot work. Cyril and I boil. People often say to me, 'you must feel the heat, being from England.' I nod bravely, never pointing out my years in Malaya. An English background seems a good excuse to complain and sweat and generally not cope with summer. But often I think of Maria Aldridge in all her corsets and layers. No ceiling fans for Maria, and I doubt they had *punkah wallahs* in Australia. If she could survive in all her finery, surely I can in my shorts and singlet.

⤛ ⟡ O ⟡ ⤜

The night I finish the cedar in the living room, I retire to bed with sore hands. I'm exhausted from my day's work, from trying to get the layers of muck off our precious wood. My arms ache, my hands ache, but most of all my fingers hurt where the nails have begun to split vertically. Bits of skin that have been covered since birth are now exposed. I've tried wearing gloves, but can't sand properly in them. I've tried clipping my nails almost out of existence, and have now resorted to putting Bandaids round each fingertip.

I flex my fattened fingers. Standards of beauty, I decide, are inversely proportional to scale of renovation. My hands are not only bizarrely Bandaided, but ingrained with fireplace blacking and tung oil. My hair is untrimmed and lank, my face has forgotten what make-up feels like, I'm too busy to walk regularly, and am eating too many biscuits with Cyril so have gained weight.

Ian, amazingly, says he likes me best this way, looking salt-of-the-earth, dedicated and wholesome. I'm not sure whether it's my altered appearance he's attracted to, or whether the concept of the 'good, hard-working woman' excites him. I suspect the latter, because I catch disturbing glimpses of fondness on his face as I work. The harder I slave, the fonder his face.

⊱─⊰⊱─◯─⊱─⊰

Benji returns and transforms the living room with 'Sweet Butterscotch' which, in reality, is more of an old mellow yellow. I'd always known the living room would be a shade of yellow. It faces north-west and gets loads of natural light through the nine tall windows. We're thrilled with the result. The cedar glows every afternoon when the sun moves round, and the air turns soft, warm and amber.

We hire a professional to sand the floors, which are grey and parched from years of neglect and from the days of the vandals, smashed windows and rain beating in. The wood is crows ash, a timber native to northern New South Wales and southern Queensland, and comes up beautifully with a proper sanding and a couple of coats of tung oil. It turns golden, like the walls. The entire room pulses with living colour. I want to spin around in there, to drink it in, to *eat* it. I can hardly bear to put furniture in the room. I kiss the walls, kiss away Esse's tears.

⊱─⊰⊱─◯─⊱─⊰

More and more I think about starting to write again. As I work on Cedar Duty, or walk Topsy in the park, or deal with toads, or water the garden, my mind is constantly nudging at the hibernating writer in me. There's a fresh bubble of excitement as I go about my duties, because I know I'm going to do it again: I know I'm going to redis-cover the pleasure of writing.

I have no idea why it has taken me so long to feel able to do this, but I do know that, for me, it is impossible to write when the will is not there. It can't be forced; it just has to happen. And when it happens, it's like being seized by something you can't control – something more powerful than self demands you push aside everything else and write till your hand nearly drops off. I realise I must battle to keep this burgeoning drive at bay until the house is finished. Gather thoughts by all means, but keep a lid on them. If I let myself commit thoughts to paper, I'll be lost, unable to stop.

Through all these plans tumbling in my head, I'm very much aware that I can't yet return to fiction. I want to. I try hard to steer my creative urges fiction-wards. I ask myself, *which century?* Perhaps the Civil War this time. Cromwell's day. It's a period that's always interested me. But it's no good. Much as I try, my brain refuses to do as it's asked. There are words blossoming inside me that demand to be put down on paper, but all of these words centre on the present, on Ian and myself and what we are doing. I feel an inescapable urge to tell our story.

Ian and Baddow House are responsible for this, for restoring my sense of stability, firming up the quicksand

I've been flailing in for the last several years. Quotes about suffering for your art, about tortured artists and so on sound like rubbish to me. I defy any person to successfully create when they're upside down, inside out, their eyes being pecked out by the crows. Struggle and oppression crowd the head, strangle inspiration, stunt creativity. Depression, I'm told, can manifest symptoms akin to dementia. I imagine this is because it takes up so much space in the head. Space which is finite. Clear out the muddle, banish the black dog, as Churchill termed it, and there is room to move, room to create, to imagine, to soar.

I want to soar again. I remember those first heady days, years ago now, when I discovered I could write. I remember exploring the sheer joy of writing, of wrangling words into sentences that pleased, satisfied, delighted. The astonishment and thrill of publication, and also the utterly humbling knowledge that someone, somewhere, deemed my words worthy of translation into other languages.

I know it's going to be hard to curb the drive in me but I must channel my creative energy into the house. I'm determined to complete this task and do it well. I'm determined to do a job worthy of Edgar's dream, of Esse's passion. Nothing must distract me.

⊱ ⊰

The next time Ian and Georgie are both away, my new found confidence gets a battering. It's around midnight and I'm half awake, though I don't know why. My eyes are shut, as they always are at night, asleep or awake. Why

se on the driveway, circa 1900. This photo was very useful when restoring the randah.

arry Aldridge, circa 1895. Sadly, nothing remains of the original garden.

Two views of Baddow House in the 1940s. The dirt track (*top*) is now the corner of Queen and Russell streets.

Negotiation day: Anne and Ian pose by the old water pump outside the scullery.

Caddow House as it looked when they first saw it. The low flat roof is the dingy, fibro kitchen soon to be demolished.

Pud at work, plastering one of a pair of old church corbels onto the exterior wall.

Top: Section of the Big Crack. A the loose bricks had to b removed, exposing the bac of the cedar panelling insid the living room

Bottom: The house encased i scaffolding – a horrifying expense

nne, jack of all trades, hard at it. But the worst job of all was sanding the cedar
ottom left).

Northern aspect of the finished house, complete with new verandahs.

Aerial view from the south, taken on Anne's horror flight. Note the box gutter dividing the main roof in two.

The new kitchen was well
worth the wait.

KATE JOHNS

The finished dining room after
Mother Mary's visit. Note the
sparkling silver.

KATE JOHNS

Anne and Ian on their wedding day. Tucked into Ian's sock out of sight is
the *skean dhu* that went with his grandfather to the Boer War.

open them and risk seeing something you don't want to see? If shadows are going to hover over me, or orbs are going to float round the room, I'd rather not know, thank you very much.

I hear a noise. It's a creak, a tweak, a footstep. I snap fully awake: a quivering sweating mass of fear. Though I'm pretty sure the noise was downstairs, which is marginally better than in our bedroom, I have no idea what to do.

If the verandahs were built, I'd be out there. But short of leaping seven metres to the ground, I'm inside, on my own, with a noise. I start to think of my father as I often do when I'm feeling spooked. If there is another side, another world, a *Hereafter*, then he's in it. And where he is, there can't be bad things.

I'm considering sneaking a hand to the phone on my bedside table to ring Ian and bleat my predicament. Not that he can do much, at nearly two hundred kilometres away. Besides, my hand wants to stay right where it is: under the blanket.

I hear something else: a tap, a light knock. Its downstairs, and, I'm beginning to suspect, outside. There it is again, louder this time. Outside. Definitely outside.

Relief melts my bones and every trace of paralysis is banished in an instant. Intruders! Burglars! Hah! No *problemo!* I leap out of bed and grab Ian's torch.

At the bedroom window, I listen, torch turned off but fingers at the ready, posed to hit the on button.

I can hear talking, whispering, girlish giggling. Kids, I think, and open my mouth to tell them to naff off. But something stops me. The girlish whispers are distant, floating up from the perimeter of the garden. Below my bedroom window the voices are male and there are several of them.

Apprehension creeps over me again. My euphoria at the realisation I am dealing with the living not the dead has blinded me to the possible dangers which are, of course, far greater than those of any lurking ghosts.

I decide to reveal my presence but not my gender. I flick on the torch and flash it round the garden. All whispering stops. I whistle for Topsy, knowing she won't come, but let them think a guard dog is a possibility.

There's a sudden awesome thud and clatter, as if a heavy missile they've thrown at the house has bounced off the exterior wall. Then I hear running footsteps. My torch picks up three male figures fleeing the scene.

I hang around for ages, going from window to window, but see and hear nothing more. How stupid we are to be scared of ghosts when our fellow humans are so much more of a genuine threat. It's never occurred to me before just how isolated we are, surrounded by the park. Windows could be smashed, screams could be screamed, and no one would hear.

⊱─◆─○─◆─⊰

There was no one to hear George Furber scream when a morticing axe struck him.

Furber was the first white man to settle at the head of navigation on the Wide Bay River. He arrived in 1847, a year before our Edgar Aldridge. He set up a trading post with a plan to ship out the wool clip from the Burnett region and to ship in supplies for the distant squatters. It didn't take him long to upset the Aborigines.

With a lack of European labour, he pressed a few of the local Aborigines into working for him. But Furber was a hard taskmaster, and apparently he didn't keep his promises. Out fencing a section of his land one day, he received the axe in the back of his head.

The wound was deep, 'glancing off the bone and slicing the skin from the back of his head and neck', according to one account. Furber knew he would die if he didn't reach help fast. So he bound up his head as tightly as he could, mounted his horse and rode the one hundred and fifty miles to the nearest doctor at Ipswich, west of Brisbane. Remarkably he survived this hideous journey, arriving in just three days with a nasty, infected wound. That he survived at all must be testament to his physical condition, determination and resilience.

After his recovery, Furber returned to Wide Bay. The settlement rapidly expanded and his business prospered. By 1851, four years after his arrival, there were forty-seven homes, ten more partially built and two hundred and ninety-nine settlers. There were five inns, several wool stores and a general store.

George Furber might have been remembered as the father of all Maryborough but, sadly, history records that the axe incident heightened Furber's loathing and distrust of the Aborigines to the point of insanity. He never left his home without a loaded pistol in his pocket, and is thought to have shot and killed three Aborigines in his time on the river. But eight years after his axe injury it was all over for George Furber, speared to death on the banks of Tinana Creek. His grave is in the park, just a short walk from Baddow House.

Old-timers say that if you stand by his grave at dusk, you feel a sense of gloom and malevolence. Others say that cameras have picked up orbs of light in the trees overhead.

A spooky place, our park, but I'm not as isolated as George Furber was that first year. My screams might go unheard, but I've a telephone at hand, the police five minutes away. I wonder whether I should ring them now and report an attempted break-in. But it seems too late, too trivial. I go back to bed.

In the morning I find a piece of bamboo, five metres long and some thirty centimetres in circumference, outside the living room wall. It's from a huge stand growing in the park adjoining our garden, dragged up here, I'm sure, to smash a window for access.

⊳⊷⊶⊙⊰⊷⊦⊲

Greg comes to reinforce the garage wall. He has a ute full of sleepers and posts. Ian is away again, but Georgie is back and she and I have been detailed to help Greg unload.

'Morning Greg,' Georgie and I call out in unison, 'how are you today?'

'No use complaining,' comes the regular reply.

Greg is in his mid-forties, a year younger than me, with very white hair that Ian teases him about. Ian likes to think the white hair makes Greg look the older of the two of them, when in fact Greg is thirteen years Ian's junior. We all shout Ian down when he gets like that.

The phone rings and I run inside. It's Ian.

A minute later Georgie runs in bleeding profusely from a cut hand. I drop the phone. 'Whatever have you done?' I ask.

'Greg jumped up on the back of the ute to unload the wood and I got a bit of an eyeful,' she explains.

'Not another one,' I say, as we wash her bleeding hand.

We've already established that some of the tradesmen don't wear underpants, though it was Ian, not us, mercifully, who got those earlier sights. One of the hazards of climbing ladders and onto the backs of utes, we realise, is the risk of unrestrained genitalia breaking free.

'So the sight made you drop the wood?'

'Mm.' Georgie winces and extracts a hideous splinter from one finger. 'It was the shock of it.'

We wonder if it is the hot climate in Maryborough that has everyone swinging free. It gives us endless scope for speculation when we are out and about to the supermarket or Station Square.

Station Square is Maryborough's main shopping plaza. We love our outings there, but have to admit it has its limitations. Christmas is approaching fast, Georgie and I know we will have to spread our wings.

CHAPTER 14

CHRISTMAS, PUDDINGS AND FLAMES

ANDREW AND ANNABEL are both still overseas. Annabel is travelling Europe and working as a 'granny nanny' – a live-in home help to elderly patients or to people recovering from operations. Andrew is still teaching in Venice. We have five children for our first festive season.

With Benji's help, Ian and I have scurried to finish one of the big bedrooms so that we can set up a kids' dormitory. This is the only room in the house in which a philistine hand has painted over all the cedar joinery. Scraping so much paint off is too daunting so we repaint it all, including the mantelpiece and hearth surrounds, in a buttery creamy colour. The walls we do in 'Blue Larkspur', which is a soft lavender blue. It all looks very French and pretty and I finish it off with a little chandelier I've found on one of my treasure hunts. There is a queen-size bed and two singles in here; accommodation for four. It becomes known as the Blue Room, for obvious reasons.

It's been a while since we've had extras to stay, with the chaos of our renovations reaching epic proportions. But with the Blue Room complete, we ease off the pace and focus on our rapidly approaching first Christmas.

We know that everyone's going to feel a bit weird. We don't expect our children to all become best mates just because Ian and I are together. The children have known each other slightly since childhood but are different ages and have vastly different interests. Ian's son, David, is a keen sportsman and rugby fan. My sons, Robert and Andrew, would rather hang out at an art gallery or literary evening than sit through a rugby match. Come to think of it, they have never in all their short lives sat through a rugby match.

The girls have more in common. Certainly Georgie and Elizabeth are both needful of the Babies' Room when they stay. Though this Christmas, Georgie shares the Blue Room with Dinie and David. Elizabeth gets the Babies' Room and Robert, with his plethora of musical instruments, is happy on his own further along the corridor.

We discover both families follow a similar routine when it comes to important rituals such as present opening, and adult children on both sides still expect to receive stockings from Santa. It augurs well for an easy time.

We place the tree in a corner of the living room where it can be seen from the bottom of the staircase and all the way along the corridor, then cover it with the usual angels, stars and lights. A big old house like Baddow, with so much dark wooden panelling, has a distinctly English feel which might be at odds with its tropical setting, but seems very appropriate for Christmas. I only wish we could conjure up a bit of snow.

With so many people involved, the mound of presents under the tree is tall and teetering. Georgie's present to me is CD-shaped. I have no trouble guessing it will be The Bangles.

Early in the morning, Elizabeth and Georgie are first to wake. We discover this has always been the way in our different households, that Elizabeth and Georgie are by far the most excitable in their respective families.

Elizabeth, as a small child, barely slept on Christmas Eve, and would spend Christmas Day feverish with exhaustion. As she grew older, she'd still wake hours before her more placid, easy-natured brothers, and pace impatiently outside their closed bedroom doors until, finally, worn down, I'd give in and say, 'all right, you can wake them up.' Some things never change.

This year the house gradually comes to life, as big children in varying states of grogginess unravel the contents of their stockings. Ian and I take lots of photos and open our own presents. By mid-morning, we're all on the bottle and starting to cook.

We nibble mince pies as we work. I've made twice my usual number, along with stacks of brandy butter. Years ago, I issued my children with a choice: 'I'm not doing Christmas pudding, Christmas cake and mince pies. That's too much fruit mince for one family to cope with. You can have two out of three.' Mince pies and pudding won every year without fail. Though this year I've also made a frozen Christmas cake: ice-cream crammed with Cointreausodden fruit, moulded into a neat dome. It smells like a boozy milkshake.

It's been a particularly hot summer. With a turkey and simmering puddings to deal with, Georgie and I nearly die as chief chefs in the airless, low-roofed, lean-to kitchen.

But the cherry red dining room looks utterly Christmassy. And it's amazing what a bit of champagne and excitement about the house can do to dispel unease. Sitting at the Glenlyon table, we take a moment to imagine the meals this table has supported, the occasions, revelry and honoured guests it has entertained. Then we toast Georgie's imminent trip to England. We toast absent friends and absent children. We toast the departed.

Everyone leaves on Boxing Day. I hug Georgie and tell her not to stay away in England for too long. But there's little danger of this, not now that Tom Carroll has entered the picture.

Ian and I think things have gone pretty well. Another milestone under our belts. We might grow complacent if we're not careful.

><+>-o-<+><

A couple of days after the children go, Ian's younger sister, Gina, and husband, Tim, call in. Tim won me over the first time I met him.

It was a few years ago. We and others of the Russell clan were staying in a cabin high on the Bunya Mountains. It was the first time I'd met most of Ian's numerous relations, and I was knocking back the wine rather too quickly.

It's a hard thing, even at the age of forty-three, to be thrown into an extended group of family and in-laws who've all known each other for thirty years or more. I felt the odd one out, the alien, different, awkward, an albatross among swans. Despite the kind efforts of some.

We barbecued dinner and sat around a long table on the deck; a beautiful night under the stars. Jokes, memories, teasing and anecdotes were flung hard and fast across the table. I clutched my wine. My wine was my friend.

Halfway through dinner, without warning, the power went off. No problem. One or two candles were found. Moonlight and stars did the rest. On, on we drank.

My tolerance for alcohol is low, which is something I don't understand. I'm a normal weight, taller than the average female. Why can other, smaller women tip booze down their throats and keep going? Isn't it all a mathematical equation? Quantity of alcohol versus quantity of blood in veins? So, loath to disgrace myself, I knew I must stop, and set down my glass to concentrate on eating food and acting sober. The evening wore on. Coming down off the booze, I began to grow thirsty. The water jugs on the table were empty. I left my chair to stumble through the black-out to the kitchen tap. No water. Strange. I returned to the table empty-handed. 'There's no water,' I told everyone.

'It's the black-out,' a voice in the dark said. 'No power, no pressure pump, no water. We're not on mains up here, dear.'

I took my seat. Picked at the food. My thirst was getting out of hand. Was I really that thirsty, or was it an illusion brought on by the knowledge that I couldn't find water? Time passed. I thought of Burke and Wills in the desert. I thought of people adrift in powerless, rudderless boats, drinking their own urine. *Get a grip*, I told myself, you are not going to die.

Ian said, 'Are you all right?'

'Yes,' I lied, 'just a bit thirsty.'

'Have some more wine,' he suggested.

'No! no.' I realised I was almost shouting, and grew hot with embarrassment.

Someone left the table. In the black of the night, I wasn't sure who it was. I heard them stumble through the dark, bang into things. A long, long time later, I heard the tripping and stumbling return.

It was Tim. 'Here,' he said, 'I found this rolling round the floor of my car.' He handed me a plastic bottle with about seven centimetres of water in the bottom. It's an act of kindness I'll never forget.

We are delighted to welcome Tim and Gina to Baddow House, proud to show them round our rotting grandeur. Halfway through the tour, they ask: 'But why are you doing this? It's going to cost a fortune.'

I'm silent. Disappointed that they don't get it, disappointed that talk has turned to money.

Ian, in his good-humoured way, laughs it off, waves his arms and says something about saving icons and giving back to life some of what we take out.

Why *are* we doing this? Let me count the whys. *Have you never wanted something so badly, your flesh has hurt with the aching for it? Has a sight never moved you to believe you could walk on water, lift a car off a child? Have you never been grabbed by a fever of inspiration, thumped between the eyes by it, known you would wither without fulfilling it?*

But I know its naïve of me to think that other eyes see as mine see, that other hearts feel as I feel. Perhaps we *are* mad, perhaps we should be conservatively stashing every little penny we can earn in safe investments instead of throwing those pennies at our dream.

I pour the tea, the fever in me concealed by the outer shell some have called *reserved*. I nibble a mince pie and sip my tea, well aware that I'm overly sensitive and defensive when people criticise what we're doing and why we're doing it. I'm a mother protecting her baby; a lioness defending her cub. I soon settle down, knowing my instincts aren't quite fair. Besides, this is Tim – Tim who I owe for life after his blind, heroic trek for water. I sit back and enjoy the short time they are able to stay.

Talk turns to ghosts. Gina and Tim also have a house with a reputation for spooks. Their most famous spook is known as the Shaker for his habit of shaking awake unsuspecting guests. Gina recounts a story from the days when Ian was married to Jenny, and they were staying at Tim and Gina's home. Ian, full of good food and wine, slumbering deeply, though aware, as everyone was, of the threat of the Shaker, woke screaming one night to the touch of a hand shaking his shoulder. It was Jenny telling him to stop snoring. He's never lived it down.

When I confess my earlier struggle to achieve a night alone at Baddow, Gina admits she doesn't like being alone overnight with the Shaker. It's always a comfort to learn that others are as daft as I am.

⊳─┼─◆▸─○─◂◆─┼─◁

I'm outside pegging washing on the line when I hear a series of loud cracks. It's a hot, dry day with a strong wind whipping about. At first I think the cracks are the sounds of branches snapping off in the wind, but soon they are too numerous and rhythmic to be explained away so easily. I grab my basket and head back to the house.

Upstairs, I hang out of a window. The cracking sounds are getting louder and I'm really confused. If I lived in a war zone I'd be seriously concerned. I run downstairs to look for Ian. He's beyond the bald, murdered poinciana tree, out by the road, digging holes in the ground for our privacy-creating hedge. It's a punishing job in the heat. The ground is like iron; a mix of bone dry clay and compacted road base that needs a crowbar to be broken up.

He looks up when I call him, his face sunburnt and streaming with sweat. 'Can you hear those noises?' I shout.

He stops, listening. On this side of the house the sound is muffled, barely there.

'It sounds like gunshots,' I say.

'Fire, more likely.'

'*Fire?* You mean a bushfire?'

'Yes.' He downs shovel and crowbar and we run around to the back of the house.

The noise is much louder here and there is smoke, which I couldn't see before. 'Call the fire brigade,' he says.

I run inside. I've never called the fire brigade in my life and my fingers tremble as I'm trying to punch the numbers on the phone. Like the dumb blonde in a movie, I hit the wrong ones and have to do it again.

'*Emergency. Fire, police or ambulance?*'

'Fire please. It's not a real emergency,' I say, 'I mean, there isn't a house on fire or anything, it's just in the park,' then curse my stupidity. Now they might take all day to get here.

'*Town?*'

'Maryborough,' I say, 'and it would be good if they could perhaps hurry up a bit.'

She gets our address, the location of the park, and hangs up. I run back outside.

Ian is near the clothes line, and lifts an arm, pointing, when I get close. I see flames running along the river bank, shooting up the massive stands of bamboo. Edgar Aldridge's bamboo. This is what is causing the loud cracking. The canes are enormous, at least ten metres high with a thirty centimetre circumference. As the heat expands inside each segmented length of cane, it explodes with a noise like a gun shot. Each towering cane burns right to the top, popping segment by segment, at the same time crashing to the ground as the base burns through. This happens over and over again until our ears are ringing.

But there is a flat grassy expanse between us and the bamboo so, with the exception of flying embers landing in the gutters or under the eaves of the house, I feel reasonably safe. We position hoses just in case, and keep a close eye on the direction of the floating embers.

Suddenly a snake of flame darts out into the grass separating us from the wall of fire. Neither of us had expected it, and we watch in horror as the flaming serpent heads straight for the perimeter of the garden.

'Don't worry,' says Young Lochinvar with his customary sangfroid, 'grass fires are easy to control. I was years with the Montville Bush Fire Brigade, I've seen this kind of thing more times than you can imagine.'

'Okay.' I'm staring unblinking at the fickle flames, ears straining for the sound of the fire brigade. I'm now seriously worried about my inept reporting of the fire and wonder if I should confess to Ian. If our garden hoses were long enough, I'd be squirting water at the flames myself.

'I'm going out to the road,' he says. 'I'll watch for the fire engine and flag them down if they're not sure how to get through here.'

I hadn't thought of that. There is no road to this part of the park. Our house and garden block the way.

'You stay here and keep an eye on things,' he says, and bolts off.

I hate the responsibility of guarding the living, writhing destructive thing that is heading our way. It teases and torments, stopping a while, retreating, running sideways then back toward me. I think it's trying to outwit me, scheming to sneak around the side without being noticed. A large area of grass is black now and the smoke is building, hurting my eyes. I wish I'd thought to shut the windows of the house, but there's no way I'm leaving my post now.

More bamboo comes crashing down. In the distance I hear the phone ring. I ignore all these things. Nothing is going to distract me. Though the fire is some sixty metres away, I can feel the heat on my face and wonder about those scenes you see on the news, of firefighters right in there amongst the flames. I don't understand how they can get so close without spontaneously combusting.

I'm considering backing right off when I hear Ian's voice, then the sound of a vehicle. Relief swamps me and I turn to see him striding toward me with a big grin on his face. The fire engine at his heels edges slowly across our lawn. It stops, men leap out and in about five minutes flat the fire is history.

Talk turns to the house and our restoration. Our firefighters are all far more interested in what's going on with us and the house than the erstwhile fire which, I'm starting to realise, was a trivial snuffing-out matter for men who deal with much more on a daily basis. But I've half an eye on the blackened ground as we talk, not quite trusting that it won't erupt again.

We thank the men profusely as they climb back into the truck. 'Any time,' they say with a smile and a wave. 'Keep an eye open though,' they caution us, 'these things have a habit of springing up.'

'No problem,' I say, amazed anyone could think for a minute that I'd turn my back. Silently I vow to stand guard for the rest of the day.

Ian returns to his hedge-hole digging.

⊱⊶⊙⊷⊰

The Christmas break over, it's back to real work. We're getting closer to finishing the interior. Bit by bit the house is transforming. We love the mellow yellow of the living room so much, we carry it on up the stairs and into the bedrooms. All the rooms in the house not already painted are now going to be yellow. It brings out both the richness of the cedar joinery and the honey glow of the floorboards.

I decide to pretty up our bedroom. It's a huge room, eight metres by six, with heavy, dark furniture including a massive walnut wardrobe we bought in an act of great extravagance when we first signed the contract on the house. There is also a cedar chest of drawers as tall as I am that once belonged to Ian's father, as well as my dressing table and a second chest of drawers. The doors, windows and architraves are, of course, rich red cedar, as is the fireplace surround, although the ornate overmantel mirror (found by me on a fossicking trip to Brisbane, glass-less and in a dozen disman-tled dirty pieces) is walnut like the wardrobe. It's a room that can take a bit of prettying without looking too girly. I buy a damask cover and cushions for the king-size bed in the same creamy, buttery colour as the walls, and cover a chair and my dressing table stool in old-rose pink velvet. Then I toss a few odds and ends around the room in the same sort of antique pink: a cushion here and there, a few bits of china I've had for years, a couple of pink flowering cyclamens on the window sill. Finally I upholster two old seagrass chairs in pink and cream toile.

It's all mangoes and crushed strawberries in our room now. In the warm afternoon light it looks good enough to eat.

But throughout the house, the newly painted walls look bare. Though we have enough furniture, cushions and objects to last us a lifetime, our pitiful art collection is lost on the hectares of wall space. My daughter, Elizabeth, suggests I explore eBay as a source of inexpensive art and prints.

I've never even heard of eBay, but over the phone she instructs me how to click on. Trillions of items for sale pop up before my startled eyes. Most are displayed with tempting glossy photos. All available from the comfort of your home. What an addictive danger to a shopaholic! Luckily both Ian and I have Self Control. There's no way people like us will get sucked into this thing. Not at all. We'll make a one or two swift, astute purchases, then hit the off button.

Within a few hours we're both hooked.

Perhaps I should explain the mechanics of eBay for the benefit of anyone else who as yet hasn't ventured there. You type in a description of your sought-after item, and up comes everything in the world that vaguely resembles it. Every sale is an auction; most have no reserve. Other buyers' bids appear on the screen alongside the time left till each particular auction is over. It might be five days; it might be five minutes. As the clock ticks down, bidding can get frantic or, sometimes, amazingly little or no bidding occurs and you get your item for next to nothing.

This never seems to happen with the things Ian and I want.

Ian has no patience, so I'm the spotter, trawling through tens of thousands of possibilities and saving likely things in 'Watch this item' on our 'My eBay' page. Ian only joins me for the excitement of the bidding.

We're supposed to be looking at art, but can't help gravitating to the antiques. Our modus operandi is to decide what we think the value of each spotted item should be and vow not to bid a cent more. But with my ready fingers hovering over the mouse and Ian's urging in my ears, it's really hard not to hit the button again and again. Especially as Ian can't bear to be beaten at anything by anyone.

We find old jugs, bowls, placemats and jardinieres. We find pieces of the dinner set I've been collecting for years: the Myott Chelsea Bird pattern, edged with dark red, a pheasant in the centre.

'I can't let that idiot beat us,' says Ian. 'Hit it again!'

Bingomichael bites the dust. The Myott plates are ours for ten dollars more than our maximum.

Bowls appear in the same set. So does *Bingomichael's* bid.

'Bloody hell,' mutters Ian. 'Hit it! Hit it!'

I do. Whoops. Twenty dollars over.

We begin to realise that my patient spotting and Ian's killer instinct are a dangerous combination. Then we discover the postage cost. Cold turkey, we abandon eBay.

But it's oh so exciting when those little parcels arrive on our doorstep. We gaze longingly at the computer. Temptation flickers.

'Of course we haven't bought any prints yet,' I point out. 'True.'

'Prints only. No other sites.'

We dash to the computer.

We buy a bundle of old botanic prints for the bedrooms in reds and pinks and creamy, buttery colours. Then we buy a couple of fake 'old masters' from Hong Kong, avoiding known works, picking only from the obscure. We end up with a Monet and a Degas, which are surprisingly easy on the eye. The Monet is signed 'Robert' at the bottom. I wonder about the unknown, talented, underpaid Hong Kong artist called Robert, whose work now adorns our kitchen wall. Everyone thinks it's a creation of my younger son.

The walls are beginning to look much, much happier.

⊱⊱⊰⊙⊱⊰⊰

I finally confess to Ian the rebirth of my need to write. He is over the moon, admits he's been longing for the day.

'We must finish the house first,' I warn him, 'otherwise it'll never get done. You mightn't like it much when I start,' I add, 'I'll have to shut myself away. No interruptions.'

'No problem,' he says, flashing his famous smile.

But I know he's going to require discipline when I need to be alone. Ian is at his happiest when we work together. If he's pruning with his chain-saw, he likes me to gather up the bits for him. If he's planting a tree, he likes me to hold the sapling trunk straight while he shovels in the dirt. When I snatch a minute to do the crossword, it's impossible to get far before I sense a presence and see his face at the window, his person at the door. 'Just thought I'd say Hi,' he says.

'Hello then,' I say.

He disappears. Ten second pass. His head pops round the door again. 'Would you like a cup of tea or anything?'

I grow cunning and do the crossword when he takes rubbish to the tip or runs errands in town. But if I'm to write another book, I'll need more than a few snatched moments when Ian's back is turned. He's going to have to learn to respect my need for solitude and quiet.

>–⋄–○–⋄–<

Sharon Christiansen calls in to visit. Sharon is the thirty-something daughter of Jan and Barry, previous owners of the house. I wonder if she, like Esse, was reluctant to leave Baddow. We show her around, aware that it must feel very strange to see other people's belongings in your old home and work being done and changes being made. She is very complimentary, and tells us we're doing a great job.

She's about to go when she says, 'Have you seen them yet?'

'Seen who?' I ask.

'Them. The ghosts.'

'No,' we both say, 'nothing at all.'

'You will,' she says. 'It's only a matter of time.'

I know I shouldn't, but can't help asking. 'So you saw things here, did you?'

'Oh yes,' she replies eagerly. 'We'd see a woman on the stairs sometimes. Mostly I'd catch glimpses of how the rooms used to look, you know, furnished as they were in the old days, but only out of the corners of my eyes. I'd hear them, too. Hear them calling my name.'

Right. Can't you just hear it? '*Sharon . . . Sha . . . ron . . . Sha . . . a . . . ron . . .*'

But Ian and I are cured of the ghost thing. We've both spent nights alone here now and have bigger things to worry about.

> ⤞⤐⊶⭘⭠⭤⥁ ⤛

Between breaks for eBay, Christmas, and for visitors, I'm still on Cedar Duty. I have the Babies' Room, the upstairs landing and passageways, and the downstairs corridors still to do. The quantity of woodwork in the house is immense. Thirty-three centimetre high skirting boards, wide architraves, all the internal windows, doors, transom windows above doors, mantelpieces, the entire staircase. It goes on and on and on. But every inch I sand is a dollar saved and I'm determined to do it.

I don't really mind sanding, especially when Ian's away. I can get absolutely filthy and don't have to worry about cleaning up for cups of tea or making dinner. I turn the CD player up extremely high and, depending on my mood, vibrate the house to either Charlotte Church, The Bangles or Queen. I sand away, lost in my thoughts.

The only thing I hate is the mess. The fine, penetrating dust, the nano-particles that infiltrate every crevice in the house, that sneak under closed doors, between window architraves, through dust sheets I've thrown over furniture, into my ears, my eyes, through my sensible face mask and into my nose, mouth and lungs. God knows what's in it. I'm counting on my very healthy immune system to chuck out anything offensive.

At the end of the day I stand under the shower and scrub

till I feel purged of the stuff. I have a glass of wine, some bread and cheese, then fall into bed, utterly whacked.

Over the years I've swum and walked on and off, made half-hearted, spasmodic attempts to keep fit, but renovating uses muscles that haven't been used since the dreaded school gymnasium where Miss Adams, determined and despotic, forced my unwilling flesh to climb ropes and vault horses. I remember trying to lie low in that gym, trying not to be noticed, *Please pick some other girl*, cowering and thinking, *When I'm a grown up, I'll be able to choose. When I'm a grown up, no one will have the power to make me do such exhausting, difficult things again.*

So now, when I'm inhaling filth, or teetering on a ladder, or sweeping and vacuuming for the fifth time that day, or sweating like an animal, dragging dead tree limbs up to Ian's ute in the tropical heat, I am happy to know that it is all been my choice.

CHAPTER 15

ANDREW'S GHOST

MY ELDER SON, ANDREW, arrives home from Italy. It's brilliant to have him back and, though we've been emailing and phoning regularly and he knows all about our Baddow adventures, he's finally going to see it for himself.

Andrew has a love of art, architecture and history, so I'm hoping he will love Baddow House and Maryborough. Fresh from the delights of Venice, however, I fear Maryborough might seem a little tame, but he does love it all and explores the town thoroughly, identifying buildings as neo this and neo that.

Andrew doesn't need the Babies' Room. Even as a little boy, Andrew had no fear of the dark or the unknown. 'What's the matter with you two?' he'd demand of his quivering younger brother and sister. 'Just because it's dark doesn't mean anything's different except that the sun has moved over the horizon.'

His words always fell on deaf ears.

Andrew never could *get* the subtlety of Night Fear. Why would there be wolves under a bed in Queensland, when the nearest living wolf is probably in Siberia? *As long as you don't count zoo escapees . . .*

Why would aliens want to abduct a little boy or girl like you two, when there are far more interesting brains out there for the taking? If there *are* such things as aliens, which there aren't, or everyone would have seen them by now. *But perhaps they like little boys and girls with half-formed minds, easier to brainwash, easier to re-educate . . .*

Ghosts? How can you believe in such garbage? With all the billions and billions of people who've died on this planet since the dawn of time, don't you think the dead would be so thick on the ground by now, that we'd be totally surrounded by them? *But perhaps they are only seen when they want to be seen . . .*

No, Andrew just didn't get it. He's the sort of sceptic who could sleep dreamlessly in such places as Hampton Court, where Catherine Howard's ghost is reputed to run headless and screaming down the gallery.

Andrew has taken the bedroom at the far end of the corridor. Elizabeth, who is visiting this same weekend, is in the Babies' Room.

It's Andrew's second night. Ian has gone to Montville so it's just the three of us. Elizabeth and I go to bed and leave Andrew tinkering on the computer downstairs.

Elizabeth always goes to bed when I do, never to be left downstairs without me. She closes all her windows and doors, as she has done all her life. When she was little, we had the routine of checking inside cupboards, closing doors tightly, looking under the bed and locking the windows. We no longer have the searching ritual, but she still sleeps better when she's hermetically sealed.

The next morning at breakfast, Andrew is casting me shifty looks. When Elizabeth leaves the room, he says, 'There's something I should tell you, Mum. Last night I think I saw a ghost.'

This is Andrew. Andrew the Unafraid. He's still unafraid, but he's speaking a very strange language. I am appalled but fascinated. I have to know all.

Elizabeth wanders back into the kitchen. Andrew and I immediately fall silent. It's an unspoken law that you do not discuss such things as ghosts when Elizabeth is present. I put on the kettle. Andrew goes to the fridge and starts shuffling food around, looking for satisfying breakfast ingredients.

Elizabeth and I sip our tea. Andrew is stirring a vast saucepan full of pasta, cheese, garden herbs and tuna. After twenty-four years, I'm still astonished at the quantity of food that fits inside my eldest son.

He joins us at the table. We're trying to act casual, normal. I'm not finding it easy, and worry that Elizabeth's perception will alert her to the fact that we're hoping to engineer a moment alone. It's really hard as Elizabeth and I tend to be together all of the time, unless her boyfriend, Simon, calls. Then she vanishes, and the office door is firmly shut.

Why won't you call when we need you, Simon? I'm getting to the point of making some pathetic, desperate excuse to get rid of her when she drains her tea, stands up and announces she's off to the shower.

'Quick, out with it,' I say, the second she's gone.

Andrew is scraping the remnants of his protein-rich pasta dish. 'When I was in the office last night, on the computer, I was typing away and I heard someone coming down the stairs,' he says, and licks his spoon.

I am riveted. 'Go on.'

When his bowl is clean enough to put away in the cupboard, he puts down his spoon, looks up at me and says, 'I didn't think anything of it. I assumed either you or Elizabeth had come down for a glass of water or something. I heard footsteps approach along the corridor and kept typing. The office door was open, the corridor light on and, out of the periphery of my vision, I saw someone walk past toward the kitchen and clearly heard footsteps. I still wasn't really thinking about it, just assuming it was one of you, but vaguely aware that it was a bit odd, as the person passing was kind of without definition and a bit dark. Not you, Mum, for sure, and even darker than Elizabeth. Or maybe my eyes were bleary from long hours on the computer and I wasn't focussing properly. Anyhow, I didn't think much of it, just kept typing.

'After a while, when no one came back from the kitchen, I thought it was strange and got up to investigate. But the kitchen light was off and no one was in there. At that point, I thought someone must have broken in – an intruder – and I started searching downstairs. You know, flinging doors open and all that. But there was no one here. That's when I thought more about the odd appearance of what I'd seen, and began to think it had been something inexplicable.'

Perhaps there's another totally logical explanation for this, perhaps we'll reason it out one day. But for now, there is one thing I am a hundred per cent sure of: Andrew does not imagine things. 'Don't tell Elizabeth,' I say.

He rolls his eyes in a *tell me something I don't know* sort of way.

'Okay, okay, stupid comment. But how did you feel?' I ask.

'I was scared when I thought an intruder was in the house, but when I found all the doors and windows were locked, I knew there couldn't be.'

'Did that scare you?'

'Not much.'

'Did you go straight to bed then?'

'No, I did a bit more on the computer first.'

I stare at this young man, my son, scarcely able to comprehend that any human being could think they see a ghost, then calmly continue tapping away on the keyboard.

'Let's keep this between just us,' I say.

'No problem.'

⊶⊷⊶○⊶⊷⊰

I tell Ian. I think I must be seeking sympathy. After all, I'm the one who has to stay here on my own one night a week, every week, and I want him to know what I have to deal with.

It's obvious to us both that I have regressed hugely since Andrew told me what he thought he saw. 'God,' I say to Ian, 'I even showed him photos of Esse and asked if the person he saw resembled her. He acknowledged it was a possibility.'

'You've got to put this from your head,' Ian tells me. 'It was probably Elizabeth getting a glass of water, as Andrew originally thought. He just didn't notice her returning.'

But I'd already thought of that. 'I subtly questioned Elizabeth in the morning,' I tell him. 'I told her I'd found a glass of water upstairs on the sideboard in the corridor, though I hadn't, and asked her whether it was she or Andrew who had left it there.'

Not me, Elizabeth had said. *I was unconscious the minute my head hit the pillow. Must have been Anders.*

It's a week before Ian has to leave and I'll be on my own again. But I grow stronger each day and by the time he goes am not too scared. 'If they are here, they love us,' I tell him.

CHAPTER 16

VERANDAHS

W E FIND A BUSINESS CARD on our doorstep: *Mike Johns. J. Corp. Constructions.* We ring him up.

Mike Johns tells us he used to live near Baddow as a kid. He describes how he and his friends would play in the creek at the bottom of the garden and dare each other to run up and bang on the door of the Ghost House. They played in the bush around here, they caught yabbies in the creek. He loves the old house and is really keen to be involved.

Mike is very tall and rangy. His appearance changes nearly every time we see him, thanks to scissors and a razor. There is long hair in a pony-tail, then there is cropped-very-short hair. There is a beard, then no beard. Then there is a partial beard – a sort of goatie – for a moment, then that is gone too. I wonder if he is going about incognito for some reason and want to tell him that as there is no one else in town anywhere near as tall as him, he has little hope of getting away with it.

Mike is only thirty-one, but has had his Master Builders' Licence since he was twenty-one. We are impressed. Clearly he is bright and capable. He is also the only person who has actually approached us to do work here instead of being hunted down and coerced.

We offer him the job of building the verandahs.

⋙—⋅◆⋅—◦—⋅◆⋅—⋘

It is sixty-five years since verandahs encircled Baddow House, and the last person to enjoy the use of these verandahs was Mr Hugh Biddles.

Hugh Biddles bought Baddow House in 1915 and lived here with his wife, Alice Charlotte, until the end of their days. In earlier years, Hugh had qualified and worked as an engineer in North Queensland, assisting in the erection some of the largest sugar mills then in the north. But before long the lure of the pearling industry took the young Hugh to Western Australia, where his brother was making a fortune.

Hugh worked hard and soon acquired his own boats but, after a particularly lucrative season, with shell and pearls worth thousands of pounds aboard his schooner, a severe storm off the coast of Broome brought his pearling days to an end.

The schooner went down in the heavy seas, and all the crew were lost but for Hugh, who spent eleven hours in the water before managing to make it to shore on a desolate stretch of coastline a long way from civilisation. The story goes that he had to walk for miles and miles along the rough coastline with nothing but a torn suit of pyjamas as protection from the tropical sun. He reached safety, badly sunburnt and suffering a chronic back injury that would plague him for the rest of his days.

Hugh returned to Maryborough, bought Baddow House, and by all accounts led a very happy – and uneventful – life with his wife, the beautiful, gentle Alice Charlotte.

Legend has it that Hugh was the one to start the ghost stories, that when the miscreant youth of town used to raid his fruit orchards, he would creep around the upstairs verandah with a sheet over his head to scare them off. I believe this is when the house first became known as the Ghost House.

Hugh Biddles' great-niece, Margaret Jacobson, still lives in Maryborough today. It is she who has told us how unsafe the verandah floorboards were when she was a child, and that she and her brothers were banned from playing on the upstairs verandah. It suits me to believe that the verandahs were pulled down because they were unfit to walk on, not because the iron balustrading was needed for bullets and missiles.

It's fascinating to listen to Margaret talk of the majestic garden with camellias half the height of the house, and of her aunt, Alice Charlotte, who loved the piano and sat in our sunny living room to play. She describes the dining room, the position of Hugh's leather-backed chairs, the meals at the big table where the children ate in obedient silence.

Her stories make me realise that the house doesn't

belong to Ian and me at all. We're just lucky enough to be occupiers, as others have been before us and will continue to do in the future. It makes me wonder who's going to live here after we're dead and gone, and whether my grandchildren will visit subsequent owners and say, *this is where Granny sat and wrote her stories.*

Alice Biddles died of cancer in 1934 and shortly afterwards Hugh's back injury worsened. He spent the final two years of his life bedridden, and died five years after his sweet Alice. He died upstairs in the Blue Room and was buried from the house.

When I stand in that room, I think of Hugh laid out at peace. I imagine him a big man, deep-chested from his pearl-diving days. But the large frame is made brittle by disease. It is shelled out and hollow. How strange to think that, but for the passage of time, there he would be. And so many others, too, in their own, individual fractions of time.

Edgar Aldridge in his brand new home, Harry in the garden, a housemaid at the copper in the scullery, Esse stepping out of the carriage, her slippered foot on the steps, a hand on the balustrade, touching where I touch now.

I'm certain that Edgar Aldridge and Hugh Biddles would be as excited as we are to witness the metamorphosis that is about to commence.

Michaelangelo said, 'I saw the angel in the marble and carved until I set him free.'

I kiss the wall and count my blessings. Right now I think I'm the luckiest woman in the world.

Are Ian and I absurd to be as excited as we are about the verandahs? Perhaps. Though renovating inside the house is giving us a huge sense of achievement as well as a beautiful place to live, the interior is happening in bits and pieces, one room at a time. It is a transformation that is creeping upon us. The verandahs, however, are huge. The verandahs will happen as one big, life-altering event and change Baddow House forever. Once again the house will look as it did in Edgar Aldridge's day. Once again it will be Aldridge's Castle – or is it our castle?

⊱─⊰⊱─⊰

The first step is to get plans drawn up. We approach architect Marian Graham. I instantly like Marian. She's a successful businesswoman in town and very professional, which could be daunting, but I sense an irreverence in her that I find attractive: a bit of sarcasm here, a raised eyebrow there. She warns us that with our heritage listing it will be a good six months from plan drawing time to building starting time. Every decision has to go before panels, committees and hearings at the Environmental Protection Agency. The EPA is the umbrella under which sits Queensland Heritage.

The aim is to return Baddow House as closely as possible to the way it used to be. Fortunately we are in possession of a stack of photographs of the house in its glory days. Some of these show close detail of the verandahs: front on, side on, roof angles, balustrading and columns. This is a huge boon.

The original verandahs on Baddow House were both upstairs and down. They were ten feet wide and three hundred and forty feet long. They included sixteen moulded brick and plaster columns, thirty-six iron pillars – each one sixteen feet tall – and there was well over three hundred feet of iron lace work. It's a mammoth job, but we know we must do it well or not at all.

The EPA is understandably keen for us to go ahead with the restoration of the Baddow House verandahs. But there are immense frustrations. We learn that we're not supposed to change so much as a toilet roll holder without permission. We have already repaired cracks in the walls, sanded and painted several rooms and peeled some wallpaper out of the entrance hall that held no historic value, being only about twelve years old.

These things, we are shocked to discover, are against the Rules. Ian and I had assumed that heritage listing means you don't alter the *fabric* of the building. You don't knock a hole in a wall to make a new door. You don't build extensions without permission. But a coat of paint? We are gobsmacked. We are told to fill in special forms to explain our reasons for having commenced work without Permission.

We must be wearing looks of rebellion, because we are then told firmly that it is within the power of the department to deny us permission to do such things as watering the garden or mowing the lawn.

Politeness restrains us from shrieking at the absurdity. Politeness, but also the sense that it would be really bad to get on the wrong side of these people. We need their co-operation.

'Not that we would be likely to exercise our authority over such particular issues as watering the garden,' the official tells us, 'but the rules are in place for good reason. Take a rare cactus garden,' he says.

We dutifully picture said spiky, prickly garden.

'To over-water such a garden might kill the cacti, hence the rules. It gives us the ability to protect whatever may chance to need protection.'

We do understand. We know there are cowboys out there who might choose to desecrate a listed property. It's just that we would have preferred a presumption of innocence until proven guilty.

We submit our plans. Marian was right. Weeks tick by. We learn that the Committee meet for decision making once a month. If you make it onto the agenda for any given month there is no guarantee that your case will get heard. Other items on the agenda might take longer than expected to discuss and resolve. If you miss out, you have to wait till the next month and hope your case will be heard that time.

Months tick by. We make phone calls. We write letters. We explain how important it is to get the verandahs back on the house to ensure its stability. We point out that every time the wind blows, more plaster drops off the outside. We point out that every time it rains, dampness seeps through the porous render and stains the interior walls we've already painted.

There's nothing more we can do, the situation is beyond our control. The wait is incredibly frustrating.

But Baddow House is, after all, a wonderful place to be, and winter in Maryborough an unequalled delight. It's impossible to believe a more perfect environment and climate could exist anywhere in the world. In winter daytime temperatures hover around twenty-four degrees, the minimums can drop into low single figures, though are usually closer to ten or twelve degrees. The days are clear, the nights are cool, not cold, the skies are blue and the air is clean, crisp and soft. With the interior of the house almost under control, and our verandah building halted by the EPA, Ian and I find the time to attack the garden through these perfect, halcyon days of our first winter.

Of course we can't touch the ground surrounding the house, but we pamper our poincianas and attend to the hedge running along our roadside boundary; feeding, mulching, watering and coaxing. I plant fistfuls of freesias between the hedge and the road. I would like this hedge to be ten metres tall and three metres thick; an impenetrable barrier between us and the outside world. This is not going to happen. The hedge is a weeping lilly pilly which, we learn, is likely to reach only two metres in ideal conditions. I threaten to rip it out and plant something else, something that will grow towering and dense, something that will block out the world with its mighty dimensions. But Ian tempers and soothes my misanthropic tendencies. He doesn't mind being spotted by passers-by – he even waves to them. I'm forced to face reality: Ian has a friendlier disposition than I. I love gates. I love barriers and seclusion. I make secret plans to plant a second hedge closer to the house when the building is finished.

Though in these days of the long wait, it is hard to believe our building will ever be finished. It is January when we first see Marian about our plans for the verandah. It is September 2004 when we get the go ahead.

After so many months of waiting, Ian and I are nearly delirious with excitement. We know that the verandahs will transform our lives. There will be hectares of space to sit and dream and watch the river go by. I imagine lots of leafy tropical plants, cane furniture and chilled glasses of Pimms. All very Somerset Maugham.

It is one year and one month since we moved into Baddow House. And after so long living with the bedlam of interior renovations, I'm relaxing in the knowledge that we are through the worst, that we are almost there. All we have to do is shut the doors and windows and the noise, mess and chaos of verandah building will be firmly out of sight and mind.

For me, just as exciting is knowing that the minute the verandahs are finished I will be able to plant my long-awaited and yearned for garden around the perimeter of the house.

For a year I've been nursing poor little cuttings taken from my previous garden. They've languished pitifully through the tropical summer in their hot plastic pots, bravely hanging on even though at times I've been too snowed under in the house to remember them. Finally they are about to be part of the garden of my dreams. I lie in bed at night planning the garden: the height, shape, texture of every corner. I make mental lists of hardy heat and sun-tolerant flowers that I can grow along the hot north-western wall, and further lists of the more delicate varieties that will survive on the gentler eastern front. All I need do is sit back and wait for completion of the verandahs.

Mike and his team have been poised to start the minute we get word, and are here the day our permission arrives.

The first task is to dig holes for the foundation pillars. An impressive machine arrives and soon we have sixteen two-metre deep, one-metre wide holes surrounding the house. Bear traps, we call them, and speculate on the improbability of getting out if we fell into one. We have guests from Montville staying the first night of the digging and, as one of them has a regular habit of fertilising the citrus trees with his own special brand of uric acid, we ban night-time rambles round the garden. We worry about Topsy, but she belies her weight and poor eyesight, and nimbly leaps any holes in her path.

After such a long wait, it is oh so thrilling to see these holes. There might be nothing above ground yet, but the holes are a sign of things to come. Men have been and broken the ground: evidence exists that we are underway.

It's tempting to peer down into them. I wonder about Edgar and Maria's second home, built on this site before our house. Surely there must be remains of those original foundations, evidence of an earlier existence. We know there were terraced gardens here, possibly Baby Joey's grave, there could be any amount of odds and ends under-ground: old coins, broken crockery, garden tools. Or, best of all, an entry to the tunnel.

At Latimer House my cousins, Pat and David, and I used

to look for scraps of interest in the garden and under floorboards. David was the patient one, best at finding things, and had his own 'museum' of coins, pottery, broken clay pipe, animal bones, a quill pen from behind a sash window, and even the rusted skeleton of an old revolver which provoked endless wondering. Was it accidentally dropped and lost? Was it thrown out with the rubbish? Or was it buried deliberately: a murder weapon concealed?

David is now an archaeologist, a specialist in archaeometallurgy, which means he's an expert in ancient metals, particularly iron and steel. He's spent a lot of time on arms and armour, and can identify anything from Ancient Greek to Saxon to modern. I'd love to have him here at Baddow with his eye and instinct for a find. He's promised to come one day, though our bear traps will be well filled by then.

The next day, Mike tells us that one of his men has defected and his team is down to two: John, the foreman, and Sarah, the apprentice. Mike will be here sometimes, we learn, but mostly he's off-site, either at home doing office work or out scouting for new projects.

I've never seen a female builder's apprentice before but Sarah is as strong as John and wears her tool belt with the swagger of a bloke. She swears and curses like one too. Topsy is terrified of her to start with, but comes round with bribes of food. John and Sarah both love dogs and Topsy doubles in size before the building is half complete.

Mind you, it is a long, long time before the building is half complete.

Bearers and joists have to be positioned first. The bearers

are huge and heavy. I marvel at Sarah's bearer-wielding power. She strides about, lifting, sawing and hammering, bracing her powerful limbs to hoist the mighty slabs of hardwood. But she doesn't show up one morning and we learn she's had an epileptic fit. John is on his own.

Sarah recovers from her seizure, but is not allowed back to work until she has written confirmation from her doctor that her new medication can guarantee no more fits. As an epileptic, building is deemed risky business. She could be up high on scaffolding when a fit strikes. She could be handling dangerous power tools, putting herself and others at risk. It's weeks before she returns.

John, labouring on his own, is a tower of strength, reliability and cheerfulness. A real Trojan. He even looks like a Trojan: all solid and swarthy with tight dark curls cut close to his head. He sings as he works and never complains about hoisting mammoth bearers single-handed.

Ian is incredibly busy at the moment. Though his Rangeview development at Maleny is complete and he's only away in Montville one night a week now, he's in the midst of buying a wood chip mill just south of Maryborough. He runs to and fro the Canterwood Mill several times a week, Montville once a week, the rubbish tip at least five times a week, besides being the General of Operations at Baddow, but he can't stand to see John left working solo and decides to help.

John is endeavouring to attach pole plates to the wall. Pole plates are hefty wooden bearers that are anchored to the house by deep bolts to support the weight of the verandah. John is swinging a sledgehammer with a strength to rival Hector's. Ian finds his own sledgehammer and goes outside.

Now, when Ian works along side the Men, he likes it to be seen that anything they can do, he can do better. Stronger, faster, more enduring – that's my Ian. He'd build the verandahs himself, if only he had the technical skills. Alas, he does not have such skills, but he knows how to swing a sledgehammer and he knows how to swing it hard.

He swaggers up to John, sledgehammer gripped in one broad fist. 'I'll give you a hand with those, mate,' he says, and clambers over the network of bearers and joists.

John is appreciative. He, too, is frustrated by the slow progress of the building. Ian positions one end of the pole plate over a bolt, takes his sledgehammer in both hands and twists his body like he's about to throw a discus.

The sledgehammer whips through the air and, with a dull thud, connects with Ian's shin. Not a sound escapes his lips. They are compressed and bloodless, but admirably silent.

'Geez that must have hurt, mate.' John is wide-eyed, shocked.

Ian flexes his knee, shrugs his shoulders. 'Not much. I'll be right.' The words sound tight, clipped, but he's already lining up his next target. More carefully, with less force, he hammers it home.

It doesn't take them long, and Ian soon makes his way back to the kitchen. The minute he rounds the corner out of sight of John, he doubles over, gripping his leg, giving in to the agony. I rush over, clucking, sympathising. His shin is black and purple, but not, we think, broken. 'A flesh wound,' I tell him, confident but unqualified. 'Swollen and bruised but not broken and bleeding. It could have been worse.'

'It was the first swing,' he laments, 'the very first one!'

✄ ⊶ ⟶ ⊙ ⟵ ⊷ ✄

CHAPTER 17

VISITORS FROM THE PAST

A GARDEN AS OLD as ours should be bursting with ancient trees – towering figs, massive camellias. We know that Edgar Aldridge was a keen horticulturist and constantly experimented in his quest to discover which plants could be grown in our sub-tropical climate. He planted sisal for rope making, sugarcane, maize and potatoes. He grew coffee, camphor, wheat, rice, dozens of varieties of fruit and vegetables, and large stands of bamboo. We're told that he won prizes as far away as London for his arrowroot. We have no reason to believe he didn't also throw his energies into ornamental trees, flowers and shrubs. Margaret Jacobsen has told us of the enormous camellias that used to grow between the house and the river when she was a child. So where has it all gone?

We don't know why the garden was all cleared so drastically – 'nuked' as we like to put it. But we know who did it.

Mr and Mrs Gilbert Stiler bought the house in 1939 after Hugh Biddles died, and it was during their reign that the verandahs were removed and the garden devastated. We've tried hard to think of a reason for such a clearance of vegetation. Were they planning a market garden? Were they afraid of snakes? Or bushfires? Certainly they ensured that there was no bush left.

The Stilers were reputed to have paid five hundred pounds for the house on what was then twelve acres of land, but they only lived at Baddow for a little over a year. Perhaps their wholesale destruction of the verandahs and the garden angered the ghosts who terrorised them out of the place.

I find it hard to imagine the Stilers as happy people. They came, they saw, they laid waste, they left. Perhaps they just didn't like the house. It was certainly the beginning of Baddow's darkest hour.

With the Stilers gone, the State Government bought the house to convert it into a migrant hostel. Somehow the conversion never happened, and the house sat empty and forlorn for years. Always stately but lonely, abandoned and increasingly derelict. Stripped of its verandahs, the walls were weathered and stained, the plaster crumbled. Windows were smashed and rain beat in, devastating the beautiful floorboards.

Local vandals did their bit, too. They stripped out five of the six original fireplaces, adorned the walls with graffiti, broke the balustrading of the internal staircase and hacked hunks out of pretty much anything a person could hack hunks out of.

No wonder the house attracted the title and reputation of the Ghost House of Maryborough.

In 1954 the 1st Baddow Troop of Boy Scouts bought the house in all its dilapidation to use as their Scout Hall. They paid just two hundred and fifty pounds for it. Live-in caretakers, a Mr and Mrs Stewart, occupied the downstairs rooms – with the exception of the main double living room which was used by the Scouts as their meeting hall. The upstairs rooms, in even poorer shape, were used for storage only.

The original kitchen at Baddow had been a separate building connected by a covered walkway. Though this was already demolished by the Stewarts' day, below ground where the kitchen had once stood, the cellar was still intact. This subterranean construction had been known as the 'hiding' room, rumoured to have been built in case of raids by Aborigines back in Edgar Aldridge's time.

It begs the question, why did Harry Aldridge and his children hide in the attic rather than the cellar, when they had their very own nineteenth century Panic Room?

One of the first questions my daughter Elizabeth – fearful of the dark and all it might conceal – asked when she came to Baddow was, 'do you have a Panic Room?' (I think she'd recently seen the Jodie Foster movie of that name, and believed every house should have one.) We don't. The cellar is no more. Occasionally our shovels hit the brick walls when we're planting trees, but these walls are only a shell now and the shell is solidly filled with garden.

We learn that the trapdoor in the cupboard under the stairs used to lead to another cellar, a brick-lined room you could stand up and walk around in. But that the wife of a previous owner found its existence a constant source of fright, a potential haven for vermin, and demanded it be filled in. We wonder how many buckets of dirt had to be lugged inside and down through the trapdoor to achieve this. For a moment Ian and I get excited and talk about excavating the dirt out again, but commonsense soon prevails.

The Stewarts tell of having to scrub down the interior walls of the house to get rid of graffiti and of boarding up the windows of the unused rooms. They describe how the overmantel mirrors above the fireplaces were all smashed, though the wooden frames were still in place, having been screwed tightly onto the walls.

It appears that the Stewarts made a huge effort to get Baddow House into suitable condition for the Scouts, but the building was too far gone and it seems no one had the means to maintain, let alone repair it.

An enterprising local builder, Mr Jack Hawes, offered to build the Scouts a new hall in town if they would do a swap. In 1960 the Scouts accepted, almost costing Baddow her life.

Mr Hawes wanted to build cottages on the land, and saw Baddow House as a source of plenty of good bricks. We'll never know why he changed his mind. I like to think that the house cast her spell over him.

Baddow House was fighting for survival. Misfortune had plagued her since the very beginning. Maria's premature death, Edgar's death, Harry's bankruptcy and his family's eviction, the Biddles' ill health, the brief but disastrous occupation by the Stilers.

Then came the indignity of abandonment, of vandalism, of near execution. How much sadness can one house bear?

Knowing how the house has suffered makes me love it even more. I kiss the walls. I kiss away Esse's tears and hope never to have to weep as she did.

><+>-o-<+><

Out of the blue we discover John and Lois Hastings, who lived at Baddow House for nine years through the nineteen-seventies. It's always exciting to meet people who have spent time at Baddow. To hear their stories adds pieces to our puzzle, sheds light on those unknown stretches. As far as Ian and I can gather, John and Lois's time was the first inhabitation of Baddow since the Biddles' that smacked of the normal life of a normal family who loved the house and garden.

It goes without saying that I ask them about the ghosts. The foolish part of me is hoping to hear lurid, scary stories, always exciting in the bright light of day and companion-ship of a group of people. But I know that next time I'm alone and the sun goes down, I'll wish I hadn't asked.

'Yes,' says John. 'I've a couple of good ghost stories for you.'

Ian and I wait with bated breath and quickening pulses.

'The first one happened when I was alone in the house. I was upstairs, just on dusk, when I heard a rhythmic knocking that seemed to come from the corner of the bedroom ceiling. There was no wind, no reason to believe any force of nature was causing the noise. I froze, listening hard. *Bang . . . bang . . . bang . . .* My heart was in my mouth. Could there be someone in the attic?'

He pauses, and I'm thinking of Harry, locked in the attic, imagining him pacing up and down, trapped, afraid, frantic for his children.

'I grabbed my torch,' continues John, 'leaned out of the window and shone its light up toward the gutter. Caught in the spotlight was a kookaburra slamming a toad against the iron. *Bang . . . bang . . . bang . . .* Hard and rhythmic.'

There's relief and laughter all round.

John holds up his hand. 'Wait, I have another one,' he says seriously.

The laughter stops. Once more our attention is all his.

'I was asleep in what you now call the Blue Room,' he tells us. 'Something woke me, though I couldn't work out what it was. I lay very still and, as I came to full consciousness, it seemed to me that the walls were moving and the room was swaying. It was as though the edges of reality were being blurred by another dimension. After a few minutes everything returned to normal, but I thought I'd better not tell Lois, knowing it might frighten her.'

John looks around at our solemn faces, then adds, 'Later that day, I heard on the news that there'd been an earthquake in the Wide Bay district.'

⊱──◇──⊰

The phone rings one day and a voice at the other end says, 'My great-great-grandfather built your house. We've heard you're restoring it and wondered if we could come round and have a look.'

The voice is that of Russell Anson, Esse's grandson. I am delighted.

They arrive and I meet Jack, widower of Esse's daughter, Barbara, their son Russell, his wife Teresa and various children.

After so long living, breathing and touching Aldridge history, it is amazing to actually meet blood relations of the family.

We go for a walk round the garden first, and explain what we are doing with the verandahs. It means so much to me that they have taken the time and made the effort to come here, that they are happy about, and approve of our restoration. I feel a great rapport with them, which only reinforces my belief that I am where I'm meant to be. I determine to give the house an extra kiss later.

When we go inside I get the strangest sensation. Feelings like this don't usually happen to me, only in my dreams. It happens the minute we are inside the entrance hall and is exciting, not a bit scary. Every hair on my neck stands upright and my scalp lifts and prickles as though it has a life of its own. I don't say anything to our visitors, but the feeling lingers with me for the duration of their visit.

We sit and drink tea, and I pull out all the old photographs we have of the house and the Aldridge family. More tingles. We talk about Esse a lot. I can see from her photographs that Esse was an exceptionally beautiful young woman. She has a sweet, heart-shaped face, huge dark eyes, and she wears gorgeous Victorian clothes, with all the pleats, lace and elegance of that era.

The Ansons tell us how devastated Esse was to have to

leave Baddow House, that before she died she told her family it would have been better never to have had it all, than to have had it and lost it.

My understanding is total. The thought of losing Baddow is unthinkable, unbearable. It is strange to feel such a link to a long-dead woman I never met, but I can't help it. There's a magnetism about her memory, and it's tugging at me. Though I'm adamant that I don't believe in ghosts in the sense that the dead can rise and walk our earth, I find myself believing that maybe, just maybe, a person can leave some essence of themselves in a place, an imprint of their existence, especially if there was great depth to their emotions.

><+>-0-<+><

My boys come up for a weekend visit. Is it coincidence that we are having a gang to dinner that Saturday night? I suspect the boys of making an extra effort to travel north to Maryborough when they know a feast is to be had.

We invite Marian Graham, the architect of the verandahs, and her partner, Adrian, plus Trevor, who will always be a particular marvel to us for finding Baddow House. We also invite Syd and Diana Collins, who own the art gallery in town, and who I have bothered a thousand times in a thousand ways to frame so much eBay art. Syd, who has the patience of Job.

I spend the day cooking curries: lamb, beef, chicken, fish and a mountain of spiced-up vegetables. By mid-afternoon, Ian returns from a visit to the tip and tells me most of

Queen Street stinks of curry. When I have a crowd, it's what I do. A habit formed from childhood in Malaya, where curry lunches were the norm at weekends. Often for the feeding of the five thousand. I can't make my curries Gurkha-hot though, as not everyone appreciates losing the skin of their soft palette these days, but I chop up loads of chillies so that my boys and Adrian can turn up the heat to their taste.

When we moved to Baddow House, the comment, *I don't suppose you'll use that dining room much, easier to eat in the kitchen,* was made too often to remember. How wrong they were. I *love* eating in the dining room. The raspberry walls tempt my appetite, food tastes better off the Myott pheasant plates, dissected by our best silverware, and wine slips easily down our throats under the halo of soft light from our enormous chandalier.

The wood of the step into the dining room dips in the middle, worn by incalculable numbers of feet: booted, slippered, bare feet. It's a tangible reminder of past dinners enjoyed in this room. If you close your eyes you can imagine the company, the laughter and the warmth. Candles instead of the chandelier. Bodies over-dressed for our tropical nights. Layered corseted clothes, up to the neck, to the wrist, to the ankle. But happy times, I feel certain.

We eat till we're fit to burst, then I bring in the puddings. Always chilled and fruity after a curry. I've made a pavlova and an open blueberry and apricot tart. Australian and Gallic, to follow the Nepalese and Malay. A multicultural mix.

Andrew and Robert help themselves to seconds of each

as Ian, inevitably, gets droopy eyes. He's up at the far end of the table, nodding alarmingly close to his bowl, too far away to kick awake. Ian, who has more vim and vigour than the Energiser bunny, winds down with a thud when he has a belly full of food and red wine, and the hour has grown late.

Everyone drifts home, and the four of us go to bed. I crash, unaccustomed to the amount of food and wine and the lateness of the hour. Out of practice.

Somewhere in the depths of my deepest slumber of the night, I'm vaguely stirred by music, and realise someone is playing the piano. It's enough to make me open my eyes and look at the clock before, drugged by food, wine and overwhelming tiredness, I slip back into sleep with the half-remembered thought that I must have been dreaming. By morning the memory is gone.

Ian and I have finished breakfast by the time the boys emerge. Robert is first and, as always, goes by way of the dining room for a quick tinker of the piano he loves. He doesn't tinker for long. He finds us in the kitchen and says, 'That's weird, I know I closed the lid of the piano last night, but it was propped up this morning.'

'It was late when we all went to bed,' Ian suggests, 'perhaps you forgot.'

Robert shakes his head. 'I always close it. Anyway, that's not the only weird thing.'

'Oh?'

'The keys feel wet, sort of sticky.'

His words make me smile. 'You must have played after mauling the remains of the pavlova last night.'

'No. I'd never do that.' He looks almost annoyed at the suggestion, as annoyed as Robert is able to look. And suddenly, a buried, dreamy thought clunks back into place in my head.

I wait until Robert has vanished with a towel to clean the piano keys then, whispering, say to Ian. 'I've just remembered something really strange. Last night, at about two-thirty, I thought I heard the piano playing. I suppose it must have been a dream.'

'It wasn't a dream,' he says. 'I heard it too.'

My stomach gives a bit of a lurch. I feel my pulses quicken. We stare at each other, the unspeakable suggestion suspended between us.

Robert wanders back into the kitchen with the towel. 'All clean,' he says, and pours himself a coffee.

I make a decision. Robert is not a child, and he doesn't scare as easily as his sister. I tell him about the music in the night and ask if he heard it too.

His eyes widen a bit, but he shakes his head. 'Though my room is further from the stairwell, I'd be less likely to hear it than you. Wow,' he says after a bit of a pause, and stares at the manky towel on the table. 'Ectoplasmic residue.'

'Ecto what?' says Ian.

'Ectoplasmic residue,' says Robert again.

'Ectoplasmic residue,' I repeat. 'Didn't you ever watch *Ghostbusters*? Or *Poltergeist*? It's that sticky wet stuff ghosts leave behind.'

But already I've had another thought. Though the music I heard was not a familiar tune, the standard was very similar to Robert's. Not a beginner. Not a concert pianist.

Somewhere in between. 'Have you taken up sleep-walking since you left home?' I ask him.

Robert takes a sip of coffee, understanding my implication in an instant. 'I don't think so,' he says, 'but then if I was asleep, I wouldn't know about it, would I?'

'Did you take a glass of water to bed?'

He nods.

'Do you think you could have come downstairs for a refill, sleep-walking, spilt some water and played a bit?'

'No recollection at all, Mum, but it's physically and scientifically possible.'

We let the case rest. And in the safe light of day, I delight in the chance to close my eyes and invoke the picture of a beautiful Esse taking her seat on the piano stool with a sweep of full skirts, settling her fine young hands on the ivory keys. Candlelight gleams on her glossy hair, catching the curve of her cheek, a hint of décolletage. Like her tears, can her music permeate the walls?

We'll never know for sure. I wonder if we'll ever hear it again.

⊱─┈◈┈─○─┈◈┈─⊰

It's one o'clock in the morning. I'm stirred from sleep by the rare sound of Topsy, the hopeless guard dog, barking.

Topsy, being a blue cattle dog, is a breed as feared by intruders as they are loved by owners. Loyal, fierce, protective and intelligent. There's something wrong with our specimen. Though she won't tolerate and tries to eat anything on four legs, she's nervous, frightened of people, except for John and Sarah who stuff her full of chips and burgers. When we're not at home, she hides. When we're in bed at night, she hides. She only barks when Ian and I are around to protect her.

The rarity of this is surprising enough to half-wake me. I nudge Ian. 'I think Topsy just barked,' I murmur sleepily.

'Probably just a possum,' says Ian, 'go back to sleep.'

Then we hear a man's voice. It's distant, out near the road. But it's raised and angry.

Ian springs out of bed. He is one of those rare individuals who snap from deep slumber to perfect clarity of wakefulness in a nanosecond. He's proud of this attribute. He sees it as manly, warrior-like, and laughs at the pathetic grogginess I suffer between the states of sleep and true consciousness. In the mornings I shuffle to the bathroom with half-paralysed feet, unable to speak or open my eyes, while Ian is out on the verandah, sucking in the morning air, surveying his domain.

I try to speak now, but I'm struggling. Ian shushes me. Was that a footstep? We both freeze, ears straining. Suddenly there is a deafening hammering. It's the knocker on the front door being banged with awesome force.

Ian strides to the stairs. I grab a torch and stagger after him. Adrenalin starts pumping, soon letting my body move freely, but my thoughts are too sluggish to realise or prevent what Ian is about to do.

I reach the bottom of the stairs and am appalled to see him grab the front door and hurl it open. He stands, framed in the doorway, legs apart, all threatening in his little shortie pyjamas.

Two men are outside with beanies on their heads and cans of rum and Coke in their hands.

At this point Ian realises that perhaps he shouldn't have flung the house wide open, but he's not going to back down now. 'Do you fellows realise what time it is?' he demands of them, as though chastising a pair of schoolboys.

Our visitors are confused by Ian's methods. They hesitate, looking taken aback. I don't think they are accustomed to being challenged by sober citizens in the middle of the night.

'It's after one o'clock in the morning,' Ian continues.

I'm standing behind him in my nightie, clutching the torch. It'd make a pretty good club. My hand tightens its grip.

'We heard this place's haunted,' one of them says.

'Yeah,' joins in his accomplice. 'We heard fifteen people got murdered here.'

Ian laughs in a sort of matey way, as if they are all in on some sort of joke together. 'Do you think we'd be living here if that was the case?'

They hesitate, undecided. Already they seem less of a threat and I'm willing to believe them just a pair of idiots who've drunk too much and dared each other to brave the Ghost House. But I'm also willing to believe that if we hadn't made our presence known, their next move would have been to start trying windows. I'm very relieved this is not one of my nights alone.

'Come on guys,' says Ian, 'it's late and we're tired, off you go now.'

They go. It's a huge relief. I know Ian will say he could

have knocked the pair of them down with one hand tied behind his back, but I'm pretty annoyed with him for his gung ho unlocking of the door.

We listen to their vehicle drive away before I turn on him.

'There could have been six of them, all with baseball bats in hand! We should have yelled at them through a window and threatened to call the police.'

I see rare contrition on Ian's face. He knows he's upset me and deserves the rebuke. But I know he'd do the same again tomorrow night. Ian is the sort of man to fight home invaders to the death before submit. If submission means life, I think I can do submission. I tell him so.

But I can see his thoughts are already elsewhere. 'Where's Topsy?' he says.

We call her.

There's no sign. We are both thinking the same thing. That rare bark wasn't one of aggression but a cry of frightened surprise. Did they then silence her? We call and call again. It takes ages before, to our immense relief, a slithering, trembling creature emerges like Golum from a hole beneath the kitchen wall. Shuddering, it creeps toward us on its belly.

We sit outside patting and soothing her. We decide to get a second dog. Perhaps a bit of back up will give Topsy more courage.

CHAPTER 18

PROGRESS, PETER AND THE POPE

SUMMER APPROACHES, and slowly, surely, our verandah grows. Sarah returns and Topsy gets fatter on her McDonald's diet. Sarah is still not supposed to drive, so is dropped off each day by her friend, Brenda. We never see Brenda get out of the car, but she's an awesome presence in the little sedan. Her arms are like tattooed hams, her shoulders bulge broadly in her singlet top. She always gives us a friendly wave before roaring off in a tyre-spinning, rubber-burning cloud of dust.

Verandah building is not the quiet, shut outside affair I'd optimistically imagined. The lawn is rendered bald and compacted by the dozens of trucks and utes that speed in and out and all over it every day. Workers come and go, deliverymen drop off materials, wives and girlfriends drop off lunchboxes, and the curious come to observe.

Ian and I both go away for a couple of days; Ian on his usual weekly trip to Montville, me on a visit to my children in Brisbane. When we come home we find all of Ian's power tools have disappeared, including a heavy duty chainsaw and brush cutter. None of these things were locked up. In fact they were left, by us, in an unlocked shed and lying about on an open porch. Still it's a nasty shock to think that someone has been lurking around, thieving, in our absence.

We glare at Topsy, the only eye-witness; useless, lovable, cowardly lump of lard that she is, and renew our determination to get a second dog. Clearly we've been too complacent. We've seen our recent night-time visitors as an aberration, and we're treating Maryborough as a sleepy little country town, populated by good, honest, salt-of-the-earth types. Too late we realise that nowhere is like that any more, and hire a lockable shipping container to sit at the end of Queen Street with all of our replacement tools and shed gear safely stowed away until we can build a proper shed.

The closest we've come so far in our quest for a second dog is a quick peek in the window of a local pet shop housing a fluffy litter of roly-poly puppies. But I don't believe the sub-tropics and such fluffy creatures go together, and say to Ian that we should hold out for something more appropriate. Some big, black devil-dog, with a broad head and powerful shoulders. Something that barks loudly. Something that will teach and embolden Topsy.

'They'll be a formidable pair,' I say.

'Unless Topsy teaches the new dog.'

I tell Ian to cut the pessimism and start scanning the local papers.

Greg offers us one of his three-year-old, home-bred Maltese terriers. Being exceedingly fluffy, small and white, it is the complete antithesis of what we're after. A tiny powder puff of yappiness.

'They might be small, but they're good barkers,' says Greg. 'Nothing'll alert you faster if someone's creepin' around.'

With huge reservations, Ian and I agree to trial the little puff, though I'm a bit scared that Topsy might eat her for breakfast.

We tie her up on the half-built verandah, afraid she might try to flee to the sanctuary of Greg's house, get lost in the process and end up looking like an Iced VoVo on the road.

'I see what Greg means about the bark,' I say after an hour or so.

'She'll settle soon,' says Ian. 'Let's give her a bit of meat or a biscuit or something.'

I discover the terrier only shuts her mouth if I'm stroking her. I sit and stroke and sit and stroke. The second I stop, she starts up again.

An hour later I say, 'do you think her throat will get sore?'

Ian gives a helpless shrug. 'It'll have to. Or exhaustion will stop her.'

We try to go about our business. I'm scared her throat will swell and close, or that she'll break brittle bones with so much vigorous barking.

Hours pass.

Ian and I are shuffling around, wondering what to do when Rhys, who's assisting Pud with the plastering of cracks on the exterior wall of the living room, strides up. Rhys is a well-spoken, well-mannered, likable young man.

'If you don't shut that fucking dog up, I'll put a bullet in its skull,' he says, and turns on his heel to return to his work.

We are silent a minute, shocked and ashamed, but suddenly very clear and decisive.

We gather up the exhausted bundle of yapping fluff and drive her back to her home.

><+>·0·<+><

The weather is totally arid for weeks, which is wonderful for getting work done, but turns the bald garden into a dustbowl. Every time a vehicle drives in or out, dust clouds billow into the house through the windows we have to leave open for power cords. From seven o'clock every morning an orchestra of nail guns, drilling, screeching circular saws, hammering, shouting, swearing and the occasional awesome *thud* as something is dropped from a great height, tunes into life.

Bricklayers come to build the core of the solid columns that will surround the house. Soon our bear traps are filled with two-metre tall, ugly, grey, Besser Block columns. They are an eyesore but we know that later, when the coast is clear, Pud plans to work his magic on them.

As the verandah gets taller, scaffolding goes up. Soon we are looking like a giant Meccano set. Large items are hauled up on ropes, swinging wildly. It's a dangerous business to venture outside these days. When the men start work on the upstairs verandah, everyone has to troop through the house and up the stairs with great boots and armfuls of trailing power tools. I hadn't anticipated this and regret having sanded and oiled the cedar staircase before the verandahs were finished.

Through all of this chaos, we mutter daily prayers of thanks to Trojan John, whose good-humoured reliability is such a steadying influence on the project. He shows up every day, whatever the weather, solid and stable. No task fazes him, however great or however small. His singing starts at seven in the morning, and doesn't finish until he goes home in the afternoon.

His early morning solos serve as a handy alarm clock for Robert and Andrew when they stay. No amount of pillows and blankets clamped to outraged ears can keep out the operatic notes, and we get bleary eyed sons appearing for breakfast earlier than they have done in years.

Though one morning Andrew still hasn't emerged and it's getting late. I'm at the point of going in to see if he is still alive, when he suddenly appears, looking slightly out of countenance. It seems John and Sarah have been working on verandah batons at his uncurtained bedroom window for the last two hours. Andrew, who sleeps naked, has been pinned beneath the sheets by their remorseless presence, only escaping when their work was done.

We go to see Peter Olds, of Olds Engineering, about making the lacework and iron posts for the verandahs. Olds Engineering has been a Maryborough icon for almost one hundred years. This seems to be a regular thing in Maryborough: father teaching son, who in turn teaches his son, who in turn . . . Expertise spanning generations. It is the same with Brian White, the joiner who makes our replacement doors and windows, and with Graham

Morrison, creator of our new gates. We are constantly astonished by the calibre of craftsmanship the town has to offer.

Peter Olds has a rare track record. Most famously, he made a bed for Pope John Paul II. In 1994, Pope John Paul had a badly broken thigh bone. When Peter heard of the mishap, he offered to make and gift a special bed to the Pope that could tilt up vertically, thus allowing the injured Pontiff to get out without difficult and painful manoeuvring.

His gift was accepted and, courtesy of Qantas, Peter travelled to Rome with the bed. He was granted an audience with the wounded Pope, who received his new bed with true papal gratitude and grace.

The latest rumour in town is that Peter has received a 'hush-hush' commission to create wheels for the Queen's new ceremonial carriage.

We know our verandah balustrading will be safe in his hands.

Armed with enlargements of old photos of Baddow House in the intact verandah days, we sit down with Peter. He looks like a craftsman of the old school. He has a kindly face, white hair, glasses on the end of his nose, smiling eyes. I think of Pinocchio's Geppetto, who loved his work so much he gave life to it.

'Do you think you can copy these?' Ian asks, pointing to a close-up of the old balustrading.

'No problem at all,' Peter assures us. He goes on to explain how they will build a die and cast all the pieces of lacework separately. According to these plans, 'We're going to need almost four hundred separate pieces.' He peers more closely at the photos, glasses defying gravity. 'You know, I have a pile of odds and ends outside behind those sheds. There just could be something similar to these. Next time you're in town, call in and have a sort through.'

But being the do-it-right-now sort of man that he is, Ian is already on his feet, eyeing the said outbuildings. He and Peter go out to explore and return in about five minutes clutching a piece of very rusty iron lacework.

Glasses are donned, photos re-examined and the lacework is declared to be not just similar, but an actual piece of the Baddow House balustrading. A piece has survived the meltdown, and we have found it. Just like that. *Too easy*, as Mike would say. The story headlines the front page of our local newspaper.

I know we are meant to be here. I don't think much happens by accident. We all have a journey and this inescapable journey is Ian's and mine. Finding that panel of lacework is just another sign. There have been plenty of signs.

➤━◆━○━◆━◅

Bills continue to roll in. Ian and I have a budget most carefully drawn up before our work commenced. Between us, we think we've been pretty canny. Estimating accurately. Overlooking nothing. But as anyone who's ever renovated will understand, unexpected problems and additional expenses crop up time and again. Mike brings us a bill once a fortnight. We learn to read the signs in his approach. Is he calling in to inspect work, or will one of those ominous white envelopes be tucked into his hip pocket?

Mike's ute rounds the corner at the end of Queen Street and brakes hard on the compact dirt of our driveway. A great black shiny noisy beast of a vehicle. It is twice the size of everybody else's utes. On the tray stands Mike's dog, Wolf, an Alaskan malamute. For those who have never seen a malamute, picture a husky, then picture it bigger than a great dane.

With all that fur, I imagine Wolf feels the sub-tropical heat. His massive jaws hang open, his tongue, the size of a human liver, lolls sideways. Topsy rushes out barking, biting at Mike's tyres, but Wolf is unreachable in the tray of his master's ute.

Mike unfolds himself from the driver's seat and strolls toward the house. He's not in work clothes. We can see one corner of a white envelope sticking out of his pocket, and fight the urge to slam shut doors and windows, or hide behind the shed and pretend we're out.

The amounts vary hugely, John and Sarah's labour being the only constant. Usually there are extras from the saw mill, from the bricklayer, the plasterer, amounts to make your blood run cold and keep you awake at night.

The trouble is, we don't want to take short cuts or compromise quality. Baddow deserves the right treatment, and we know, for all our shuddering dread of the bills, that Mike is giving us the job we wanted.

⋄⋄⋄⋄⋄⋄

For a long, long time the verandahs are full height and size, but a skeleton only. Mike doesn't want the floorboards and lacework added until the very end, to protect their finish from possible damage and from being splattered when Pud and Benji repair and paint the exterior of the house. He thoughtfully gets his men to put sheets of plywood down on the bearers and joists so that the verandah can be walked on while things are being finished off.

The day the men put the ply down on the upstairs bearers, Ian and I fling open the French doors the minute we are alone. For the first time we can step outside upstairs. It's exhilarating. We are seven metres from the ground, up in the canopy of the jacaranda trees. 'I'll be able to pluck the blossoms,' I say.

'Me Tarzan, you Jane,' says Ian.

Ian hates to stop work before dusk but, today, I make him. This is a milestone not to be missed. We go downstairs, grab a bottle of champagne and two glasses and return to our tree house.

I look at Ian and know that there is no place on earth that either of us would rather be than sitting together on the splintery plywood with our backs against the wall of the Babies' Room; hot, dirty and tired, soaking up the wonder of this historic moment.

Every atom of me is totally relaxed, totally happy. I'm not thinking of the labour and trials behind us, nor am I thinking of the hard work ahead. Right here, right now, I'm just filled to overflowing with the unadulterated pleasure of the moment. It might be the eye of the storm, a few snatched minutes of peace before it all starts again, but it's a moment of absolute joy.

From our new vantage point, we watch the sun dip over

the trees on the river bank, turning the eucalypts amber and the grass emerald. We see the familiar white egrets skimming their reflections on the water. The tide is high, so the river looks swollen and fresh. It's easy to imagine the tall sailing ships coming into view, their tentative progress slowed by the need to drop lines and test depth. Amazing that such ships navigated so far up-river. We think about those first days before our house was built, when Edgar lived in his simple hut in the village of Wide Bay of a few hundred souls, and imagine the effect the sight of a ship's mast would have on that little bunch of hopeful settlers. How the cry would go up, and everyone would cluster at the water's edge. A ship meant supplies, new folk, and news from home that could bring joy, hope or grief. I feel so spoilt by my weekly letters and phone calls from my mother in England.

How she would love this place. I close my eyes, sip my drink and listen to the orchestra of birds in our garden and surrounding park. I can hear the chatter of lorikeets, the call of the whip bird, plus a chorus of other indistinguishable sounds, punctuated occasionally by the raucous hysteria of the kookaburra. So many different voices, so many different songs. It's almost deafening.

I know I must press Mother to visit us, but not now, not until we're finished. A rough and ready building site is no place for her. But one day, soon, when we have freed the angel from our marble, I will prise her out of the security of her Cotswold village and bring her here.

I make the mistake of telling the EPA that we have found the original piece of balustrade. I'm excited about it. I think we'll earn great favour from them for finding it.

We discover that the original balustrading is shorter than modern building regulations demand if your verandah floor is more than one metre from the ground.

I'm all for nice high balustrading, especially upstairs. I hate heights and never lean against balcony railings. The height solution seems simple. The original lacework was screwed directly onto the verandah floorboards. We need an extra fifteen centimetres. We will sit our new lacework on a wooden bar fifteen centimetres from the floor, in the fashion of many verandahs in Queensland.

The EPA are appalled. We are not allowed to do this. The original lacework was attached directly to the floorboards with no bar. Direct attachment it must be.

We point out that this is illegal as it contravenes modern building regulations.

Heritage will not budge.

'We can't break the law,' we say.

Heritage consider the problem and tell us to gain our extra height by stringing taut wire from post to post above the lacework. Now it's our turn to be appalled. This is an 1883 house! Stretched wire above the lacework is totally out of keeping. We are determined to refuse. We do refuse.

But Ian and I have been at this game for a while now. We grow cunning. For some reason, the EPA's written demand to use taut wire instead of the wooden bar, only refers to the downstairs verandah. Have they forgotten we have an upstairs?

If downstairs is the only issue, we have a solution. We build a garden wall around the perimeter of the house, creating a raised flower bed, thereby lifting the ground level to less than a metre from the verandah floor. Our balustrading can now be any height. Indeed we don't even need balustrading for these new levels. We attach the replica of the too-short original to the floorboards.

Everyone is happy.

We put the upstairs lacework on the bar.

I am happy.

CHAPTER 19

FLOODS, RAIN AND THE GATHERING STORM

T HE ROOF HAS TO BE replaced. It's a complex roof
with different levels, several peaks, separate hip
sections over the upstairs bay windows and –
horror of horrors – a major box gutter that runs across the
centre of the roof, dividing it into two broad gables. A box
gutter is deadly but unavoidable when the shape of your
roof doesn't allow all the rain to run outwards. Half of the
rain that falls on our roof runs into the centre then travels
along the box gutter until it reaches a gutter on an outer
eave where it can finally enter a downpipe and escape.

Box gutters fill with leaves and trap water. They corrode,
erode and leak. There is no way that we can avoid a box
gutter on the new roof. Our hearts sink.

We've been told we might get another five years out of
the roof, but we'd be mad not to replace it now, before the
scaffolding is taken down from the verandah restoration.
Scaffolding costs are horrific. You pay a huge sum of
money to have your scaffolding erected and another huge

sum to have it dismantled at the end of the job. So, though it's tempting to say *sod the roof, we're sick of renovating; if there's another five years in it, let's do it later,* we know that if we don't do the roof now, we will have to pay a second round of erecting and dismantling fees to the scaffolder down the track.

But wait, there's more: each and every day the scaffolding surrounds your house, you also pay a huge sum. Just for it to be there. Scaffolding rent. This makes us very impatient to get the roof finished. Our roofer, Wayne, likes to work alone. He's comfortable working solo and can get things done his own way in his own good time. But we dream of a team of ten showing up and finishing it all in a few short hours. The days drag excruciatingly. Every day that passes makes our scaffolding bill look more and more like the national defence budget.

But slowly new roof begins to replace old. With shouts of warning, battered, rusty red sheets of iron are frisbeed to the ground. We all duck and dodge, knowing we could lose our heads from a badly aimed sheet. Topsy lies low.

The new box gutter is stainless steel, never to rust; the new roof is powder-coated dark grey, never to be repainted.

It's summer and too hot to stand on the roof. We worry that Wayne's feet will get scorched through the melting soles of his shoes. Greg gingerly scales the scaffolding to help paint the flashing at the base of the chimney stacks. Even with a thick towel folded beneath his backside, he can't sit on the heat of the roof. But he refuses to give up, refuses to let us down. He comes back very late every afternoon when the sun's rays are weak and low, ties himself to a chimney, and works on.

➤━◆➤━○━◆━┥◄

Our second Christmas approaches and everyone stops for a couple of weeks. Ian and I are nearly insane about the cost of the scaffolding, but mercifully the scaffolder grants us a half-price discount in scaffolding rent for the holiday period when no one will be working on the house. No one except us and Greg, because Mike has made a brilliant but unwelcome suggestion.

He advises us to paint the rafters and batons of the verandah roof over Christmas, so it will be done before the verandah roofing iron goes on. 'Otherwise you'll never avoid slopping paint all over the iron.' Great. Just how we wanted to spend our Christmas.

Greg paints rafters and we paint batons until we are painting in our dreams at night.

Ian's children come up for Christmas and we stop. They haven't been up for a while, and a seed of worry has been growing in both of us, that the more they realise how close their father and I have become, the less keen they are on our relationship. We know that more than anything they want Ian to be happy, but it's hard for them to acknowledge that he might have deep feelings for a woman who is not their mother. They need to believe that their parents' relationship was unique. Any evidence that challenges this, they don't want to see.

Annabel and Georgie are both back from Europe, so all

four are able to be here. My three, who take it in turns to spend Christmas with me and their father, are with their father this year.

Ian and I hope to have a fun and productive time during which fears and doubts are allayed, and everyone feels as relaxed as they did in earlier days.

My pleasure in seeing Georgie back from England is wholehearted. I've really missed her and I believe we slip back into our old ways without any trouble, which in turn helps the others to feel at home. Like last Christmas, she and I are chief chefs again, and now that we have put an air conditioner in the kitchen and two ceiling fans in the dining room, everything is much more comfortable.

We all eat, loll about, open parcels and drink champagne. Ian buys me a statue of Beethoven for the dining room. I give him a cedar shelf for the office. It's so easy to find presents for each other with this house to fill. Ian's girls and I have raided Sussan's as usual, so there are pyjamas, slippers and dressing gowns for the women of the house. David has new golf clubs. They leave on Boxing Day.

Ian and I think it's gone well, which is a great relief, seeing as we hope to tackle the delicate marriage issue before too long. Some parents might choose to stand up and tell their adult children outright when and how they intend to re-marry. Some might decisively point out how it is possible to both remember and cherish the past, while looking to the future and moving on. But neither Ian nor I want to upset anyone's sensibilities.

Right from the beginning of our relationship, we've taken the tactful path to try to make it as easy as possible for all concerned to adjust. We don't cuddle and carry on in front of the children, nor do we talk openly about our feelings for each other.

We've crept on eggshells.

Perhaps this has been our mistake. Perhaps they would have a better understanding of how much we mean to one another if we had been more openly demonstrative. Perhaps we've given the impression that we don't feel close to each other at all, that we are inhabiting Baddow as a couple of middle-aged companions who've long since lost the ability or need to love.

But Ian and I are new at this. There are no classes to tell us how to handle our specific situation. Even if there were, every family, every personality is different. No doubt plenty of others looking in on our situation would itch to tell us what we should and shouldn't be doing. But it is not an easy thing for Ian to look his children in the eye and tell them what they don't want to hear.

It's a confusing time, muddling along, hoping for the best. There is only one thing in all the confusion of which Ian and I are dead certain. Stumbling and erroneous we might be, but we have done the best we knew how to do in the circumstances.

>-+-+>-0-<+-+-<

My children come up on 27 December. It's the twenty-fifth anniversary of my arrival in Australia, which calls for further feasting. Unfortunately there are more roof batons to paint. It's hard to work at such a Bacchanalian time of year, but we rouse ourselves and find extra paint brushes for all hands.

It's scorching outside, wielding our brushes, and the paint is doing its best to dry on the bristles and solidify in the tins. We work hard and fast, Ian and I well aware that if we don't get it done while my children are here, there will be so much more for us to do later. It's a massive relief when the final brushstrokes are complete.

Elizabeth has spent the last two months in East Timor doing voluntary hospital work. Having her safely home is yet another reason to celebrate. As a parent, I wish my daughter would sit safely by my side and not feel driven to do adventurous things. But as a human being I am grateful, and admire her desire to make a difference, to be a useful member of the human race.

Elizabeth is not a doctor, she is not a nurse, but so desperate are the hospitals in East Timor, they will take anyone and have them do anything. Elizabeth's legendary lack of sqeamishness stood her in good stead as untrained, untutored, she was left to stitch women up after childbirth in a land of no anaesthetics, dodging legs and feet trying to kick her in the head as she wielded her needle and thread, going about the bloody, painful task. She assisted in amputations, again undertaken with no anaesthesia, and she watched children die, witnessing the distress of broken parents.

The convent adjacent to the hospital gave her sleeping accommodation in her own small cell, and in her spare time she entertained the orphans in the care of the nuns. She still sends presents to her orphans and the nuns.

Elizabeth's safe return home seems a far more relevant

cause for celebration than our belated Christmas or the twenty-fifth anniversary of my arrival in Australia.

We create a wonderful feast on my anniversary night. Our toasts are many and varied. Again I'm bursting with gratitude for my children's good-natured acceptance of this new life at Baddow with Ian. I try to express my gratitude to them, to let them know how easy they have made the transition for me. Friends who have done the step-family thing tell me that boys are usually more accepting of change than girls. *As long as they've decent food in front of them. As long as they've the familiar comforts of life, boys will be happy.* It's us females, apparently, who tend to be the complex little horrors. So perhaps I should be extra grateful to Elizabeth.

Robert was never going to mind. Robert, who'll take to the streets and march for any cause he believes in, who defends the underdog and despises injustice to the extent that Elizabeth and I have to take care in his presence not to make catty remarks along the lines of: *Check out the colour of that woman's hair . . .* or *wasn't Orlando Bloom appalling in Kingdom of Heaven?* Such comments are likely to trigger a *for God's sake, you two, don't be so unkind. They're doing the best they can.*

I could join a polygamous cult, grow a second head, turn into an alien, and Robert would nod and say, 'that's fine, Mum, you must have your reasons.'

Andrew would be much the same. Non-judgemental. Accepting. Perhaps, as Andrew usually has his head in a book, he wouldn't even notice.

Yes, I can see that if any of the children were going to have trouble accepting change in my life, it wouldn't have been the boys. But Elizabeth has been fine. Better than fine. She's effusive, delighted. 'When are you guys going to get married?' she keeps asking me.

Holidays over, children go and Ian and I are back on full scaffolding rent again. The roof is still not done, the situation infuriatingly out of our control. We can press and cajole till we're blue in the face, but we can't make it happen any faster. Greg introduces us to a capable young man willing to help with the roof, but we are told that he can't be put on, as insurance won't cover him. The scaffolding is starting to look like a permanent fixture.

The first night Ian is away after Christmas, rain is forecast. I'm not too worried, as I've been assured things are secured at the end of every working day, either with bits of new roof or tarpaulins.

I'm woken from deep sleep by a cracking thunderstorm. I barely have time to wonder if the roof is all right before the ceiling of our bedroom turns into Niagara Falls.

I flick on the lights and scramble for buckets, towels and mops. It's hopeless. There are far too many cascades to be contained in the few buckets I can find. I run to Robert's bedroom and tip out piles of his belongings that are stored in old solid plastic toy boxes. I make rows of my buckets and boxes and throw every towel in the house onto the floor in between them. I turn off the lights when I realise water is pouring down through light fittings and over the wall switches. I can't get the bedroom torch to work, and stumble down the black stairwell to fetch another.

The water is coming down in an area about two metres by two metres, right at one end of the box gutter. I realise the new section of guttering is failing us and fume at the builder and roofer who have left it that way.

Early in the new year Pud comes to fill the exterior cracks with his magic mud and Benji begins to paint the walls. They start on the chimney stacks up in the stratosphere and work their way down until they're doing the columns that fill the bear traps.

Benji uses a special paint, Rock Coat, with a stretchy quality, so that if fine cracks appear in the plaster, the elasticity in the paint allows it to expand like skin, without tearing.

Watching Pud at work on the sixteen columns, I decide his is more than a trade; more than a craft. Pud is making art of our home. He finds a chunk of broken old verandah column amongst the rubble in the garden and cuts a template from the profile of its moulded edge. Then, one by one, he coats our ugly, grey columns with plaster. Adding layers, building their shape, using his template to mould the plaster of the bulky upper part to match the originals. It's the sort of job that could easily end up looking like a melting ice-cream cone, but his work is flawless. It takes a full day to create each column.

At last the roof is finished and the scaffolders come to remove the Meccano set from the house. It's a wonderful moment, both to see an end to the bills and to see the house revealed with its magnificent verandahs.

In yet another indignity, the murdered poinciana tree is nudged by the scaffolders' truck as they leave, and loses a great chunk of bark. Ian rushes over to inspect the damage but is heartened to glimpse green wood deep within this new wound. Evidence that the tree is not quite dead. He goes into a renewed frenzy of mulching, watering and hugging.

'Perhaps next spring,' I say.

By the time Pud and Benji have finished their work, we've been at the verandahs for almost seven months. It's been a massive feat to fit them around such a large, uneven, bulging, bowing house, where no measurement was level, no angle true. Mike tells us they have taken three thousand man hours, used two and a half kilometres of steel reinforcing, three kilometres of bearers, joists and rafters, four kilometres of decking, four hundred powder-coated balustrade panels, twenty thousand hand-driven nails and five hundred bolts. Amongst other things.

⊳−⊷−○−⊶−⊲

We have to oil the verandah decking. Ian and I research this carefully. We don't want to have to redo the four kilometres again. Ever. Sikkens Cetol decking oil is the advice of the experts, but we flinch when we're told how often we have to apply it.

'Surely there is something more permanent on the market?' we plead.

Debbie from Earles Paints in Maryborough shakes her

head. 'Three coats now and you do it again in six to twelve months. That should get you a couple of years.'

It's a pig of a job. Greg cuts in with a paint brush round the edges. I do the main part with a mop. It's back-breaking, hand-blistering, monotonous and hateful – and the oil rots the plastic nodules that attach the sponge to the mop. I have to buy about ten new sponges for each floor of the verandah. At one stage, sick of rotting mops, I fling it all aside, grab the sponge in my bare hands and finish off on my hands and knees. It's a month before the colour fades from my fingers.

But it's amazing to stroll around the verandahs when we are finished. Verandahs that have not been intact for more than sixty-five years. At first we pad around in bare feet and yell at Topsy if she dares to close in on our pristine, richly glowing boards. But gradually we grow more care-less: shoes are worn, dogs are permitted, furniture is arranged and, lastly, huge terracotta pots are shoved into place upstairs and down.

Ian lugs countless sacks of potting mix that weigh as much as I do, up the internal staircase. I want to plant bougainvillea in giant terracotta pots upstairs so it can clamber over the balustrading. I visualise a riot of cascading colour all around the upper level. I visualise the hanging gardens of Babylon.

'You might get sick of these things,' warns Ian. 'Remember how thorny they are.'

'I won't,' I promise, and swear to keep them trained, pruned and perfectly under control.

Ian shrugs. 'If you're sure.' And lugs more sacks of potting mix upstairs.

The upper verandah is a wonder. We look out over the park on two sides, the river on another. We are as high as the tree canopy surrounding us, and catch the slightest puff of breeze.

But we are too busy to dally over our breezy view for long. We are desperate to move on and get the kitchen done, because a momentous event is occurring in October, just six months away.

Mother is coming.

In her day, Mother lived in Malaya, Hong Kong, Singapore and Brunei. She's travelled back and forth from Asia to England countless times. First on troop ships and later on planes. For thirty years, she packed up and moved house every couple of years as my father's regiment was transferred from one country to another. She's endured nightmare flights at a time when it took days to get from Singapore to London. She's done this pregnant and with toddlers. She's been off-loaded in strange countries when there's been engine trouble. She's been forced to camp in Middle Eastern hotels between sheets still warm from the previous occupants, and she's sat up half the night to keep the fleas and bed bugs off her baby (I'm grateful for that one). Always with stoicism. Without complaint.

But now she is retired from her Life of Upheaval. She no longer cares for travel. She no longer cares for inconvenience. She is too elderly; her years demand respect. She will not like to stay in a house without a proper kitchen.

A sense of urgency creeps into our work.

The days and nights begin to cool as we head into autumn. It's wonderful to sleep under a quilt again, though one night, snug beneath the quilt, I dream of floods. I dream of a swelling Mary, bubbling up and over her banks, lapping along the grass with relentless encroachment until she's swallowing trees, cars and houses. Our house is on an ever-shrinking island. I run upstairs and watch in horror as the lawn disappears inch by rapid inch, and the water creeps onto the verandah steps. It's impossible to drag everything upstairs on my own, but I try, heaving tables and chairs up the steep cedar staircase and into the bedrooms. Soon I'm in ankle-deep water as I run from room to room, probably screaming, because the next thing I know there's an elbow in my ribs and a voice in my ear saying, 'Wake up, you're having a bad dream.'

Ian and I have been hearing tales of Mary River floods since arriving in Maryborough.

All Wharf Street goes under . . . all but the tops of the roofs . . .

It gets up the City Hall steps . . .

All the way to the door of St Paul's . . .

Inside the School of the Arts building . . .

They take boats down Kent Street . . .

The place looks like Venice . . .

As for Queens Park . . . nothing left there . . .

It's easy to dismiss a lot of what you hear as old-timers trying to scare new-timers. But since my dream, I've become gripped by the fear of Baddow House flooding. The river looks so close, and if the water rises as high as they say, it's easy to believe it could reach the house.

We need to know for sure, so we visit Jamie Cockburn at the Maryborough City Council.

'I don't think so,' he tells us, 'but I'll fetch you a flood plan.'

Ian and I practically snatch his hand off when the plan is proffered. We scan its contents with bated breath.

A flood plan marks the highest point on your land, and uses contours to show the heights of the past floods. Our house is on the highest point at thirteen metres. The 'Great Flood' of 1893 peaked at twelve point eight metres.

There's a collective sigh of relief. The river has never been inside our house. It's been horribly, frighteningly close once, more than a hundred years ago, but the floods of 1955, 1974 and 1999 look like pups compared to the 'Great Flood'.

I grow fascinated by the 'Great Flood' and visit the Historical Society, now occupying the School of the Arts building, to read all about it.

In the days preceding this flood of floods, the catchment area for the headwaters of the Mary – which happens to be our old green hills of Montville – received, in a four-day period, seven feet of rain. Seven feet! I think it must be a misprint. But no, I'm told, it's quite accurate. Coupled with king tides and enough rain in Maryborough to raise the local water table, the effect was disastrous.

To make matters worse, bad weather had knocked out some telegraph poles between Maryborough and Gympie, the nearest town upriver, so there was no warning.

It was the first week of February, 1893, when the river rose and bulged, and rose and bulged. No one thought it could possibly rise any further. But it did. The banks broke and water spilled out across paddocks, parks and into the streets of the town. And it kept rising.

Schooners broke anchor and – along with houses, barns, horses and cattle – were swept away down river. Terrified animals clambered to safety on the roofs of floating houses. The land at the water's edge was a chaos of panic-stricken dogs, fowl and cattle. The ground beneath them was alive with snakes. Distinction between wild and domestic creatures no longer existed: all were trying to escape the deadly torrent.

Fifteen brave men were selected to try and save the Maryborough Bridge. They were stationed along the bridge and, armed with long poles, endeavoured to keep the debris from stacking up. They kept up their efforts all day and into the evening when, with a deafening crack, the bridge gave way. The men dropped their poles and scrambled to safety. All survived.

But others were not so lucky. Many lives were lost, along with more than one hundred and thirty houses.

It makes horrifying, fascinating reading, but it's a relief to know that we'll be high and dry if such a catastrophe happens again. Though it's not long before old-timers start to tell us of an Aboriginal story of a terrible flood long before white man came. A flood that covered all the land for many, many miles around. Everything was submerged except one hill, where the present Maryborough hospital stands. Ian and I do calculations and realise that such a deluge would put our roof well and truly underwater.

But we have more immediate things to worry about than

legends of the ancients. One day Ian tells me, 'I have to go away next Sunday.'

'Oh? What's happening?'

'It would have been Jenny's and my thirtieth wedding anniversary. The kids want to have a lunch gathering back in Montville to mark the occasion.'

I am silent. I think this is strange, seeing as Jenny is dead. And I think this is hurtful to me. Perhaps if we were married, I wouldn't mind so much. But circumstances do not seem to be permitting Ian and me to enjoy any wedding anniversaries of our own and it is hard, therefore, to see him going away to celebrate his marriage to someone else.

Ian and I long ago vowed not to interfere or be difficult with matters concerning each other's children so, though I hate it, I make no attempt to stop him.

I analyse myself at length. Am I jealous? Would another, more generous-spirited human being think it was great that Ian could share in such a happy day with his children? I'm a parent too and understand how vital it is to have special moments alone with our respective families. From the beginning, Ian and I both recognised the importance of this and we've ensured that it happens. But, whichever way I look at it, I can't reconcile the idea of him celebrating a wedding anniversary with his late wife. Especially as it rubs salt in the wound of having to wait ourselves.

The day arrives and I am slightly mollified by Ian telling me that he means to take the opportunity to have a good talk to his children about us. Topsy and I wave him off, trying not to feel too desolate.

The day drags. I don't get anything done but just hang

around, watching the clock and wallowing in stupid self-pity. I know I should get outside, do some gardening, enjoy where I am. I try to remind myself how lucky I am to live here. But nothing works.

I wonder if it has occurred to Ian's children that I might not be feeling great about this. I try to imagine myself in their shoes. It's true that I phoned my mother in England on the day that would have been her fiftieth wedding anniversary, had my father been alive. I ring her on his birthday too. They are never maudlin calls, more a case of raising our glasses to him and drinking a toast.

But no amount of reasoning in my head lets me imagine myself organising a get-together for what would have been their wedding anniversary, while leaving her new partner at home alone – if she had a new partner.

Perhaps it is harder to lose a mother than a father, harder to come to terms with the loss. I know I'm fortunate to still have my mother, just as my own children are fortunate to still have both of their parents. Perhaps divorce is easier to come to terms with than death. Perhaps this is why my own children have no problem accepting Ian in my future.

Though it could be argued that children of divorced parents might nurture secret hopes of their mother and father reuniting. Had this been the case with my children, then my making a life with Ian must surely demolish those hopes once and for all. For children of a widowed parent, the reuniting option doesn't exist. Wouldn't this make the parent's moving on a less complex issue? I wonder about all these things, my brain going round and round in circles till I'm dizzy with over-analysis. None of it eases the misery of the day.

Ian returns. We eat dinner then slump in front of the TV. I ask the inevitable question: 'Did you get a chance to talk about our future?'

He's silent.

'Did you?' I prompt.

'I talked about us and marriage. Yes.'

'And?'

'Do you really want to know?'

'Yes,' I say. I'm still feeling far too masochistic to deny myself the details.

'They have reservations about you.'

'Oh?'

He turns to face me. 'Well if you really want to know, they had quite a lot to say. They think you talk too much and talk over the top of people. They say they would have far more respect for you if you went out and got a job. And they are upset because, while you make them feel unable to talk about their mother in front of you, you go on about your father all the time.'

Suddenly I'm not talking too much any more. Suddenly I'm not talking at all. These missiles are so acutely hurtful and unexpected, all I can do is stare in dumb shock at Ian, as I try to digest the words.

It's impossible to think straight, my brain is a collision of reaction and emotion. I'm overturned, inside out, giddy, shaking, sick to the stomach, because I truly believed we all liked and respected each other, that we were all moving forward to a happy future together. I'm especially shocked about Georgie, who had spent so much time with me and of whom I had grown so fond.

How could the matter of our marriage be upsetting enough to have provoked this response? Shouldn't our initial moving in together – that first indication that we meant to make our future a shared one – have been seen as the bigger step?

For a moment I can't work out how I feel. Angry, I decide and, with my anger, discover I have regained the power of speech. 'Go out and get a job?' I start. 'What the hell do they think I've been doing since we've been here? I work all day every day. I sand and paint, sand and paint till my hands bleed. And besides that I'm apprentice to every trade in the house, I'm the foreman when you're away three days a week, I oil verandahs, I'm the courier, the paint collector, the tea lady, the gardener, the cook, the dog walker and everything else I haven't mentioned.'

'Yes, I know,' says Ian. 'You've done so much. I explained that to them.'

'And I've done all this at the expense of my writing. My writing is my work. But I've put it on hold so we could finish the house. Make a home. *Our* home.'

I fall silent for a minute, catching my breath. I do know I talk too much. It's been a problem since childhood. Ask my mother. Ask my school teachers. I seriously doubt the affliction will ever leave me. *Chatterbox* they called me when I was little. I don't even bother discussing this with Ian, I know I'm guilty as charged and, besides, overriding everything in my head at the moment is the accusation that they are unable to discuss their mother when I'm around.

Suddenly I'm about to talk too much again. The words trip off my tongue, stumbling over each other in their haste to get out. 'How could they say that?' I almost shout. 'Don't you remember when Georgie lived here? Don't you remember how we talked about Jenny all the time? Ask Georgie what we talked about every morning when we walked around the golf course. And while we worked, painted, drank, ate, drove, watched TV, pretty much *whenever. You* were here, *you* heard us!'

'Yes,' says Ian, 'I heard you.' He's very subdued, looking down into his drink. I realise I'm shooting the messenger and stop.

In the ensuing silence, my anger subsides. It's replaced by another, far more painful emotion. I am hurt by this. Really hurt. And I know it has set our future back by miles.

'It's not about you,' says Ian. 'This would have happened whoever I was with. Remember that. It's not about *you.* Don't take it as personal.'

I suspect he's right, but it's hard not to be hurt, hard to take it on the chin, turn the other cheek. Had there been resistance to my relationship with Ian in the beginning, I would have better understood. But so much time has passed, so many happy days have been shared, and so much has been achieved that I'd grown complacent. I know I should ignore it, school myself not to care. The problem is, this turn of events doesn't just affect me, it affects Ian and the quality of our life together. How can I expect Ian to be happy when those nearest and dearest to him are not?

It's hard to see a horizon clear of trouble and, suddenly, I'm experiencing an almost overwhelming urge to bolt. Immature, no doubt, but I just can't bear the thought of more conflict in my life. I'm of the opinion our capacity to bear conflict is finite, and believe I've had enough in recent years to last me this lifetime and beyond. I tell Ian this; tell him that I'd rather live at peace in a cave on my own than have to deal with fresh conflict.

But it's awful to see Ian this unhappy. Searching for a sense of perspective, I again try to see it from his children's point of view. Though I am, of course, older than Ian's children, I *do* know what it's like to lose a parent at a premature age. In fact my father was a similar age to Ian when he began to develop Alzheimer's disease. I try to imagine my mother with a new partner. I try to imagine how I would feel. For the umpteenth time in recent years, I wish my sister Jane lived close at hand. I ring her in England, pour out all the details and ask her how she would have felt if Mother had met someone else. The conversation fails to soothe me because Jane feels exactly as I do. Her sense of injustice burns as mine does. But for now there's nothing more I can say, nothing I can do. I just have to wait and hope that time will soothe everybody's negative feelings to the extent that we can talk about it. Perhaps I'll be able to talk to Georgie. Surely Georgie would find it impossible to look me in the eye and say she wasn't able to talk about her mother when she was here? Surely she can't have forgotten so much?

And in the meanwhile, we have work to do. There is a kitchen to build. A garden to create. This is not a time to fall about moping.

CHAPTER 20

RESOLUTION

C ATS' CLAW CAN GROW thirty centimetres in a week. The little spikes on its tendrils rip your hands, it doesn't respond well to any poison we can discover and if you pull at it, it just breaks off at ground level because lurking beneath the ground are huge, potato-like tubers. If each plant was attached to only one tuber, perhaps they could be dug up, but they lie cunningly connected like strings of sausages, running deeper and deeper underground. Most of these tubers are about the size of a sweet potato, but we have read of one six metres long that was discovered beneath a concrete slab.

Cats' claw snakes round and round tree trunks, over itself, round and over, over and round, until its mass is greater than that of the tree inside. We hack through the deadly coils and find poor slender, squeezed trunks deep within. Some are dead; some are clinging to life but as weak as weeds growing in a cellar.

Hacking, I've decided, is great therapy for the confusion

and disappointment I'm feeling right now. I tug aggressively at a stubborn rope of cats' claw and a massive clump of it lands on my head. I shake it off but bits end up tangled in my hair, and fine particles are in my eyes and mouth, and stuck to the sunscreen on my face.

I'd always thought that if you behaved in a certain way, if you did this, then that, then the next, it would all add together neatly, like a mathematical equation, to give you the desired result. In other words, that you should be able to control your life if you are capable of controlling your actions, words and behaviour. Then I remember the lost friend from my Montville days, and tell myself: Well, there's an example of my bestowing unconditional respect and affection on another human being, only to have forces beyond my control overthrow everything.

It's a bit shattering to realise how vulnerable outside forces can make us. I think of the white feather in the movie *Forrest Gump*, floating at the mercy of the breeze and decide I'm feeling a bit feather-like myself right now. Life is puffing me this way and that, and there's not a great deal I can do about it.

I glance over at Ian who is, as usual, stolidly working at twice my speed. His pile of shredded cats' claw is massive and his face is bright red and sweaty. I realise that this new shift must be much harder on him than it is on me, and feel a huge surge of affection for him. He looks up, gives me a wide grin, and suddenly I'm not feeling quite as feather-like any more. I attack the vines with renewed vigour.

We have, of course, talked till we're blue in the face since the pillars of our future were so abruptly shaken. Ian believes it is only a matter of time before everyone comes around. His children are young, all under thirty. He believes maturity will open their eyes and soothe their pique. Over and again he tells me they need *time* to learn to accept the idea of sharing him with someone else.

This I understand, but *time* is more of a luxury than it used to be. Starting out in your twenties with a partner, there's the expectation, the hope, that you could get as many as sixty years together. For Ian and me, at fifty-eight and forty-six respectively, the expectation is so much less. There's a sense of needing to hurry up with the problem solving, so that we can enjoy as many trouble-free years as possible.

I swing wildly from wanting to find the patience to let the months – the *years* – slide by until that hopeful day when everyone might be happy, to wanting to yell at the world, *Don't you realise we are consenting adults and can do as we damn well please?*

Today is a wanting-to-yell day, and the cats' claw is bearing the brunt of my frustration.

We're still cutting a swathe through it when the new pup, Lottie, barks and we look up to see a man walking toward us across the lawn.

Lottie has come from Charlotte Plains, sister-in-law Robyn's sheep station out west. 'Real Outback,' Ian tells me. Robyn is married to Ian's elder brother, Reid, and we recently visited their property near Cunnamulla. I'm just so grateful to Robyn for giving us Lottie. Lottie is a beautiful black kelpie, all slender, lithe and slippery. My children call her 'the eel'. Lottie is sensitive and gentle, but she's brave.

She plays outside in thunderstorms, and she barks lustily at strangers.

Unfortunately, when Lottie barks, Topsy figures there's danger at hand and lies low or stays close. She's under Ian's legs now as the stranger approaches across the lawn. I notice he's holding a camera.

We stop work to greet him. He apologises for interrupting us and explains that his mother, who suffered from dementia, died in the garden here several years ago. He hopes to take photos of the site.

I remember the white cross we saw on the pathway that first day with Trevor. I gesture in that direction. 'We found a cross out there on the path,' I say. 'Are you sure you are in the right place?'

'Yes, it was here, just here,' he tells me and points to where we are standing. 'At the time it didn't seem right to put a cross in your garden, so we put it outside in the park where she had been wandering.'

We assure him he can take as many photos as he likes.

'It was a very distressing time,' he continues, 'we think she must have seen the lights of the house and tried to get up there but, as you know, it's been such a jungle here. She was dead for a week before she was found. It was the hottest week of the year.'

I'm stunned that a body could lie here undiscovered by the inhabitants of the house. Especially if it was so hot.

Later, when the man has taken his photos and gone, we sit on the grass and talk about it. I discover that Ian knew, but kept it from me, thinking I might be upset.

I am, a bit. No one likes to think of dead bodies being

discovered in their garden, but mostly I'm distressed because it reminds me of my father, who died of Alzheimer's disease. He had some wandering episodes too, although he was always found pretty much straightaway. Dementia patients can be great escape artists.

It's a common misconception that Alzheimer's sufferers become confused but docile and 'vegetable-like'. Nothing could have been further from the truth in my father's case. He was restless, agitated, paced the house all day and wouldn't sleep at night. That he didn't escape more often is only due to my mother's vigilance.

At twice the size of my mother, he wasn't easy to manage; to dress, to feed, to bath, to contain. Mother was determined to keep him at home. His doctor prescribed daunting quantities of sedatives and sleeping pills. Nothing seemed to work; his metabolism demolishing whatever he was given.

Nothing slowed him: storming from room to room, up and down the stairs, wrenching taps, flooding the house, uprooting plants, turning furniture upside down. Mother tried hiring a night nurse so that she could lock herself in another room and get some sleep at night. But he would batter the door down to find her.

At the Alzheimer's respite centre in Stratford, other patients were terrified of him. He was an incongruous sight among the frail, elderly ladies shuffling along corridors with their Zimmer frames: a powerful man, former Boxing Captain of Sandhurst, well over six feet tall, built like a rugby forward, four times their body weight, bearing down on them with a look of fierce determination on his face.

Given Mother's insistence that she could keep looking after him at home, the doctor made her take down all the *kukris* and military swords displayed on the walls of their house. 'I'm not suggesting he would,' said the doctor, 'but you never know.'

When at last he died and I stood before the congregation at his funeral, I recited some words of Shakespeare's that, to me, summed up those final years my mother and father had together.

> *Let me not to the marriage of true minds*
> *Admit impediments. Love is not love*
> *Which alters when it alteration finds,*
> *Or bends with the remover to remove*
> *O no! It is an ever-fixed mark*
> *That looks on tempests and is never shaken . . .*

I sit on the lawn, all covered in sweat and cats' claw debris. My father would have loved this house. I can almost hear him saying, 'Don't clear all that garden up before I get there, leave some for me to do.' How he would have enjoyed tackling this jungle with his *kukri*.

A *kukri* is the hefty curved knife carried by all Gurkha soldiers, famous for inspiring great fear into enemy hearts. With Father a Gurkha officer, Jane and I grew up on Gurkha legends and lore. The one I liked best was that once a Gurkha has unsheathed his *kukri*, it cannot then be re-sheathed before first drawing blood.

Father bequeathed a titanic respect for the Gurkha people to us.

Ian gave me a *kukri* a couple of years ago; a good, sharp, working *kukri* that I have, until now, propped up on the mantelpiece in the living room. I fetch it and use it to clear cats' claw where the old lady died. The only blood it will draw today is that of the cats' claw.

⊱────◦────⊰

Georgie rings. I feel awkward, tongue-tied. It's some months since the day Ian revealed his children's feelings about me, and this is the first contact I've had with any of them since. Perhaps I should have been the one to call, to extend the olive branch, but have felt neither the ability nor the desire. So much easier to stick my head in the sand, pretend that everything's normal. I think Georgie is brave to be the one. We're stilted at first, though gradually warm up. But even then, there's a morass of unease just below the surface. I tell her I don't understand what's happened, why there's been such a negative shift. Georgie admits she would have hated to be on the receiving end as I was. We decide it would be productive to get together for a good talk. Just the two of us.

When Ian is next away, Georgie drives up to Maryborough through hammering rain and arrives exhausted. It's a three-hour drive from Brisbane and she couldn't leave till after work. I'm touched that she is willing to go to so much trouble to see me and feel a little more optimistic.

I pour her a glass of wine, and we curl up on sofas in the living room as we've done so often before, and talk. I tell her I realise how easy it is to say things about people when you don't think your words will get back to them.

'But don't you think it is better that you *do* know how we feel about you?' she asks.

I don't, actually. I think blissful ignorance would have been preferable, but I just sip my drink and say, 'Perhaps.'

My anger is long gone, I just want every trace of conflict and hurt to evaporate, and I want to release Ian from the purgatory he's currently in so that we can move forward. 'But I was very surprised to discover you all felt that way', I reiterate. 'I honestly believed we were really happy together.'

There's a moment of silence. We swig our wine.

I say, 'If you were fifteen years old, I'd skirt about the issues, strive for tact, but you are twenty-eight next month, old enough for me to be honest.'

She nods.

I take a breath. 'Okay. Don't you remember how you and I used to talk about your mother?' This I have to ask, because I believe the accusation that she was unable to discuss her mother when I was around to be so completely misplaced. I repeat a few of the stories about her mother that Georgie and I shared in her time at Baddow before she went overseas. Childhood anecdotes: mother and daughter hysterical with laughter when a boulder slipped down a rockface and clipped the wheel of their car; Jenny's tears when Dinie, the eldest, first started boarding school; Jenny chastising Georgie for speeding. The who-looks-like-whom games she and I would play: *you've got your Dad's feet, your Mum's smile,* I'd say. *She's got your Dad's smile, your Mum's nose, he's got your Dad's everything.* Laughter.

Especially the chin. Wear your sunglasses, Georgie, I'd tell her. *Because you have your Dad's eyes. Cover them up and you'll look just like your Mum.* It was fun, a game of laughter and happy memories. There were confidences too. Deep confidences.

'Yes, I do remember,' she admits, 'but there were times I felt uncomfortable.'

'I never minded talking about your mother, you know. It's never been a problem for me at all. Just because a person is no longer living, I don't expect their time on earth to be wiped from conversation or thought.'

I remind myself not to use the death of my father as an analogy. I hate this – hate feeling that I must try not to mention him. So, with a silent apology to Father, I pluck another loss from my memory, and go on to describe a lesson I learned on the importance of talking freely about people who have died from a friend who had lost her husband. She told me that sometimes people would cross the road when they saw her coming, because they didn't know what to say to her or how to behave around her. Should they offer condolences, or should they not mention the subject at all?

What she wanted was for people to include her husband's name in normal conversation, as they would have done when he was alive. She told me I was the only person she felt truly at ease with in those early days, because I seemed to suffer no discomfort when talking about him. That I had managed this was quite inadvertent, but I have never forgotten her words. Perhaps it is one of the reasons Ian and I grew so comfortable together so quickly.

I then go on to remind Georgie how much I like her mother's sisters who have both visited us at Baddow, and how her mother's niece has been befriended by my sister in England. I'm trying to show how our families have meshed, but don't press it, because I believe she has conceded an inch and I don't want to push things.

She asks me if I need to speak to David, Dinie or Annabel as well.

'If they are happy to have you representing them all, then no,' I say. 'But if any of them feel they want to talk to me individually, I'm happy to listen.'

So, with Georgie as ambassador for all four, and me representing me, we press forward. I try not to feel out-numbered. We drink a bit more then touch on the *why don't I go out and get a job* issue. I'm not so bothered by this any more. My indignation has dissolved. I can see it was a state-ment made through ignorance of just what has been going on here at Baddow. Georgie tells me that Ian has made clear to them how busy the renovations have kept me.

I wonder whether to try and explain to her the anguish of not being able to write for so long, and how the renova-tion of Baddow House was first my excuse for not writing and then my cure. I decide against it, doubtful that my own private agonies are relevant. Besides, we're making progress, starting to unwind, and I'm loath to drift from the true purpose of our conversation.

We press on. Georgie explains that they are happy about their father and me being together; it's the idea of marriage that upsets them all. 'We don't want Dad to have to be alone,' she says, 'and we realise we're lucky. We realise you could have been worse, you could have been one of those gushing sorts of women. We just don't want you to get married. We don't ever want there to be another Mrs Russell.'

As I've never had an intimate discussion with her brother or sisters, I feel bound to ask if it is just she who feels this way, or whether it is all four of them.

'All of us,' she says. 'We all feel the same.'

I'm not doing so well at understanding this. I suspect there are a few cells missing in the *willing to sacrifice all for the good of others* part of my brain. Sometimes I want to yell, *You have your Tom, you are about to make your happy future together. Why should your father and I be deprived of ours?* But I never do. This is the immature, impetuous, unkind me bubbling to the surface, and I don't like it.

Astrology is not my thing. It's a bit like ghost stories. You tell yourself, *surely sane people don't really believe in all that?* But it's fascinating and alluring nevertheless. A friend once told me that as an Aries I am likely to be childish and impatient. Aries people, apparently, stamp their feet and carry on when they don't get what they want. Some of the worst tyrants of the world, including Hitler, have shared my star sign. It's a sobering thought. I'd rather have been born quiet, sweet and patient, but forewarned is forearmed. Knowing that I might be programmed to exercise those ugly 'me first' traits, I must endeavour to ward them off before they surface.

I try to explain that the fact of our being older doesn't make our wants and feelings, our desire to make a commitment to each other, any less than a couple of her own age.

She perks up at this point and tells me that, though there has been no official proposal or announcement yet, she and boyfriend Tom have started looking at engagement rings.

I ask her if it has ever occurred to her that her father and I might have done that sort of thing.

She looks surprised. 'No,' she says, shaking her head.

It's tempting to ask how she'd feel if Tom's relatives told her they didn't ever want to see her as Tom's wife. Would she step down graciously, or would she fly in their face and marry him anyway?

But I don't, of course. I just feel pressed down by sadness, and by my sense of grief over our lost friendship. In the months she spent at Baddow, Georgie grew to mean a great deal to me. She entered my life when I most needed a friend, and when that friendship was offered I soaked it up, blossomed with it. I can't understand how something that felt so genuine can just . . . evaporate.

We talk for hours, and matters *do* improve. Though I'm conscious the entire time of the oceans of damage that still need to be healed, it's hard not to slip back into our old ways of just plain enjoying being together. As long as we steer clear of Ian, relationships and marriage, we find ourselves laughing and joking. That Georgie and I have had a kindred spirit thing happening from the start is obvious to me. Equally obvious to me is that our relationship is only challenged by two things: the fear of her mother's memory being pushed aside, and by the threat of her losing an ounce of Ian.

Later, I point out to her that she only seems to develop negative feelings toward me when she's away from me. Together we have fun. Apart she has time to dwell on the fact that her father is away from her old home, up in Maryborough with Another Woman. She agrees that it's the case.

'We'll just have to see more of each other then, won't we?'

She laughs.

As the older one, I know I ought to be the wiser. I'm not at all sure that I am, but I do know that Georgie needs to believe that nothing is going to undermine her relationship with her father. Nor is anything going to cheapen her father's memories of her mother.

I suggest Muddy Waters Café for lunch the next day. Muddy Waters is usually a success.

Georgie returns to Brisbane the following afternoon. We hug and kiss and her parting words are, 'I think I can get used to the idea, just give me a bit of warning before it happens. About a month.'

'No problem,' I call, waving her off.

We wait a year.

CHAPTER 21

CROCODILES IN THE PARK

'WE NEED TO CLEAR THE jungle between the house and the river,' Ian announces one morning over breakfast. 'Now is a good time, before we're busy rebuilding the kitchen.'

My heart sinks. I suspected this was coming. Though I know that the end result will be a welcome transformation, I am very much dreading the back-breaking labour that will be involved. But there is no delaying Ian when Ian is on a mission. 'All right,' I sigh resignedly. 'When do we start?'

This particular jungle is the Sleeping Beauty forest we struggled through that very first day almost two years ago with Trevor when we were trying to sneak glimpses of the house.

There are perhaps three okay trees we can leave, but the rest is a tangle of overgrown leucaena (grown in some places as cattle fodder but should be banned from the face of the universe as far as I'm concerned), various scrubby, shrubby noxious weeds and the inevitable cats' claw.

Leucaena grows straight up like a tree, with fluffy foliage on top. On its own, we'd be able to thread our way amongst it and dodge the prickly shrubs, but the whole area is trussed up tight with decades of growth of cats' claw. Think of a ball of string and then multiply it over a couple of football pitches.

Stage one of Ian's plan is a detailed reconnaissance. We squeeze into the jungle, crawling and clambering, reconfirming what we already know – that this job is going to be a nightmare. I've stupidly not worn long pants and my legs are getting scratched. I want to go back and change, but am loath to be thought a wimp. Especially as Ian and the dogs are coping so brilliantly. Ian, also in shorts, strides ahead with great sense of purpose. I imagine the thick hairs on his legs offer the sort of protection my bald legs are without. The dogs frolic and pounce on scraps of life that call this jungle home. Everyone is happy and hairy except me.

But to my surprise and relief, we happen upon an unexpected path and suddenly the going gets much easier. We can at least move freely while we take our mental notes. Ian leads the way over grass, sticks and scrubby weeds that have been nicely flattened down. It gives us a chance to catch our breath, inspect our wounds and be sure of our direction. We carry on for some ten minutes when Ian suddenly stops dead. 'Go back,' he says.

'Why?'

'Just do it.'

I hear the alarm in his voice that he's trying to conceal. I retreat. He gives me a head start, then follows, whistling the dogs and throwing worried looks over his shoulder as he goes.

'What did you see?' I call back.

'Just keep walking,' he says. 'Right up to the house. *Topsy! Lottie!*'

'They're with me!' I yell, 'You're scaring them too.'

My imagination is running wild. What has he seen? I'm annoyed that he won't tell me, like I'm some little petal to be cosseted, but I'm not going to stop and argue about it here. I wonder if he's seen a body or something. It would be really bad to have a second person die in the garden.

As soon as I get back up to the top, I turn to face him.

He's standing straight and serious, looking all manly and authoritative. 'Crocodiles,' he says, before I even have to ask.

'What?' I shriek. 'You saw *crocodiles?*'

'No, not as such. But that flattened path, it was part of their slide. I should have realised sooner, with all the grass down in one direction like that.' A kind of knowing yet faraway look passes over his face. 'I know crocodile territory when I see it. It's those years I spent in North Queensland. A man learns these things.' He pauses, gives a little shake of his head. I can see there's an element of disappointment, of having let himself down. 'I should have realised it sooner,' he admits. 'It was only when I saw the nest at the end that it hit me.'

I can't believe we have crocodiles in the garden. I make a mental note not to tell my mother. 'Were there eggs or anything in the nest?' I ask.

'No, no eggs. But there was quite a large flattened area where the crocs turn. They must be pretty big specimens.'

'I'm surprised the dogs didn't smell them.'

'Mmn. It's probably why we've never been able to coax the dogs into the river.'

'What are we going to do?'

'This close to a residential area? I'll have to report it to the Department of Parks and Wildlife. I'll ring them now.'

We hurry inside.

'This is Ian Russell of Baddow House.' Ian's telephone voice is full of authority today, full of know-how.

'I want to report the presence of a crocodile or crocodiles on our land. Yes . . . yes, we are close to the river . . . well no, I didn't actually see them . . . but I am familiar with this sort of thing. I spent many years in North Queensland, you know.'

I can hear a note of indignation creep into his voice and I know he has a sceptic on the end of the line.

'It was quite obviously the slide of a large crocodile. No other animal leaves that sort of track. Very well, very well. Thank you for your time.'

Click.

'They didn't believe me,' he says.

'They thought it was a crank call?'

'No. Worse. They humoured me like I was some kind of idiot. They insisted there had been no sightings in this part of the river for a long time. Decades. We'll just have to keep watch. Take some photos perhaps.' His face brightens with this thought. I sense his need for action and grow alarmed. 'You're not going down there again?'

But he's already reaching for the camera.

We have photos of squashed grass to study. We talk about it endlessly. When Ian's son, David, comes up for the weekend, we tell him our news, but swear him to secrecy so that the girls aren't frightened.

We're delighted that David has made this trip to Baddow, though none of us mention who has said what about whom, David's smiling countenance and sunny nature assure me that he's not harbouring any negative feelings.

With our increased number, we decide to make another reconnaissance trip to our crocodile territory.

We tie the dogs up in the garden. It's really quite frightening; creeping along, senses alert, poised for flight. But the flattened path doesn't look quite as flattened this time. Little stems and bits of grass are starting to pop upright again. It's lost the ominous look of a recently and well used path. We dare to press on to the 'nest'.

Words fail us when we reach it. There's a ring of rocks – more of a rectangle really, a few burnt twigs, a pile of dirty magazines and a couple of empty Coke cans. We shuffle around for a while, kicking at a twig here, a Coke can there.

On the path back up to the garden, I strive for something to say, and offer: 'That rectangle of rocks was a bit weird, almost like it could have been a grave or something.'

'Oh come on,' Ian snaps, 'it was just a kid's camp and you know it.'

Though Ian's sense of humour never deserts him for long, I silently vow to be good and not tease him about it. It's going to be hard. I'm smiling already.

The next day we commence clearing what is now known as 'Crocodile Patch'.

><+>-0-<+>-<

Our bonfire is the biggest I've ever seen. A mountain of leucaena, cats' claw and other, nameless, weeds towers between the house and the river. Ian and the dogs are really excited. I'm a bit worried about sparks lodging under the eaves of the house and have positioned strategic hoses.

For days we've had a Drott, which is like a small bull-dozer, ripping up the jungle, and for days Ian has been side by side with the Drott, wielding his chainsaw and machete. He's looking a bit like a survivor of the Chinese 'death by a thousand cuts' torture routine, but I know he's at his happiest when doing this sort of thing.

There's a wild gleam in his eye and extra spring in his step as, armed with the necessary fire department permit and a jerry can of fuel, he advances on the ten-metre-high mountain.

I'm backing off, one eye on the mountain, one eye on the quickest route to the hoses when, with a thunderous roar, the pile erupts. Even at my distance the heat is intense, and I retreat further. Ian is up close to the fire, poking at it with huge branches and hurling more debris in. The dogs bark and scuffle with each other.

It burns and burns. And burns and burns and burns. I bring tea and sandwiches down to the site. Between mouthfuls, Ian hurls more debris into the towering inferno. His face is black with what I hope is soot, not singed flesh.

The day wears on. I bring tea and cake down to the site. Ian continues to find debris to feed the roaring mass.

Night approaches and the flames look spectacular against the violet shadows of dusk. The dogs are exhausted, but lie faithfully near Ian, who's looking blacker than the night sky. I can only spot him by the whites of his eyes.

But the heat *is* subsiding, the mountain becoming a slumped, glowing mass. We decide it's safe to go to bed.

It takes a week for the last glowing embers to die. It takes two *months* for the ground below the surface to cool down enough to support life. We learn this the hard way, with the loss of several young trees planted on the spot.

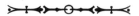

CHAPTER 22

KITCHEN

THE ORIGINAL KITCHEN AT Baddow was a separate building between the house and the street that had been connected to the main house via a covered walkway. We know it had a cellar, courtesy of the Stewarts, caretakers during the Scouts' time, and historian Tom Ryan, who was present during an excavation of the kitchen some ten years ago. But the cellar is now no more than four subterranean walls, filled with soil and rocks, that we drive over every day to enter the garage.

After the original kitchen had been pulled down, Mr Hawes, the builder who recognised the significance of Baddow House and halted the planned demolition, built a wooden lean-to against the southern wall to provide a makeshift kitchen. We imagine it was only ever intended to be temporary. This structure not only survived but was used for decades – even enlarged – turning the southern face of the house into a serious eyesore.

The design of this extension is appallingly inappropriate

to the original part of the house. The lean-to's roof is low, flat and expansive enough to kick a football around on. More recent alterations have seen the exterior walls cheaply clad with split logs in a ghastly parody of a settler's hut. The flyscreens are torn, panes of glass are slipping out of windows and the whole structure leaks like a sieve.

Inside, everything is cracked, stained and depressing. The fibro walls wobble when you touch them and are peppered with holes as though the Karate Kid has run amok. And it's dark. A black hole so dingy we need lights on all day, even in our bright Queensland summer. Unfortunately this charming construction stands in the only place a kitchen could go, so we need to demolish it before we can start building a new one. Which means being kitchenless altogether for as long as it takes Mike Johns to build it.

'How fast can you be?' we ask Mike.

He kicks at the dirt and looks at the sky. 'Demolition will only take a week. We'll have you in your new kitchen within two months.'

We believe his optimism.

I'm not looking forward to being kitchenless but I know we'll survive. It's amazing what you can put up with if you know it's only temporary.

'There *is* one problem,' says Mike.

'Only one?' says Ian, all smiley and jokey.

'Yes, you'll lose access to your bathroom.'

We hadn't thought of this. There is only one bathroom in all of Baddow's vastness. It occupies the top floor of the Keep and is accessed via the main upstairs corridor and a little annexe that is the upper part of the vestibule. The vestibule is the entry to the kitchen and will also have to come down. So our bathroom door will open onto a gaping chasm some seven metres deep and over a metre wide. It is a distance we could jump – and if it was on the ground floor, I'd be happy to jump it. Ian declares he's happy to jump it anyway. My vertigo-esque tendencies make me sweat just thinking about this. I've a horrible feeling Ian means what he says so quickly forbid it.

'We can put a plank across,' suggests Mike.

Great. Now we get to walk the plank seven metres from the ground in the pitch dark if we want to go to the loo at night.

Mike sees the look on my face. 'It will be safe,' he assures me. 'It'll be a plank with walls and it will be anchored.'

'Like a bridge?'

'We have the technology.' This is one of Mike's favourite sayings. Whenever we ask if something is possible or not, he gives us a calm, confident look and repeats his mantra. Perhaps he watches a lot of sci-fi when he's not at work. But he's not looking so calm and confident now. 'You do realise we will have to disconnect the power?' he says.

This is nothing. We've had plenty of power interruptions already. 'No problem,' I say, 'how long will it be this time?'

'For the duration of the building.'

It takes a minute to sink in. I must be looking as if my IQ has taken a nosedive, because when Mike goes on to explain, he uses kindergarten terms. 'Your meter box is on the old kitchen wall,' he says slowly. 'Your power will have to be disconnected from the road and the meter box will be removed. You can't install the new meter box until the new kitchen walls are built.'

I suspect Ian knew this but had chickened out of telling me. 'They'll put a temporary powerboard in the garden,' Ian says to me now, with the Must-Pacify-Anne look he wears when he's worried I'll get cross. 'They'll have to, because Mike and his men need power for their power tools. We'll just run extension cords out to their power-board if we need power for anything.'

If we need power?

I regroup. The only way to deal with the chaos of reno-vating is to accept these nasty surprises with good grace.

'Okay,' I say. 'But I can't live without a fridge.'

'You can have the fridge,' they assure me.

'And the washing machine,' I quickly add.

I don't fancy trips to the riverbank to beat clothes on a rock, especially now that I'm clued up on the crocodile and shark situation.

In the end, I'm allowed two extension cords with enough adaptors to give me the fridge, washing machine, kettle, toaster, TV and crockpot. We have no other power whatso-ever: no computer, no heaters, no lights. We creep round with torches at night. Thank God we are no longer scared of the ghosts.

>─┤◆>─O─<◆┤─<

It's March when they begin. I'm starting to count the days till Mother arrives. We still have six months, which seems like loads. Two months till we're in the new kitchen, that's

May, which gives us four months to tidy up, plant my cottage garden and do all the last-minute touches. Cyril shakes his head and predicts July at the earliest.

The old kitchen is down within a week. Then the ground is prepared by an excavator. Trenches are dug for new plumbing, new sewerage pipes and – thanks to a brainwave of Calvin's – to bury the power lines from the road to the house. 'You may as well do it while it's all dug up,' he points out. It's one of those ideas you slap your head over and say *Why didn't we think of that?* We've despised the looping, drooping overhead power lines since we first saw the house.

Then it pours with rain for two weeks. With our network of trenches, the front garden is looking very much like France in 1916. Ian puts duckboards down for us to walk on. Progress slows. John and Sarah dodge showers and work in ankle-deep water.

However our new kitchen *is* emerging. We do Besser Block walls, render, then press shallow lines into the render to match those on the original house. These lines give the illusion that the house is built of massive stone blocks, rather than rendered bricks. Whatever Edgar Aldridge did we are determined to follow. A roof skeleton appears one day, trusses are hoisted, batons hammered down and electrical cord threaded through in readiness for the great day when our power will be restored.

But weeks are ticking by, and we begin to fear that Cyril's prediction of July is somewhat optimistic.

I plunge into a kitchen design frenzy with cabinet maker Brad Weiss. Brad doesn't say much from behind his thick beard and when he does speak it comes out in reluctant-sounding monosyllables. I'm a bit worried at first, because I have precise and unusual ideas for the kitchen. I want it to look as though it has been there for as long as the rest of the house. I want its proportions and style to match the original architecture.

But I soon discover that Brad is tuned in to my way of thinking. We understand each other totally and design cupboard doors that resemble those on an antique dresser. We find huge stone tiles that look as close to old flagstones as you could hope to find. We paint the cupboard doors terracotta, then add a coat of spearmint green, thin enough to see hints of the red beneath.

More weeks tick by. Every night I cook in the crockpot in the office. We grow unutterably sick of sloppy food. Dirty dishes are dealt with in a bucket. After dinner each night I carry a glowing fluoro tube and my bucket of dishes outside to the old scullery. The glowing tube sits on top of the fridge we've crammed into one corner, and I wash up by its pale, translucent light. It's winter now, and I'm lashed by a cold, southerly that whips through the old iron louvres. There are no panes of glass in the scullery and when it rains, the wind slings freezing raindrops through the gaps in the louvres and into my face as I work.

We do at least have hot water, thanks to some nifty work by Calvin, so can luxuriate in hot showers at the end of each day. This is a real bonus, because at one stage we were told that hot water would not be possible until the power was reconnected. At the time, we bravely vowed to bear cold showers, but that was before we knew it would all take so long and stretch well into winter.

Extension cords snake everywhere. It's impossible to clean the floors properly. The fridge in the old scullery is for food, the booze fridge is on the verandah. One morning we discover the latter has been emptied overnight. The guard dogs slink shamefully past at breakfast. The thief returns the following night, but Ian and I are not completely stupid, and have not restocked the booze fridge. The thief makes off with a lone can of Coke.

Once a week we get pizza delivered. Never in my life have pizzas been so welcome, though the delivery boys seem a bit nervous about delivering to the Ghost House, especially as said house is always plunged in complete blackness every time they come. Afraid they will start refusing to deliver, I tip heavily.

Our weak, battery-run fluoro lantern gives out a pathetic pallid glow that can't be seen at all from the front, so each week I look out for the delivery car's headlights and stand ready at the door, money in my hand, trying to look wholesome and normal, not at all like a crone from the Dark Ages with outstretched hand, luring the unsuspecting into her vile lair. Some of the delivery boys are braver than others. One lad doesn't get out of his car until I walk out to the road with my lantern.

Pizza and cash are exchanged with a smile and thanks from me, but with a grabbing of money and hasty retreat from the delivery boy. A spinning of tyres. A burning of rubber. 'Till next week!' I call out.

Ian and I devour our pizza by weak lantern light. Not quite manna from heaven, but as far as my stomach is concerned it's the highlight of the week.

There's a spooky incident a couple of months after we lose our power. It's midday. Broad daylight. Ian and I are sitting in the office going over the usual; re-examining kitchen plans, fretting about money, lamenting the slowness of the building, when our computer printer starts making its grinding-into-a-switched-on-state noises.

We stop talking and stare at the printer. It goes quiet.

'Did you hear that?' I ask Ian.

'Mmn.'

'Not my imagination then?'

'No.'

There is no power connected to the house at all. Our only source is the builders' temporary power-board in the garden. The computer cords lie inert on the floor under the desk. They might as well be a million miles from the power-board outside.

A thread of memory surfaces. Was it the Christiansens? I can't remember. But someone at some stage in our time here has told me that our office is one of the 'haunted spots' of the house. And it was while sitting before this very computer, after all, that Andrew thought he'd seen his ghost.

'Don't be ridiculous,' says Ian, swift to take on the role of sceptic. I regret voicing my thoughts. It's a good place to be, secure beneath the mantle of scepticism. I dive under with him.

But, secretly, the office commands new respect from me. From now on, I enter with all senses alert. What am I expecting? A powerless computer flickering into life, voices from the long dead hammering their message across the screen? And if so, what would they say to us? *Welcome . . . kindred spirits . . . welcome . . .* or maybe *get out . . . this is my house . . .* GET . . . OUT . . .!!

⊱━◆━○━◆━⊰

Finally, halfway through June, power is restored. It's quite a Biblical moment. 'Let there be light!' says Calvin, and flicks a switch. After three months of creeping round with torches through the long, dark evenings, it is extraordinary to see warm, golden light flood the house.

I've read that suicides are more common in parts of the world where inhabitants are subjected to lengthy periods of darkness. Sweden, for example, so far from the equator they get a good twenty hours of darkness in winter months, has really grim suicide rates. Not that I'm suggesting Ian and I have suffered greatly from our lack of light, but when the power is restored, we skip about like spring lambs. We can't get enough of it and are really wasteful, having the lights on in all the rooms of the house every evening for days.

At last I can wind up all the extension cords, give the floors a good wash, turn on the computer, check approximately five hundred emails, and warm us with a fan heater while we watch TV.

Benji returns to paint. Everyone is aware of the pressure of Mother's arrival and Benji works like a fiend, abandoning other customers. 'Mother Mary is the priority,' he says. It's a phrase often echoed at this time.

Ian and I spread out all the new window frames on the

verandah and paint them before installation. When they are in, they are too stiff to be locked properly. Cyril comes to the rescue yet again, dismantling them, shaving bits off and refitting them with careful, patient hands.

Ian has saved the old facia boards that were pulled down with the gutters when the roof of the house was removed. He has discovered that they are seasoned red cedar. Parts are rotten, but enough survives for Cyril to make open shelves for the kitchen and a mantelpiece to fit around the cook top that has Ian whooping with delight.

Everyone thinks I'm mad when I produce pale pink cut glass knobs for the doors and drawers. But all later agree that they're great. I know I'm being patronised but let it go. There is no comment from the team when I produce the pink toaster. I think they're pretending not to have noticed.

We are in our new kitchen. I can hardly believe it. Suddenly there is space and more space, cupboards, shelves, an oven, a big, deep sink, clean broad bench tops, natural light and a table and chairs.

Ian attaches his 'wine gun' to the wall above the cedar mantelpiece. At a glance you'd swear it was an old rifle and suspect Ian of being a mad keen gun enthusiast. But this is actually a bottle of wine.

The story goes after the Second World War ended, a digger bought the bottle as a souvenir in Italy before he came home to Australia. He never opened and drank his prize and, after he died, his widow sold it to a second-hand dealer. It looks like a gun, feels like a gun, but is made of glass. If you tip it back and forth you can hear the liquid gurgle and see the cork in the nozzle.

Ian is an even more obsessed collector than I am, but our collections blend well. You need a few anvils, dingo traps, copper urns and old pots and pans hanging around the place to dilute the mass of pretty china I can't live without. So our new kitchen is an eclectic mix of rose-patterned teapots and branding irons, delicate plates and dented pewter tankards, camp ovens and boomerangs.

It's the same when you wander the rest of the house. You'll see a bowl of fresh roses alongside a stuffed crocodile; a pair of bronze, claymore-clutching, kilt-wearing Scotsmen sharing space with etched ruby glass goblets; a 'blunderbuss', *kukris* and empty shell cases alongside antique hand-painted vases.

Though in the living room, where the bi-fold cedar doors can divide the space in two, Ian has claimed one half of the room and I've claimed the other. There is a noticeable lift in colour in my half, which I fill with fresh flowers and flowering pots of orchids – lilies and begonias when they are in season – and a noticeable concentration of more manly items in Ian's half.

'Rikki-Tikki-Tavi' takes pride of place. Rikki-Tikki-Tavi is a stuffed mongoose fighting a cobra that I picked up in a junk shop in Brisbane. Ian's favourite story as a boy was Kipling's *Rikki-Tikki-Tavi*. This eponymous mongoose lives in the garden of an English family in India. When a cobra slithers in to threaten the little English boy, Rikki-

Tikki-Tavi pounces, bravely fighting and killing the cobra, saving the lives of the child and his family.

Taxidermy is not my thing. I am decidedly unkeen when Ian suggests putting a stag's head in the dining room. The idea of eating with a beheaded head stuck on the wall beside me seems revolting. But when I see Rikki-Tikki-Tavi for sale, I know I can bear it for the excitement it will give Ian. Especially if Rikki-Tikki-Tavi is confined to Ian's end of the living room: the 'Gentlemen's Room', which looks increasingly like the port and cigars region of the house.

Collecting, arranging and re-arranging our belongings is an immensely satisfying and entertaining pastime, but we must stop. We only have a month till Mother's arrival, and need to set our sights on the garden.

A massive stack of aged mellow bricks sits waiting. They are the remnants of an old industrial kiln, found by a piece of great good fortune following a long, frustrating hunt for something to pave the path and patio around the kitchen.

We also find Charlie.

Charlie was born a cockney but has lived in Australia for more than thirty years. He is small and sparsely built, wiry, energetic and blessed with a keen, creative eye. We know our paths, walls and patio will have perfect curves and proportions.

Charlie knows Mother Mary is coming. He's ready and waiting to start paving the moment he gets the go ahead.

Charlie rivals Cyril for tea-drinking capacity and christens me Lady Coronary, for the number of biscuits I produce and ply them with. During tea breaks, Charlie fascinates us with tales of life behind bars. Not that

Charlie's ever been locked up himself, but his wife, Rae, is head of the education program at the local gaol; the Maryborough Correctional Centre, to be more correct. It's located a few kilometres out of town and houses some three hundred prisoners, including some real nutters by the sound of things. Charlie has worked there occasionally too. He's run art classes and landscaping classes for the prisoners. He's even been savaged by a police dog during a training exercise in the prison yard. This earns him such nicknames as 'Biscuit' and 'Chum' amongst the gaolbirds.

Charlie lives up to expectation. We soon have a patio, paths and low curved walls of warm aged bricks. It transforms the garden.

Finally I can plant my waiting collection of flowers and shrubs. I have gardenias and camellias for the raised garden bed along the eastern wall. In front of them I cram dozens of annuals: snapdragons, petunias and stocks, to fill the gaps until my shrubs grow fat enough to fill the beds. Along the hot north-western wall I put lavender and roses, daisies, verbena, cosmos, forget-me-nots, and allamanda and climbing roses to creep over the verandah columns.

They'll need my tender loving care for a while until they get their roots down a bit, then should be able to withstand the gruelling summer heat.

Through all of this Ian and I, with Greg's help, start laying turf on our barren lawn. It's hot heavy work but the reward is instant, like laying a beautiful carpet over a wreck of a floor.

Ian drives out to the local turf farm and collects one batch at a time on the tray of his ute while Greg and I ready the bare soil with water and fertiliser. When Ian returns, the three of us heave the pieces of turf into position. All are cut to a size and weight that can be lifted one at a time. It's back-breaking work – my arms are jelly within the first half hour – but it's oh so exciting to see the garden transform. We work at a rate of about a hundred and fifty square metres a day. It takes ten days spread over almost three weeks.

The clock is ticking. It's only a couple of weeks before Mother is due. But on a day when Ian is in Montville, Charlie and I get a bit carried away and use our leftover bricks to create a big circular bed in the middle of the back lawn. We dig up a recently planted pink bauhinia tree from the perimeter of the garden, and drag it up the hill to the centre of our circle. I make a mental note to keep Ian and his poisonous spray kit away. I don't want my bauhinia sharing the fate of Ian's poinciana, which is still sitting leafless and forlorn out at the front of the house. I fill the rest of the circle in with snapdragons, dianthus and pansies until it is jammed full and a rainbow of colour.

Charlie and I stand back, muddy, sweaty and liberally coated with fertiliser, delighted with our efforts and hoping Ian will approve this latest addition.

He does.

><+>-0-<+><

Now that we have our *paradise found*, Ian decides it would be a real treat to view things from the air. There is a little airstrip in Maryborough, a flying club and a few light planes which can be hired out. Flying has been one of the loves of Ian's life. Though he hasn't piloted a plane for almost thirty years, one of the highlights of his adventurous youth was being at the controls of a tiny piece of winged aluminium and hurtling through the stratosphere.

Me, I'm not so keen. Flying has never featured as a favourite thing to do, more a necessary evil to bear. There are two factors at play here: one, I've never quite got over the tendency to airsickness that made me such a trial to my sister when we were young; two, I think it's pretty scary, zooming along eight thousand metres above the ground. I'm not keen on boats either. Terra firma is where I like to be. Two feet firmly planted, thank you.

The smaller the plane the more I hate it. The smaller the plane the more you get tossed about, the more you feel every unexpected twitch of the atmosphere. Vulnerability inversely proportional to size of plane: this is my unshakable belief.

Ian presses and cajoles. 'You'll love it when you're up there. The jacarandas are in full bloom, it's going to look amazing.'

'I don't know,' I say, 'perhaps next year.'

'Why next year?' says Do-It-Right-Now Man.

'Well it would be really bad to die when my mother is due. Just think how disappointed she'd be.'

'For God's sake, don't be such an idiot. You're not going to die. We'll go on a clear day, not a breath of wind.'

I recount several cases of small planes going down on clear days. These are the sort of statistics I store up to use on occasions such as this.

Ian presses and presses. 'When you see the house your nerves will disappear. I promise.'

'I do remember,' I reluctantly concede, 'that when I went snorkelling in shark-infested waters off Heron Island, I did forget all about the sharks once I saw how beautiful the reef was.'

'There you go,' he says. 'It'll be the same.'

'Maybe.'

But he's already reaching for the phone, booking Roy Gibson, a local pilot for the next day. 'It'll be a four-seater,' he tells me, 'because I'd like to take Bob Harper, the photographer, with us. Wouldn't it be great to have some aerial shots done with a proper camera? After seeing the house, we'll fly over the wood chip mill, then have a look at Fraser Island, before coming back.'

'Can I sleep on it?'

'Sure you can. With Bob coming, I've told Roy we need the four-seater whether you join us or not.'

I wake in the morning with a knot of dread in my belly. Ian is bouncing with cheerfulness. 'I'm so glad you're doing this, that we can share the experience. And I'm really proud of you,' he adds, with an arm round my shoulders, 'because I know you don't find these things easy.'

Thus, it seems, I am committed.

I don't feel too bad at the airport. The day is clear as promised, not a breath of wind, not another plane in sight, no flocks of birds or bats, and the land around Maryborough is totally flat. No mountains or canyons or other natural features likely to cause up or down draughts. I tell myself it will be no worse than a cable car ride, and it is only for an hour. How bad can one hour be?

We find Roy in the hangar, tinkering with the plane. 'Is *that* our plane?' I whisper to Ian.

'A Cessna 172,' he says with barely suppressed excitement.

The plane is the size of a mosquito. I can't believe four people are going to fit inside. And I can't believe its engine, assuming it has one, will have the power to lift four people off the ground.

Bob, our photographer, approaches with a cheery wave. He explains that he'll have to be in the front with Roy to get clear vision for the photos. 'You'd better sit behind me, Anne, because I have to push my seat right back for the camera angle. Ian can sit behind Roy where there'll be more leg room.'

Ian says that he doesn't mind the lack of space. A leg room debate commences.

'You'll like it better behind Roy,' Ian tells me. 'Bob's side of the plane doesn't have a door, just a doorway.'

End of debate. I scramble in behind Roy's seat. Then Ian gets in and the plane nearly topples sideways. He puts an arm round me, grinning. 'You'll love it once we're up there, I swear. And don't worry, Roy tells me the plane has just had its one hundred hour check.'

Sitting in the belly of the mosquito, I get a sense of the surreal. I can't believe I'm doing this, therefore I'm not. I'm not here at all. It's a dream, and soon I will wake in our beautiful king-size bed, stretch, yawn and contemplate the day.

The propeller hums into life. The mosquito vibrates. We taxi across the tarmac.

A cable car ride, I tell myself, and it will be over soon.

Within ten seconds of take-off, I know I'm in trouble. A tight band of fear constricts me. Every muscle and sinew clenches into total rigidity. Ian's arm maintains its circle of my shoulders. The wind through the open doorway, roars loudly enough to drown out conversation. Ian smiles and points, occasionally shouting in my ear when he spots a landmark.

I realise I can't bear it, won't be able to bear it, but I am trapped so have no choice but to bear it.

Ian is shouting and pointing. 'The house . . .' I hear, but can't look. Roy is circling our home so that Bob can get unobstructed photos through the opening. There is no way my eyes can travel in that direction, the sight of Bob hanging out into space is more than I can handle.

The circling gets tighter, lower. The plane gives a bit of a lurch. To my horror I feel tears spring to my eyes. Ian has spotted them and squeezes my shoulders. I'm now sobbing but, as Bob and Roy have their backs to us, I'm hoping to get away with it undiscovered. I struggle to regain control, taking deep breaths, gripping the one and only wall of the plane as though my life depends on it.

I know I'm ruining Ian's flight, but had no idea it would be this awful, this unmanageable. I lean towards Ian's ear. 'I don't want to go to Fraser Island,' I say, the only words I utter for the duration of the flight. He nods.

I start to feel ill. I'm not sure if it is pure motion sickness, or whether it is compounded by terror-induced nausea. I try closing my eyes, but feel worse. The best is to stare straight ahead.

We are almost at the woodchip mill. Bob has been

booked to photograph this also. Roy circles the mill, Bob clicking away. The circling is ghastly, the plane tilted at an angle so unnatural I feel as though the merest puff of wind could flip us over. Round and round we go. I'm clutching the wall, leaning into it, staring straight ahead. Roy's eyes are on Bob's activities most of the time. *Watch where you're going!* I want to shout. Not that the traffic is heavy. We don't see another plane the whole time we're airborne.

All the way back to Maryborough, I'm rigid, fighting nausea. By the time we make our approach to the airstrip I think I'm going to be sick into the hat on my lap. I take deep breaths. We touch down neatly. Roy is a skilled pilot. We taxi to the hangar, hop out. I'm stiff all over, muscles pulled from my neck to my calves. I shake hands with Roy and Bob, murmur my thanks, and tell Ian I'll meet him by the car. In the privacy of the far side of the car, I drop to my knees and vomit onto the grass.

Ian is really nice to me for the rest of the day. He grovels and waits on me hand and foot. My nausea doesn't clear till the following morning.

CHAPTER 23

MOTHER MARY – AND MARRIAGE

WE DECIDE TO HAVE A party before Mother arrives, to thank everyone who has been involved in our project over the two years. She is due on Saturday 1 October, so we arrange the party for the preceding Sunday. This will give me five clear days after the party to clean the house, arrange flowers, perfect her bedroom, polish the silver, prune the upstairs bougainvillea that's thornily growing at an alarming rate, fill the fridge with wholesome food, bake a cake and anything else I can think of to make me look like a domestic goddess.

The day before the party, Georgie and Tom surprise us with an overnight visit. After dinner, when Georgie and I clear the plates from the dining table and take them to the kitchen, there is a hushed, urgent conversation occurring in the dining room. Georgie and I are oblivious, rinsing plates, deciding what to have for pudding, but, out of our sight, leaning forward across the table, Tom is asking Ian for Georgie's hand in marriage.

It is the most exciting news in our extended family for ages. Seldom do you see a pair who, from first glance, you can tell are perfectly matched. Georgie and Tom are peas in a pod. Their wedding is set for the following May.

The next morning we have to drag our thoughts away from Tom and Georgie and apply ourselves to the serious task of getting organised for the party. I have treated myself to the services of a caterer from town so there's no cooking to do, but there's still plenty awaiting my attention: flowers to arrange, furniture to dust, floors to sweep, cushions to plump, a bar to set up on the lawn. Finally I tether a big fat pink ribbon from pillar to pillar across the top of the verandah steps.

There is Mike and his team, all the other tradespeople who have been involved: plumbers, bricklayers, roofer, concreters; Marian, the architect, and her team; a National Trust representative; Peter, from Olds Engineering, who has just completed the Queen's new carriage wheels; Brian White, the joiner; taciturn Brad of the kitchen; and Charlie, Greg, Cyril, Benji and Calvin, along with all the spouses and girlfriends. There is the Mayoress and the press; Trevor, without whom we would never have found the house; Jan and Barry Christiansen, who've driven the four hours from Toowoomba; and there is our guest of honour, Margaret Jacobson, great-niece of Mr Hugh Biddles. Margaret is going to cut the ribbon.

We number about seventy people.

We throw the house open and everyone wanders about upstairs and down, showing their admiring families all the crazy things they had to do here and, in the case of those who were employed in early days, seeing the finished product. Greg, indispensable as ever, mans the bar with his wife, Karen. The booze flows.

Ian gets up and thanks everyone. He's great at this sort of thing, singling everyone out, getting our true gratitude across. What has started out as a thank you party for the workers suddenly feels like a re-birth of Baddow House, a fulfilment of Edgar Aldridge's dream. Ian expresses this, and makes the point that we couldn't have done it without the help of every person present. Calvin steps forward to say that no one minded going the extra yards for us, which is truly moving.

I'm feeling too damp-eyed to speak, but now it's Mayoress Barbara Hovard's turn. Her words are a heartfelt thanks from Maryborough to Ian and me for saving Baddow House, such an important Maryborough icon. Finally we call Margaret forward and hand her the scissors. She snips, the pink ribbon flutters away and cameras click like mad.

We party into the night.

⊱┈◈┈○┈◈┈⊰

Mother's plane lands on time, and I whisk her up the highway for the three-hour trip to Maryborough. We arrive midmorning and Ian is waiting to greet us.

Everything has been pruned, polished and primped into perfection. Except for the silver. I ran out of time. It's lurking, shamefully unpolished, in the dining room. But it's dark in there and her eyes aren't what they used to be. I'm hoping to get away with it.

Before we go inside, Ian beckons us over to the poisoned poinciana tree in the middle of the front garden. He's grinning and pointing. We peer close. Sure enough, all along the poor denuded branches are plump little green swellings. 'It's a sign,' he says, beaming at us.

And so it is. Like the phoenix rising from the ashes, it is reborn after what had seemed a certain death. 'Very symbolic,' I say, and look up at the white walls of our finished home.

Ian catches my eye and flashes another smile. 'Very,' he agrees.

We put Mother in the Blue Room, Hugh Biddles' room. I don't tell her that his corpse lay in state there until the cortege arrived to take him to the cemetery. It's a spacious sunny room with a couple of armchairs and I know she'll love it.

She stays for six weeks. We get visits from Cyril, Greg, Benji, Calvin and Charlie, all coming to pay their respects. I explain to her how hard they've striven to finish off in time for her arrival.

She spots the silver on day two. We sit and clean it together. It takes all day and our fingers are stained and weary.

We do a lot of talking. She says how much my father would have loved and appreciated what we've done here, and how happy he'd be to see Ian and me together. 'When are you going to get married?' she adds.

I explain.

Mother is tolerant, non-judgemental, but I'm her child. She's piqued, a bit cross with Ian for not sorting everyone out. Though she can see how happy we are together, and this gladdens her heart when I've obviously been a worry to her for far too long.

Most mornings are spent lolling in the deep shade of the western verandah overlooking the river; sipping tea, nibbling scones. Throughout the day we move around the verandah seeking shade as the sun moves, and by the afternoon we are on the eastern side watching the kookaburras fly back and forth to their nest in the Canary Island palm tree. Lottie runs across the grass beneath them, jumping and biting at the sky. Topsy, old and fat, lies at our feet.

Since the age of nine, I've lived on the other side of the world from my mother. When she was in Malaya, I was in England at school. When she and my father retired home to England, I flew to Australia. There have been countless visits over the years, but this is not the same as being able to call in on a regular basis. It is not the life that we planned, it just happened. So you learn to adapt to make the most of the time that you have together, appreciating those moments, storing them up.

Every week since I was nine years old, I've received a letter from my mother. Every week for almost forty years.

At school, each morning after breakfast, we boarders would file past a board where the day's post was pinned. Every morning every girl hoped to receive a letter. Some never did. Once a week, there were two blue airmail envelopes waiting – one for Jane and one for me. Away but never forgotten.

When I came to Australia, her letters continued. Through all the baby rearing years, the children at school years, through to the end of my first marriage, the years of my father's illness, my time in the wilderness, and on into my life in Maryborough. There is something immensely comforting in peering into the letterbox to discover one of those blue envelopes, that familiar scrawling hand.

But it is better – wonderful – to have her here in the flesh, and a joy to sit back and drink in everything we've accomplished. She tells us how proud we should be. And we are. We are more than proud. When I stand back and look up at our home, feeling so strong and whole and well, I have the mad idea that the angel we've freed is a guardian angel, *my* guardian angel, who has been calling me since the day I stepped out of Trevor's car – a gratifying, voluptuous thought.

My children all come up to stay, and Mother and I do a couple of trips. I take her to Adelaide for a reunion with her cousin, Dede, and we stay in Brisbane for a few days, visiting the children and doing the Botanic Gardens and antique shops. It's a hotter than normal spring and, at her age, Mother is feeling the heat.

'Next time, Mother Mary,' I say, 'you must come in August. It'll be much cooler then.'

She is amused by her new name, started by Benji, Cyril and the gang, but not distracted from my transparent attempt to squeeze a commitment out of her to come again. She's cautious about making one, hating the thought of another journey, far too comfortable in her Cotswold life.

Mother's tiny village of Long Compton is a hotbed of Bridge-playing, curry-eating, tea-drinking widows. They are also all garden enthusiasts, go on regular coach trips together, go the theatre, the cinema, drive each other to doctor's appointments, to dentist appointments, to chiropody appointments. And they all, even the Bishop's mother, avidly devour my romance novels. (I suspect that in village circles I am known as the Australian who writes racy stories.)

I persist in my efforts to lure her back another time. Even when we're at the airport, putting her on the plane. I point out the simplicity and comfort of today's journeys compared to those of yesteryear. I point out that, listed as 'needing assistance', she is met at the door of the plane by a smiling airport employee with a wheelchair, ready to whisk her straight into Jane's capable hands. 'And next time,' I add enticingly, 'the garden will have grown beautiful. Next time the poinciana will be huge.'

She hesitates a second or two. 'Next time,' she says and, with a wave, she's off.

⊱⊰⊱⊰◦⊱⊰⊱⊰

Ian and I are officially engaged. I'm wearing a delicious pink sapphire and diamond ring on my left hand. How Ian found a ring just that right shade of pink is a wonder, and testament to his keen hunting and gathering skills. He slips it onto my finger at a decidedly unromantic moment while we're checking emails.

Friends tease us, calling me the Bride, Ian the Groom, nudging and winking like we're sweet young things. *When? When? When?* everyone keeps asking. 'After Georgie and Tom,' we say.

But I learn that our engagement provokes a few more

tears when Ian tells his children. Half of me frets and worries when I hear this sort of thing. The other half knows I should ignore it all, hold my head up and get on with my life, which is a wonderful life in all other respects.

When I'm with friends and family who care enough to remind and prompt me to maintain a positive outlook, it's easy. But when I'm alone or feeling outnumbered, the fretting part of me makes unwelcome appearances.

'It'll be all right,' says Ian. 'Give them time and all will be well. Remember, it's not you. They would feel this way whoever I was with.'

A couple of weeks later Ian's mobile phone rings. I don't usually answer his mobile, but he's gone to the tip and the ringing is persistent. I pick it up. It's Georgie. This is the first time I've spoken to her since our engagement. I explain that her dad is out and that I'll ask him to call her back when he gets home. She thanks me and hangs up. Two minutes later the phone rings again. 'I know I didn't say anything about you and Dad,' she says.

'That's OK,' I tell her. 'I know it's a difficult time for you.'

She goes on to explain that she's disappointed in me for not having made the effort to see her and her siblings, for not having somehow paved the way for Ian to break the news to them. She adds that she believes that her father has been pushed into it.

I don't trust myself to speak. Even if I could swallow my outrage, I suspect that anything I might say in the current climate would be taken the wrong way. It's a brief, tense, miserable phone call.

Perhaps the children are so incredulous that their father might want to marry any woman who is not their mother that they can't help but imagine I've manipulated him into it. Perhaps they *need* to believe it, as a coping mechanism. But such a belief is hardly going to win me any favours.

I'm not sure what to do. There have been moments over these last months when I've questioned whether it's all too hard, too heart-breaking. A life alone, free of complications, beckons temptingly. But then I look at Ian and know I can't do it. There seems to be no good solution, no happy ending. What we're doing is hurting others, but if we step back, we hurt ourselves. I run it all over and over in my head, torturing my brain. I want peace and happiness for everyone, but I don't know how to achieve it.

>-+-+>-0-<+-+-<

The Maryborough Heritage Awards are an annual event. It's a black tie dinner, with entertainment and an MC on stage reading nominations, declaring winners. It's like being at the Oscars, we're told. We nominate all our guys.

There are various categories, but unfortunately some of our nominees are running against each other. Peter Olds is against Brian White, the joiner, for the Manufacturer's Award. Cyril, Greg, Calvin and Pud are running against each other for the Service Provider's Award. Benji's on his own for the Painting Award. As is Mike for the building.

I fill in the nomination forms and write glowing accounts of their work. They call in to sign the forms. Pud brings us a present. He's made an exquisite, neo-Grecian wall moulding of Diana the Huntress with a running wolf at her heels.

I absolutely love it and know exactly where it needs to go. Ian is away, so Cyril and I attach it to the wall. A final nightmare job for Cyril who's carried out so many already.

He smears the back of the moulding thickly with about a gallon of Liquid Nails. 'Are you sure you won't change your mind about where you want this?' he asks.

'I'm sure.'

'Once this is up, you'll practically have to knock the wall down to get it off.'

'I'm sure,' I repeat.

It's large and heavy. We use our combined strength to place it against the wall and push hard. It doesn't stick. We take it off and Cyril adds still more Liquid Nails.

This is repeated three times before we feel any kind of decent adhesion. We daren't let go. We keep pushing as hard as we can. 'We could probably take turns,' I suggest eventually.

Cyril nods. 'I'll do the first shift.'

I release the moulding and go to put the kettle on, make tea, then hurry back.

'I'll give your arms a rest,' I say and with one hand on Diana, the other on the wolf, start pushing again.

I do short shifts, Cyril, whose arms are three times as thick as mine, does longer shifts.

'How long do you think we need to do this?' I ask.

'Usually dries in just five minutes,' Cyril tells me. 'But this thing is heavy and we put a lot of goo on.'

It's on one of my shifts, while Cyril has his back turned

and I'm starting to relax a bit, that I feel the unthinkable happening. '*Cyril!*' I yell. It's a panic-stricken, unladylike shriek.

He's back in a flash. Diana and her wolf have migrated about a metre south. It's almost impossible to slide her back up into place again because the Liquid Nails mixture is very close to dry. Cyril's earlier words give edge to my panic; *Once this is up, you'll practically have to knock the wall down to get it off* . . . I'm visualising Diana, interestingly oblique for ever and ever, about thirty centimetres from the floor. But we sweat and heave and she starts to creep back up the wall, millimetre by millimetre.

At last, she's back in place. We both press her to the wall with all our might. 'I should get some bracing,' says Cyril.

'Please be quick,' I say.

He sprints for the shed and comes back armed with a plank of wood, jamming it against the opposite stairs and into Diana's midriff. After about two hours we dare to let go, but sit and watch for signs of slippage. The bracing is in place for twenty-four hours.

We invite Pud back to have a look.

'No problem fixing it to the wall?' he asks.

'Not at all,' I say airily, and fancy I see a twinkle of appreciation in his eye.

>─◆─○─◆─<

Finally, *finally* I start to write, almost five years since I last put a creative pen to paper. It's impossible to put it off another day. I buy a stack of school exercise books, pick up my pen and let it happen. *The Ghost House of Maryborough*, I scrawl across the first page, then write till my eyes are nearly hanging out of my head.

People are always amazed when I say I *write* my books, literally, with a pen onto sheets of paper. But I long ago discovered my inability to create onto a computer screen. It's more than off-putting to stare at that static screen, upright at a desk chair for hours on end. I love the feel of pen travelling across paper, of shaping the words with my own hand. And there's the added bonus of being able to write in comfort. I can sprawl on the sofa, the bed, or recline on the wicker chaise longue on the upstairs verandah.

Of course the time comes when my handwritten work becomes a mess of scribbled, edited additions and alterations, of paragraphs re-ordered and chunks re-arranged. My pages also grow increasingly congested with doodles and decorations; created when my mind is languid and my pen is restless.

When my work reaches this disordered state, reluctantly I migrate to the office, settle myself at the computer and type it up. Usually I'll run through it all once on the screen to pick up simple errors, then I print out my first draft. Clean and tidy. Easy to read. Once more I can abandon the computer, pick up my pen and write until my printed sheets are a mess. Then it's back to the computer to key in the alterations. Print it out. Write some more. Print it out. Write some more. It's the only way I can work.

I've chosen Ian's weekly trip to Montville for this momentous beginning, which gives me two days to get a good start before I have to train him not to interrupt me constantly.

'You can interrupt five times a day – even ten,' I tell him when he returns, 'but not one hundred.'

He's very meek, trying oh so hard to be good. I hear his booted feet tiptoeing along corridors. It's hard to tiptoe in such clodhopping boots. I see his face at the window. He's on the verandah, peering in, but darts away when I spot him. I sense a presence and look up to discover him, bootless and silent, at the office door. 'Would you like a cup of tea?' he asks.

I lay down my pen. It's impossible to get cross. 'Very well.'

Over tea he says, 'I just wondered how you were going. Are you happy with your progress?'

I reach for a Tim Tam. 'Yes, very happy. But I'm going to have to get Sally Henderson to have another talk to you.'

He hangs his head.

Sally is a friend from our Montville days who has just written a book about her experiences with elephant conservation in Africa. Sally has her husband, Jeremy, well under control. Sally, as Ian is well aware, is a woman who knows how to lay down the law and get her work done. Already she has explained to Ian the importance of uninterrupted time to write. 'When Anne starts writing, she must be allowed to shut the door and lock you out. No interruptions. And you can't expect her to do any housework,' she adds, wagging a threatening finger at him.

Her decisiveness makes me smile. I don't mind the housework, as I do have some help already. But I am glad of Sally's words, glad for Ian to be hearing this from someone else.

He makes a genuine effort to do as he's told, but I soon

learn to get most of my writing done during the two days he's away each week.

It's hard to describe how much it means to me to be able to write again. Though I've been able to throw my creative energy into the house and garden, it's not fulfilling in quite the same way as writing.

With the restoration of a home and garden, the bones already exist. You take four walls; four very shabby walls in our case. You repair and adorn them. You give strength, stability and beauty to them. And they return the favour by providing a comforting, warm and inspiring place to live.

Writing, on the other hand, begins with a void. You stare at a starkly white sheet of unmarked paper. Your pen hovers over it for a delicious moment before the thrill of the first touch. And every word you put down is your own choice, your own arrangement, your own self. It's seducing, revealing, not for the faint-hearted. It lays you bare.

Sometimes the words drop like gems from your ready pen, sometimes they are hard-won, wrangled and agonised over. Either way, the result is the same: you are replete and content, the satisfaction of expressing yourself almost meditative, so deeply relaxing to me that I sometimes fall asleep as I write.

I'm more grateful to Ian than I can express, and grateful to Baddow House, for being part of my life and making this possible.

The Maryborough Awards Night arrives. Baddow House wins four awards. Benji for intrepid painting, Brian White for his artful joinery, Pud for his amazing plastering, and Ian and I receive a special 'Award of Excellence' in appreciation for all the work done to save Baddow House.

Ian wants to say a few words, but there are rules to keep the microphone away from the general public, even award recipients, otherwise the night drags on too long, putting the good burghers of Maryborough to sleep over their pudding. Every time Ian gets near the stage and within grabbing distance of the mike, he's thwarted.

The night is almost over, and Ian's on the verge of rugby tackling unsuspecting MC Syd Collins when Mayoress Barbara Hovard steps in and lets him have a turn.

He duly thanks everyone involved in our project, the town, the mayor, the tradesmen, expressing how fortunate we are to have found so much talent and experience in Maryborough. He goes on to say how lucky we were to find the house, to be the ones to have the opportunity of restoring it, and how amazing it is to be able to call Baddow House home. 'I had the pride,' he says, 'Anne had the passion.'

The night is over.

⊱─❖─⊰

Georgie and Tom have an engagement party. With Dinie's thirtieth also on the agenda, Georgie and Tom's wedding in May, as well as our own wedding to plan, it seems to be the time for parties.

I arrive at Georgie and Tom's engagement party stripped
of confidence. I haven't seen Ian's children for a few
months, not since I started wearing their father's ring, and
haven't spoken to any of them since the day Georgie called.
I have no idea how they will react to me.

Georgie is glowing and beautiful in a little black dress
and high, high heels. Her face is radiant with her Tom at
her side and I just want to pick her up and hug her tight. I
wish the timing was otherwise, that differences had been
resolved before the magic of this night for her.

Sipping my drink, making small talk, gravitating to the
few familiar faces in the crowd, I think about what she said
to me over the phone and worry that I should have talked
more with Ian's children, been more open. When I'm miserable I tend to clam up into silent reserve. Some might see
this as haughty, aloof and unbending. And so it is an
immense relief when, first Annabel congratulates me, then
David comes up halfway through the party, apologises for
not having acknowledged our engagement earlier, and tells
me how pleased he is for us. He tells me how much his
father means to him – that to see his father happy is more
important than anything in the world. He tells me that he
is right behind us.

It's a start, a brilliant one. I'm walking on air, and so is
Ian when I share this with him. Which I do immediately.
It's a weight gone from our shoulders as we step forward,
move on, skip through the other celebrations until it's time
for our own.

We are to marry in St Paul's Anglican Church, site of Maria Aldridge's belltower. Long ago we decided that we didn't want a circus. We want it short, quiet and sweet. 'Just us,' we say to Father Ian Trainor, resident vicar of St Paul's.

'You will have to have two witnesses,' he tells us.

'Okay,' we say. 'Just us, plus two.'

Ian, as a widower, is seen as a sinless victim of circumstance, welcome in any church. As a divorcée, I get a bit of a grilling. Father Ian is very kind and tactful, but he does have a duty to carry out. I'm to be made to understand about commitment and the sanctity of marriage. Permission has to be gained from the Bishop to allow me to be married on consecrated ground.

Permission is given with all the grace and speed we could have hoped for. We fix our date – exactly five and a half years after our first nerve-racking date.

A week before the wedding, I read an article in the paper about the new *Omen* movie, a remake of Gregory Peck's 1976 classic. This is a story about the coming of the Antichrist, born into this world as a human child. In the first movie, Gregory Peck and wife unwittingly raise this child, believing him to be their son, until all hell breaks loose, evil things happen thick and fast, and Peck has to kill the child to thwart Satan's Plan. This devil child has a birthmark on his head in the form of 666. Triple six, we learn, is the number of 'the Beast'.

My newspaper reports that many women around the world with babies due this year on the Sixth of June are begging their doctors to induce them early. For this year, it will be more than just the sixth day of the sixth month. This year, the date will the sixth of the sixth of the sixth. 666. This all rings a bell in my head. Suddenly I realise this is our wedding day. I rush to tell Ian.

The funny side strikes us pretty much straightaway. Let them induce their babies early. Let them stockpile food and crucifixes, hang garlic and wave incense. Let them build their survival domes in the United States. We have a wedding to attend.

Ian's sister Ann and her husband Ted drive all the way from Miles to be our two witnesses. They arrive mid-afternoon and laugh to discover that Ian and I have already hacked into the wedding cake Kerry Lyons, a friend from Montville, made for us.

Throughout the day the contents of the Maryborough florist shop transfer themselves bunch by bunch into our house, including a bouquet from Ian's children. The delivery-man starts to get a bit sick of Topsy and Lottie who rush out at him every time he arrives, then try to savage the tyres of his van when he drives away. But we don't try to stop them. Topsy, it seems, is learning important lessons.

We are touched that so many people are thinking of us and wishing us well. All the children ring, mine and Ian's, as well as friends from both ends of the planet. The phone starts ringing at dawn and doesn't stop all day, so what else is there to do, really, but eat cake?

We hack into it again with Ann and Ted, and drink tea before showering and changing.

I wear a black skirt and short purple suede jacket. Ian is far more flamboyant in his father's kilt and sporran. It's a bit moth-eaten, but luckily the moth holes aren't in any dangerous places. He buttons up the silver studs on his waistcoat and tucks his *skean dhu* into one ancient tartan sock. At the last minute I panic that I'm unbride-like, so grab a pink lisianthus from one of the bouquets filling the house.

Ted is smart in his St Andrew's tie and Ian and Ann's father's tartan waistcoat – also moth-eaten. Ann is very glamorous in all black except for her mother's red velvet-trimmed jacket and the heirloom necklace she wore to her own wedding.

It's almost dusk when Ted drives us to church. He won't let Ian sit in the back with me. 'Not until you're married,' he says.

Ian and I are pathetically nervous. We can't blame stage fright, as we have an audience of just two. We decide the momentousness of the occasion has finally caught up with us.

Father Ian greets us and introduces us to his wife, Maureen, who is going to take some photos, then we all troop to the small Warriors' Chapel at the side of the church. My Ian is pretty excited to be getting married in the Warriors' Chapel. There's an extra swish to his kilt as he approaches the altar and the *skean dhu* glints in the candlelight.

Ann and Ted flank us as we say our lines. Sweaty hands clasped, my ring goes on, and all of a sudden we are man and wife. Maureen's camera clicks away and, arm in arm, we walk down the aisle.

As we exit the church, there's a wonderful pealing of bells from Maria's tower. Mayoress, Barbara Hovard, in an incredibly kind and thoughtful gesture, has arranged for the bell ringers to come on our night. We stand outside the tower, awash with emotion and the poignancy of the moment as Maria's music peals across town.

Barbara appears out of the twilight. She has tears in her eyes and, as she walks away, calls out, 'Maryborough is so glad you came here!'

'And we're so glad we came to Maryborough!' shouts Ian.

EPILOGUE

O UR RENOVATIONS MIGHT be complete but, all of a
sudden, life is getting busy again. We are inun-
dated with people wanting to know our story. The
Maryborough Herald covers us with photos on a six page
spread. The *Fraser Coast Chronicle* is next, then Wide Bay's
Revive magazine, which focuses on my writing of Baddow's
story. A Queensland Heritage publication features us, and
so does *Country Style* with a feature written by a talented
young journalist, Kate Johns.

I seem to spend a lot of time primping the house for
photographers, which is easier said than done. We are far too
big for the sort of quick cosmetic job I used to do on my
previous house when visitors were due. The best I can
manage here is to arrange a few flowers and disguise the
worst of the mess in a very sweep-it-all-under-the-carpet sort
of a way. Beyond that, visitors have to take us as they find us.

A few days after the wedding, my three children come up
for the weekend and we create a wedding feast to consume

in our festive-coloured dining room. Some very special champagne slides down our throats, a gift from Ian's nephew, and we eat our favourites: roast pork in honour of Ian, cherry tart in honour of me. The children are full of questions: *Are you going to be Anne Russell now?*

'Well yes,' I say, 'I suppose I am.' I never did return to my maiden name after my divorce, and it would seem inappropriate to use the name of my first husband when I'm married to my second. It feels a bit strange to carry a different name to my children, but something I know I'll get used to.

Two weeks later, Ian and I are working in the back garden when we hear a car tooting, then another. Lottie and Topsy rush like snarling cannonballs to the front of the house. We follow, expecting to find raffle ticket sellers or Jehovah's Witnesses, but it is Ian's children, along with Georgie's husband, Tom, and David's girlfriend, Courtenay.

'We've come to take you out to lunch,' they say.

It's a total, wonderful surprise, planned by Georgie, and I can read the emotion and relief on Ian's face. We go to Muddy Waters, where our waitress, noting the air of excitement and happiness at our table, asks what we're celebrating.

'Oh, various things,' I say, and we all clink our glasses.

━━◆━○━◆━━

A few weeks later we are nominated for the Queensland National Trust Awards, and travel to Brisbane for the night.

The Queensland Governor, Quentin Bryce, is there to

present the awards, and looks fiercely skinny, yet elegant in her suit and immaculate make-up. There are drinks and nibbles and quite a crowd. I'm surprised to find myself a bit nervous as we take our seats to watch the presentations.

Our names are called. We've won an award and suddenly we're on our feet heading for the stage. The Governor shakes our hands, presents our certificate and Ian reaches for the microphone. He speaks briefly, then wraps up by saying 'Carrying out such a big renovation job can be a stressful exercise, put pressure on relationships, cause arguments.' He pauses for effect, playing the crowd. 'Not so with us. We went into this as financial partners and came out as man and wife.'

The crowd love it.

'We were rather more than "financial partners",' I hiss as we take our seats.

Ian shrugs. 'Who cares? It was a good line.'

And it was.

⊳⊢◇⊷●⊶◇⊣⊲

Never would we have imagined generating so much attention when we first sighted the grim-looking house with Trevor three years ago. It's wonderful to be patted on the head and told well done, but the biggest prize for us is our sense of achievement, our memories of the work and the delight we now share in our home and each other.

But though we are pleased with ourselves and our efforts, we never forget it was Edgar and Maria Aldridge's dream that started it all.

When we get home from the National Trust Awards, we go to the upstairs verandah. It's a beautiful winter night, the air is soft and calm with a gentle breeze to keep the mozzies away. The moon is full, a perfect white orb reflecting on the river, flooding our domain with its translucent light. We can see the garden clearly, the dog house, the flower borders, the bougainvillea cascading thornily over the upstairs balustrading. I can even make out my second-year seedling pansies and snapdragons in Charlie's circular bed.

Across the river there's a sparse ribbon of lights: houses on the other side where once there would have been total darkness. I can only imagine what it must have been like all those years ago, the great distance that separated this spot from the known world: an isolation that must have been as exhilarating as it was daunting.

I wonder if Edgar was able to find any pleasure in standing here, once his Maria was taken from him. I hope so, even if his own time left was short. I know that others must have done so: Harry and his Lappie, their children, Esse, May, Daniel and Harry Junior. Hugh and Alice Biddles before illness and injury struck them down.

Only now can I come to grips with the love these people must have had for Baddow House. Like a relationship between a man and woman, my early passion has settled into a warm, enduring feeling that seems unshakable, as theirs must have been. I suspect Esse felt this more keenly than most, but these days it's her many happy years that sit with me, not her tragic moment of eviction. I've lost all my fear. As we love the house, I know the house loves us. I believe it's breathing easy now, saved from extinction.

I believe Baddow House will continue to return the favour and look after us as it has indeed been my muse and, together with Ian, my inspiration and my cure. And I'm grateful. Deeply, abidingly grateful.

I find myself wishing Baddow could really be the Ghost House of its reputation. The thought of seeing the bearded Edgar stroll into the office or passing the beautiful Esse on the stairs warms me. I want to believe they are with us because, suddenly, I am very sure I want to share all this with them.

ACKNOWLEDGEMENTS

I AM INDEBTED to so many people for the making of this book. Starting at the very beginning: Edgar Aldridge, thank you for having the courage to leave your safe home in Essex, England and take a chance on a new life in Australia. Thank you also for being astute and determined enough to prosper, to fulfil your dreams and build Baddow House.

Thank you Maryborough, and to all those who helped you blossom through your first century, thank you for luring Ian and me here with your astonishing bounty of old and beautiful buildings.

Thanks also to Trevor Spohr, for knowing that Ian and I would find Baddow House irresistible despite its frightening state of dilapidation. Without you, none of this would have happened.

To all our helpers: Ron Monteverde for the under-pinning; architects Marian Graham and John Nash; David McLeod for engineering; Calvin Hannam for electrics;

Tony 'Benji' Benecke for intrepid painting; Peter Polley for floor sanding; Graham Morrison for the gates; Mike Johns and John Sama for making the restoration of the verandahs happen against such immense odds; Peter Olds for his reproduction of the balustrading; Brian White for his timber joinery; Neville 'Pud' Cockburn for his skilful and ingenious plastering; Brad Weiss for the kitchen; Paul Fairlie for tiling; Wayne Linthwaite for the roof; Charlie Hurcombe for creative paving; Russell Donovan; Greg Dennis for his loyalty and being our jack-of-all-trades; and, of course, Cyril Streat for solving a thousand impossible problems; thank you does not seem sufficient praise.

To my test audience, those who read the manuscript and told me not to change a word, thank you so much. You gave me confidence, courage and peace of mind.

Thanks also to my agent, Lyn Tranter, for your belief and support, and for quashing the *but who would want to read about me?* doubts.

To everyone at Random House, a big thank you, especially to Katie Stackhouse who worked tirelessly to make this book happen, even when she was supposed to be enjoying an overseas family holiday.

And lastly but most importantly, Ian, who lived every moment of these pages with me, and who shared the excitement of our story coming to life, thank you for supporting me through thick and thin, in good times and in bad, thank you for being exactly who you are.

LOCHINVAR

O, young Lochinvar is come out of the west,
Through all the wide Border his steed was the best,
And save his good broad-sword he weapons had none;
He rode all unarmed, and he rode all alone.
So faithful in love, and so dauntless in war,
There never was knight like the young Lochinvar.

He stayed not for brake, and he stopped not for stone,
He swam the Eske river where ford there was none;
But, ere he alighted at Netherby gate;
The bride had consented, the gallant came late:
For a laggard in love, and a dastard in war,
Was to wed the fair Ellen of brave Lochinvar.

So boldly he entered the Netherby hall,
Among bride's-men and kinsmen, and brothers and all.
Then spoke the bride's father, his hand on his sword,
(For the poor craven bridegroom said never a word,)
'O come ye in peace here, or come ye in war,
Or to dance at our bridal, young Lord Lochinvar?'

'I long wooed your daughter, my suit you denied; –
Love swells like the Solway, but ebbs like its tide –
And now I am come, with this lost love of mine
To lead but one measure, drink one cup of wine.
There are maidens in Scotland more lovely by far,
That would gladly be bride to the young Lochinvar.

The bride kissed the goblet: the knight took it up,
He quaffed off the wine, and he threw down the cup,
She looked down to blush, and she looked up to sigh.
With a smile on her lips and a tear in her eye.
He took her soft hand, ere her mother could bar,-
'Now tread we a measure!' said young Lochinvar.

So stately his form, and so lovely her face,
That never a hall such a galliard did grace;
While her mother did fret and her father did fume,
And the bridegroom stood dangling his bonnet and plume;
And the bride-maidens whispered, ''Twere better by far
To have matched our fair cousin with young Lochinvar.'

One touch to her hand, and one word in her ear,
When they reached the hall door and the charger stood
    near;
So light to the croupe the fair lady he swung,
So light to the saddle before her he sprung! –
'She is won! We are gone, over bank, bush and scaur;
They'll have fleet steeds that follow,' quoth young
    Lochinvar.

There was mounting 'mong Graemes of the Netherby clan;
Forsters, Fenwicks and Musgraves, they rode and they ran:
There was racing, and chasing, on Cannobie Lee,
But the lost bride of Netherby ne'er did they see.
So daring in love, and so dauntless in war,
Have ye e'er heard of gallant like young Lochinvar?

                                    Sir Walter Scott